READING SARTRE

Jean-Paul Sartre was one of the most influential philosophers of the twentieth century. The fourteen original essays in this volume focus on the phenomenological and existentialist writings of the first major phase of his published career, arguing with scholarly precision for their continuing importance to philosophical debate.

Aspects of Sartre's philosophy under discussion in this volume include:

- Consciousness and self-consciousness
- Imagination and aesthetic experience
- Emotions and other feelings
- Embodiment
- Selfhood and the Other
- Freedom, bad faith, and authenticity
- Literary fiction as philosophical writing.

Reading Sartre: On phenomenology and existentialism is an indispensable resource for understanding Sartre's philosophy. It is essential reading for students of phenomenology, existentialism, ethics, or aesthetics, and for anyone interested in the roots of contemporary thought in twentieth-century philosophy.

Jonathan Webber is Lecturer in Philosophy at Cardiff University. He is the author of *The Existentialism of Jean-Paul Sartre* (Routledge, 2009) and translator of Sartre's book *The Imaginary* (Routledge, 2004).

READING SARTRE

On phenomenology and existentialism

Edited by
Jonathan Webber

LONDON AND NEW YORK

First published 2011
by Routledge
2 Park Square, Milton Park, Abingdon, Oxon, OX14 4RN

Simultaneously published in the USA and Canada by Routledge
711 Third Avenue, New York, NY 10017

Routledge is an imprint of the Taylor & Francis Group, an informa business

© 2011 Jonathan Webber for selection and editorial matter; individual
contributors for their contributions.

Typeset in Goudy by
Taylor & Francis Books

British Library Cataloguing in Publication Data
A catalogue record for this book is available from the British Library

Library of Congress Cataloging-in-Publication Data
Reading Sartre : on phenomenology and existentialism / edited by
Jonathan Webber.
p. cm.
Includes bibliographical references and index.
1. Sartre, Jean-Paul, 1905–1980. 2. Phenomenology.
3. Existentialism. I. Webber, Jonathan.
B2430.S34R43 2010
194--dc22
2010008825

ISBN 13: 978-0-415-55095-6 (hbk)
ISBN 13: 978-0-415-55096-3 (pbk)
ISBN 13: 978-0-203-84414-4 (ebk)

CONTENTS

CONTENTS

CONTRIBUTORS

Christine Daigle is Associate Professor of Philosophy at Brock University and Past President of the North American Sartre Society. She is the author of *Le nihilisme est-il un humanisme? Étude sur Nietzsche et Sartre* (2005) and *Jean-Paul Sartre* (2009), is co-editor of *Sartre and Beauvoir: The Riddle of Influence* (2008), and has published articles on the ethics of Nietzsche, Sartre, and Beauvoir.

Andreas Elpidorou is a doctoral candidate in philosophy at Boston University and Visiting Scholar at the University of Pittsburgh. He is writing his dissertation on the nature of perceptual content.

Matthew C. Eshleman is Associate Professor of Philosophy at University of North Carolina Wilmington. He is the author of a series of articles on Sartre and Beauvoir, focusing on their theories of freedom, bad faith, and normative justification.

Sebastian Gardner is Professor of Philosophy at University College London. He is the author of *Sartre's Being and Nothingness* (2009), *Kant and the Critique of Pure Reason* (1999), *Irrationality and the Philosophy of Psychoanalysis* (1993), and numerous papers on metaphysics, aesthetics, and psychoanalysis in European philosophy since Kant.

Azzedine Haddour is Senior Lecturer in French at University College London. He is the author of *Colonial Myths: History and Narrative* (2001), editor of *The Fanon Reader* (2006), co-translator of a collection of Sartre's essays, *Colonialism and Neocolonialism* (2001), and author of various articles on Sartre and postcolonial theory.

Anthony Hatzimoysis is Assistant Professor of Philosophy at the University of Athens. He is the author of *The Philosophy of Sartre* (2010) and editor of *Self-knowledge* (forthcoming) and *Philosophy and the Emotions* (2003). He has published a range of articles on the nature and knowledge of emotion.

Robert Hopkins is Professor of Philosophy and Head of the Department of Philosophy at The University of Sheffield. He is the author of *Picture, Image and Experience* (1998) and a range of articles in aesthetics, epistemology, and philosophy of mind, focusing on beauty, depiction, testimony, perception, and imagination.

Andrew Leak is Professor of French at University College London. He is a former President of the UK Sartre Society and former editor of *Sartre Studies International*. He is the author of *The Perverted Consciousness: Sexuality and Sartre* (1989), *Jean-Paul Sartre* (2006), and numerous articles on existentialism, literature, and critical theory.

Katherine J. Morris is Fellow in Philosophy at Mansfield College, University of Oxford. She is the author of *Sartre* (2008) and editor of *Sartre and the Body* (2010), and has published a range of articles on the nature of embodiment and the philosophy of psychiatry and psychoanalysis.

Sarah Richmond is Senior Lecturer in Philosophy at University College London. She has published articles on phenomenology, psychoanalysis, and feminist philosophy, focusing on the nature of lived experience and drawing particularly on Bergson, Klein, and Sartre.

Alan Thomas is Professor of Ethics at Tilburg University and Director of the Tilburg Hub for Ethics and Social Philosophy. He is the author of *Value and Context: The Nature of Moral and Political Knowledge* (2006) and numerous articles in philosophy of mind, moral psychology, and the metaphysics and epistemology of moral value.

Jonathan Webber is Lecturer in Philosophy at Cardiff University. He is the author of *The Existentialism of Jean-Paul Sartre* (2009) and translator of Sartre's book *The Imaginary* (2004). He has published articles on moral psychology and applied ethics, focusing on the nature and ethical importance of character and personality.

Kenneth Williford is Associate Professor of Philosophy at The University of Texas at Arlington. He is co-translator of Sartre's book *The Imagination* (2010) and co-editor of *Self-representational Approaches to Consciousness* (2006), and has published a series of articles on the nature of consciousness.

Dan Zahavi is Professor of Philosophy and Director of the Center for Subjectivity Research at University of Copenhagen. He is the author of numerous books and articles in philosophy of mind and cognitive science informed by twentieth-century phenomenological philosophy, including *Self-awareness and Alterity* (1999) and *Subjectivity and Selfhood* (2005), and is co-author of *The Phenomenological Mind* (2008).

PREFACE

Reading Sartre is no easy task. Although much of his substantial oeuvre is characterised by a brisk lucidity, his philosophical writings tend to involve dense, entangled, abstruse passages at crucial moments and the gradual development of his own idiosyncratic terminology as he struggles to articulate his comprehensive and systematic account of our existence in all of its dimensions. Yet these writings have proved fertile ground for readers with a wide range of theoretical interests, yielding valuable insights and perspectives in return for exegetical and argumentative labour. This is especially true of his philosophical output of the 1930s and 1940s, his most clearly phenomenological and existentialist works which form the basis of the rest of his career. Part of the aim of this book is to provide a snapshot of current scholarly engagement with these works and the contribution this is making to various discussions and debates. In so doing, it documents inevitable interpretive disagreements among those currently working with Sartre alongside much agreement across their diverse intellectual styles and commitments.

The contributions to this book range across the breadth of Sartre's philosophical concerns in the first decade or so of his published career, including the nature of mind and its relation to the rest of reality, the ways in which we understand ourselves and one another, the moral and political dimensions of interpersonal interaction, the nature of communication and aesthetic experience, and the nature of philosophy itself. Sartre's thoughts on these topics are deeply interwoven to form a single fabric. As a result, they run through this book in such a way that the chapters cannot be categorised under general headings without breaking many of the threads that hold the book together and thereby misrepresenting Sartre's thought as a mosaic of distinct ideas. This is why the chapters have been arranged by alphabetical order of author, an editorial decision that might at first seem simply lazy but is rather aimed at presenting a fair portrait of his work in this period and encouraging the various currents of contemporary thought represented here to influence and benefit from one another.

This book is the culmination of a series of workshops held at Cardiff University and the Institute of Philosophy in London during the summer and autumn of 2009 and will be launched with a conference at Sartre's alma mater, the École Normale Supérieure in Paris, in the autumn of 2010. This project was funded by a Research Networking grant from the Arts and Humanities Research Council of the United Kingdom, for which we are all grateful. We would also like to thank Aberdare Hall at Cardiff University, Barry Smith and Shahrar Ali of the Institute of Philosophy, and Jean Bourgault and Gilles Phillipe of ITEM-ENS Équipe Sartre for their help in organising the events, and all the participants of the workshops for their helpful discussions of earlier drafts of the chapters of this book. Thanks are also due to Matthew Eshleman, Jeremy Smyczek, and Suzi Wells for their help with the final stages of the editorial task and to Matilde Webber for being so well behaved that these final stages could be completed in reasonable time.

1

THE ETHICS OF AUTHENTICITY

Christine Daigle

What saith thy conscience? Thou shalt become what thou art.
Friedrich Nietzsche, *The Gay Science* §270

One of the most problematic parts of Sartre's philosophy is certainly his ethics. No ethical treatise followed the famous announcement in the last lines of *Being and Nothingness*. There are only a few essays, e.g. *Existentialism Is a Humanism*, *Anti-Semite and Jew*, and *What Is Literature?*, that tackle ethical problems of one kind or another. The attempt at writing an ethics was abandoned after filling ten notebooks from 1947 to 1948. The *Notebooks for an Ethics*, two out of the ten notebooks that were published posthumously in 1983, contain an attempt at an ethics, one that Sartre retrospectively deemed a failure. The abandonment of the project has inevitably led to some speculation as to its cause. In his *Sartre, le dernier philosophe*, Alain Renaut explains it by pointing to the publication of *The Ethics of Ambiguity* by Beauvoir in 1947. Since this essay, according to Renaut, responded directly to the call for an ethics that concluded *Being and Nothingness*, there was no need for Sartre to continue working on his own answer. Because Beauvoir successfully elaborated an ethics on the ontological basis provided by *Being and Nothingness* the job was done and Sartre could devote himself to something different. I want to challenge this.

I have argued elsewhere that it is possible to reconstruct a Sartrean ethics if one carefully reads his essays of the 1940s along with the *Notebooks for an Ethics* (see Daigle 2005 and 2007). I think that Sartre is unfair to himself when he judges the content of the *Notebooks* to represent a failed attempt at an ethics. That he will later turn toward an ethics that emphasizes more the socio-historical location of the individual does not mean that the ethics of the 1940s is to be dismissed. In fact, I think it can be argued that the later ethics is merely an extension and complement of the earlier one, albeit a much needed one. That said, the sorry situation that is made for the individual in *Being and Nothingness* does not seem to provide much ground for an ethics. If authenticity is the ethical ideal one must aim for, and that is indeed the key of Sartre's ethics, it is not clear how the for-itself that

1

emerges out of the ontological treatise is in any position to attain it. Sartre needs to revise some of his views for this to happen. I will argue that Beauvoir's intervention, in 'Pyrrhus and Cinéas' and *The Ethics of Ambiguity*, is crucial in that regard. Her different appropriation of Hegel and Heidegger and her understanding of situation led Sartre to the path of conversion and reciprocity that are key to authenticity and the possibility of an ethical life. I will proceed by first explaining Heidegger's notion of authenticity as it permeates much of Sartre's and Beauvoir's thinking on the topic. I will then explain the conundrum of bad faith in Sartre as well as his views on interpersonal relations and authenticity. Following this, I will turn to Beauvoir's understanding of authenticity. This will reveal that Beauvoir's contribution was key to Sartre's development of an ethics of authenticity as we find it in the *Notebooks for an Ethics*.

The problem of authenticity: the case of Heidegger

What is authenticity and why is it a problem? It is important to clarify the nature of the concept that Beauvoir and Sartre tackle. To do so, it is important to keep in mind that both were interested in Heidegger's phenomenology. While this is not an essay on Heidegger, I think it is crucial to consider, even if very briefly, what he had to say about authenticity in order to better understand Beauvoir's and Sartre's own dealings with the concept.

In *Being and Time*, Heidegger talked about authentic and inauthentic *Dasein*. Notably, he refused to give the concept its traditional ethical spin. Authenticity and inauthenticity are modes of being for Dasein as it relates to being and to the world. Inauthenticity is a kind of being-in-the-world for Dasein whereby Dasein is 'completely fascinated by the "world" and by the Dasein-with of Others in the "they"' (Heidegger 1962: 220). Authenticity, by contrast, is the kind of being-in-the-world whereby Dasein is self-aware of itself as the being that is a being-there, that is a being that is present to being. Dasein is aware of its relation to the world. Similarly, as we will come to see, the authentic for-itself in Sartre will be the one that will also understand its relation to the world as one that creates the world and the values contained therein. Heidegger explains that '*authentic* existence is not something which floats above falling everydayness; existentially, it is only a modified way in which such everydayness is seized upon' (Heidegger 1962: 224). Heidegger insists that authenticity and inauthenticity are merely modes of being for Dasein and that no one mode is better or more desirable than the other. Rather, they are tied together and equiprimordial. He thus claims that his views are only descriptive and not prescriptive. Interestingly, however, the structures or modes of being that he identifies as being inauthentic are all the most immediate experiences that Dasein has of its being-in-the-world, namely facticity, fallenness and existentiality.

Dasein is inauthentic when it dwells in its own facticity (its being-in-the-world), when it lets itself be fascinated by the they (being thrown into the world, Dasein is a *Mitdasein* or Dasein-with) and when it is oblivious to its own being-toward-death. The experience of dread, which accompanies the experience of oneself as a being-toward-death – but can also be brought up by other, everyday experiences – is one that uncovers nothingness for Dasein.

Being-toward-death plays a key role with regards to authenticity in Heidegger. Once Dasein makes of his own death something existentially relevant, it is in an authentic mode. That is, it has uncovered its own possibilities and their finite nature. The idea of possibility is the key here: death has to become a genuine possibility for us. It does so in the mode of authenticity and through anticipation. Anticipation or anxiety is a particular mood that leads one to the authentic mode where one is freed from illusions, the illusions of inauthenticity, and where one realizes that one truly is a being-towards-death.[1] The ultimate possibility is the termination of one's Dasein.

In any case, the two modes of being-in-the-world of Dasein are not equivalent. Although Heidegger is careful in refraining from qualifying authenticity as better or more desirable, the whole gist of these sections of *Being and Time* is that Dasein has to be authentic. Thus, authenticity is not merely an ontological category but an ought. Dasein may let itself be trapped in inauthentic modes but must aim toward authenticity as a mode of its own being. The ontological yields an ethical demand, that of authenticity.[2]

Sartre on authenticity

Sartre's handling of the problem of authenticity is different from Heidegger's while being informed by it. The point at which he comes closest to Heidegger's ontologization of the problem is in *Being and Nothingness*. Indeed, the chapter on bad faith tries to deal with the concepts of bad faith and good faith in strict ontological terms, not introducing an ought the way Heidegger inadvertently did in *Being and Time*. Using the terms 'authenticity' and 'inauthenticity' was bound to put Heidegger in a difficult position, and it did. It is quite conceivable that Sartre uses 'bad faith' and 'good faith' in order to avoid the ethical pitfall that Heidegger was faced with. The terms 'authenticity' and 'inauthenticity' simply carry a heavy ethical baggage. Using 'bad faith' and 'good faith' is intended to help think about the problem in an ontological manner.[3] Sartre warns us at the end of the chapter on bad faith:

> If it is indifferent whether one is in good or in bad faith, because bad faith reapprehends good faith and creeps to the very origin of the project of good faith, that does not mean that we can not

radically escape bad faith. But this supposes a self-recovery of being which was previously corrupted. This self-recovery we shall call authenticity, the description of which has no place here.

(B&N: 94)

Thus authenticity is not good faith and inauthenticity is not bad faith, although it is very tempting to read them as such. The waiter is in bad faith when he pretends to *be* a waiter. Ought he to realize that this is not how he ought to conceive of himself? Not in this section of *Being and Nothingness*, where Sartre is describing a mode of being. While I think that Sartre's linguistic precautions have not been sufficient to rescue him from the ethical pitfall, this is not a matter I wish to pursue at great length here. There is plenty of debate on what exactly Sartre is trying to achieve and whether he achieves it in the chapter on bad faith and other scholars have addressed these issues better than I would.[4]

But let me try this. What is bad faith? One is in bad faith when one denies that one is a being for-itself. The waiter is deemed to be in bad faith because he fancies he *is* a waiter in the strong ontological sense. Existentially, the woman at the rendezvous is all mind. She experiences herself as divorced from her body. Now, ontologically that is impossible since, as a for-itself, she is an embodied consciousness. No consciousness can be conscious *of* without the body. She nevertheless experiences herself, at that moment, as pure mind. Her body is then a thing, an object from which she is separated. An ontological impossibility becomes an existential reality. To thus conceive of oneself at odds with one's ontological being is to be in bad faith. Bad faith is not an ontological concept although it points to the failure of one's existential being to correspond to one's ontological being. Bad faith is a phenomenological existential concept that extends into an ethical one. In fact, I want to go so far as to say that it is always ethical since there is an underlying claim operating here, namely: that one ought to be what one is, that is, a being that is what it is not and is not what it is.

It would not be surprising if the chapter on bad faith had an ethical import, as I think it does. After all, this chapter and its supposed strict ontological dealings with bad faith and good faith can almost be seen as an interlude in Sartre's overall ethical approach to the question of authenticity since it is preceded and followed by inquiries into the concept from an ethical point of view. Already in his literary writings of the 1930s he is investigating the problem. It is a theme in *Nausea* (1938) with the figure of the *salaud* and it recurs in 'The Childhood of a Leader', one of the short stories published together as *The Wall* in 1939. In *Nausea*, Roquentin despises the bourgeois of Bouville whom he calls *salauds*. The salaud is in bad faith as he, much like the waiter to come in *Being and Nothingness*, plays at being the bourgeois he *is*, enacting his predetermined role conscientiously and exercising his rights and duties, themselves also set and fixed. Similarly, in 'The Childhood of a Leader', after a little wandering and existential – authentic? – musings, Lucien discovers who he really *is*. Sartre says 'And now, indeed, that was exactly what Lucien was: a huge bundle of rights and responsibilities' (TW: 204). He has a right to exist, his existence takes the form of an in-itself: he *is* Lucien, he *is* a Leader. He is in bad faith.

Sartre's ethical concern with authenticity continues in his *War Diaries*. It is then as much a personal concern for being authentic as a theoretical concern for understanding the mechanisms by which one may become authentic. At the time, he is reading Heidegger and the language he uses in his diaries is informed by this reading.[5] Not only is he borrowing Heidegger's language but clearly also some of his views on authenticity. Thus he says that authenticity is to be obtained only through historicity. He defines it as one way for the individual to be situated, to understand oneself as a situated being. He says: 'Authenticity is a *duty* that comes to us both from outside and from inside since our "inside" is an outside. To be authentic, is to fully realize one's situated being, whatever that situation may be' (WD: 53–4; my emphasis).[6] Authenticity will be gained through assuming one's free situated and historical being. However, this gain will have to be perpetually regained as one persists in one's free project. If that does not happen, one will relapse in inauthenticity.

The diaries' sketches on the notion of authenticity find their way into *Being and Nothingness* but not in the chapter on bad faith. As explained earlier, the chapter on bad faith is dedicated to an ontological exploration of the notion of bad faith. Later in the treatise, in the section 'Freedom and Responsibility', he explains what responsibility is, again, from an ontological point of view. What he says there is reminiscent of his definition of authenticity in the *War Diaries*. He says:

> The one who realizes in anguish his condition as being thrown into a responsibility which extends to his very abandonment has no longer either remorse or regret or excuse; he is no longer anything but a freedom which perfectly reveals itself and whose being resides in this very revelation. But as we pointed out at the beginning of this work, most of the time we flee anguish in bad faith.
>
> (B&N: 577)

Thus anguish is equated with authenticity. Authenticity is, as in Heidegger, to be obtained through the anguished discovery of oneself as a free, responsible, situated being. However, contra Heidegger, Sartre does not think that this anguished discovery entails an understanding of oneself as a being-toward-death. Indeed, he rejects this notion vehemently, leading him to assert that Heidegger points to a solution but fails to provide it himself. For Sartre, authenticity is the discovery of oneself as this being that seeks to be God, yet fails to be it. As said earlier in the book, 'the being toward which human reality surpasses itself is not a transcendent God; it is at the heart of human reality; it is only human reality itself as totality' (B&N: 114). But this totality is one that is what it is not and is not what it is. It is a project that constantly aims to be one with itself, to be a for-itself–in-itself. The final word of *Being and Nothingness* is that the for-itself is a being that desires to be God and that flees anguish in bad faith. It seems to make authenticity extremely difficult, if not altogether impossible to attain.

Thomas Anderson has argued that for Sartre's ethics, in general, and for authenticity, in particular, to be possible, there is a need for a conversion (Anderson 1993). According to him, the for-itself must abandon the desire to be God. This entails a rejection of the ontology of *Being and Nothingness*. Anderson finds this conversion at work in the *Notebooks*. While Anderson's analyses are helpful, I agree rather with Yiwei Zheng's reading of the conversion presented in the *Notebooks*. He explains that it is not necessary to reject the ontology of *Being and Nothingness* in order to be authentic. In fact, he thinks that the ontology has to be preserved and that an ethics can be elaborated on its basis. According to this ontology, the for-itself desires to be God. We cannot not desire to be God. If we did, we would be in bad faith and inauthenticity again. Authenticity requires that one embraces oneself as a being for whom the desire to be God is a feature of one's being. According to Zheng, what happens however is that 'in authenticity we come to view the value of being God as subordinate to some higher value – freedom' (Zheng 2002: 133). In authenticity, one realizes that the desire to be God is what drives us to actualize the free beings we are. Seeing things under the right perspective, one is authentic, and 'in authenticity there is a willing of the unreflective project' (Zheng 2002: 138). The for-itself understands himself as this free project that aims to be what it is in the mode of not being it. To be authentic is to understand that one is a finite, contingent and ignorant point of view on the world and that because of that one creates a world. Sartre explains that the

> authentic man never loses sight of the absolute goals of the human condition. He is the pure choice of his absolute goals. These goals are: to save the world (in making being be), to make freedom the ground of the world, to take up creation for his own use, and to make the origin of the world absolute through freedom taking hold of itself.

(NE: 448)

This project has to be embraced reflectively. The for-itself's project is gratuitous at its heart. But as willed by the for-itself as an expression of his freedom, it is justified. 'It is this double simultaneous aspect of the human project, gratuitous at its core and consecrated by a reflective reprise, that makes it into *authentic existence*' (NE: 481). Through this process, one accepts responsibility for oneself and for the world that one has created. But the *Notebooks* also go further. One must convert to the notion of freedom as superseding the project to be God but one must also convert to the Other.

The conversion to the Other and to one's intersubjective being is problematic in view of the picture that Sartre has drawn of interpersonal relationships in *Being and Nothingness*. While I do not wish to analyse this in detail, some explanations are in order. Sartre acknowledges that we are both a being for-itself and a being for-others. He recognizes 'Hegel's brilliant intuition [which] is to make me depend on the Other *in my being*. I am, he said, a being for-itself which is for-itself only through another. Therefore the Other penetrates me to the heart' (B&N: 261). Immediately after this, though, he announces that Hegel must be rejected since he introduces only a cognitive relationship with the Other. He then proceeds to the famous analysis of the look with its whole emphasis on the negative aspect of the existence of others. The Other looks at me, he robs me of my world, he objectifies me, he alienates me. The look is inauthentic in that it objectifies the Other but a consciousness that encounters an other in the world cannot help but objectify that other. The Other is an object in the world for me. When he is a subject, when he exercises his freedom by looking at me, I bear the brunt of his freedom rather than recognize it in reciprocity. The freedom of the Other alienates me and deprives me of my own freedom. 'My being for-others is a fall through absolute emptiness toward objectivity' (B&N: 298). Further, in the section 'Concrete Relations with Others', Sartre describes failed relationships between consciousnesses. In the third section of this chapter he writes: 'The "we" is a certain particular experience which is produced in special cases on the foundation of being for-others in general. The being-for-others precedes and founds the *being-with-others*' (B&N: 436).[7] But the we-object and the we-subject he describes are alienating and not authentic instances of *Mitsein à la* Heidegger. Thence follows the famous damning statement: 'The essence of the relations between consciousnesses is not the *Mitsein*; it is conflict' (B&N: 451).

How will one convert to the Other if the conversion is to happen on the basis of the ontology of *Being and Nothingness*? The conversion to the Other is essential to authenticity. Sartre says so much himself in the *Notebooks*. But, as Eva Lundgren-Gothlin pointed out, in the *Notebooks*, 'Sartre simply assumes that men can behave generously and unselfishly toward each other. The conflict is no longer inevitable' (Lundgren-Gothlin 1994: 901). This shift requires some explanation. T. Storm Heter has proposed a very interesting one in his 'Authenticity and Others: Sartre's Ethics of Recognition'. He argues therein that authenticity entails recognizing others in a Hegelian fashion. He points to the definition of authenticity that Sartre provides in *Anti-Semite and Jew*. In that essay, Sartre explains that authenticity entails two conditions: (1) lucid consciousness and (2) accepting responsibility. Heter proposes that these two conditions are based on an implicit third condition i.e. that one respects and recognizes the freedom of others (see Heter 2006: 22). As he says, 'The third condition of authenticity adds a rich social dimension to authenticity and answers the subjectivist worry' (Heter 2006: 28). Heter further argues that while *Anti-Semite and Jew* describes non-mutual recognition, *What Is Literature?* describes mutual recognition. He thus wants to consider both essays as each shedding light on one of the two faces of the same coin. According to Heter, *The Notebooks for an Ethics* endorses the ethics presented in these earlier essays while focusing on the notion of the appeal, 'which is Sartre's term for the phenomenon that makes mutual recognition possible' (Heter 2006: 35). He thus concludes that 'authenticity requires embracing the inter-subjective nature of one's identity' (Heter 2006: 38).

While I have no qualms with this conclusion, I do have reservations about the underlying claim made by Heter. The point of his article is to show that Sartre's ethics is not Kantian in nature but Hegelian. As he says, Kantian ethics rests on demands emerging out of the categorical imperative and, as he demonstrated, Sartre's ethics rests on the appeal to the Other. Heter argues that it is thanks to his incorporation of Hegel's notion of mutual recognition that Sartre can rest his ethics on the appeal. However, I like to pay attention to what Sartre himself says of *Being and Nothingness* and its relation to Hegel: he did not see the dialectic at work in it; he was not working much on Hegel at the time and although he does refer to and refute Hegel in many places, he certainly did not use the Hegelian master–slave dialectic in all its aspects (IRPG: 9–10). I agree with Lundgren-Gothlin's assessment in that relation: 'Sartre borrowed from the first part only of Hegel's master–slave dialectic, where the two consciousnesses simultaneously try to dominate each other' (Lundgren-Gothlin 1994: 899). Thus, his selective appropriation of Hegel cannot be the ground for him to devise a reciprocal recognition of freedoms as is necessitated for authenticity. I argue instead that what is required, is the mediation of Beauvoir and her emphasis on the Heideggerian *Mitsein* as well as her full appropriation of the master–slave dialectic as entailing a second moment wherein the conflict is transformed into mutual recognition.

Beauvoir on authenticity

The notion of authenticity and the ethical problem in general are themes that permeate the whole Beauvoirian corpus. However, it is in her writings from the 1940s that she explores them at length: in 'Pyrrhus and Cinéas' (1944) and *The Ethics of Ambiguity* (1947), but also in *The Second Sex* (1949) in the context of understanding the experiences of woman. Her approach to the problem of authenticity is informed by her appropriation of Hegel and

Heidegger but also by her reading of Marx, which I won't be concerned with.[8] I will proceed chronologically and trace the concept of authenticity as it is devised in successive texts.

In her 'Pyrrhus and Cinéas', Beauvoir tackles the notion of authenticity in a very Heideggerian sense. Interestingly, this is the essay where she stands closest to Sartre. She uncritically adopts the ontology presented in *Being and Nothingness* and seeks to elaborate an ethics on that basis. Thus she claims that the human being is a project, a being that is what it is not and is not what it is, a being who must transcend himself all the while wanting to be. However, her appropriation of Hegel and Heidegger sets her on a path that distances her from Sartre. Following Heidegger, she explains that the human being is the one that unveils being. It is the ontological and ethical duty of the individual to unveil this being and generate the conditions for the unveiling to happen. One is thrown into the world and unveils the world that one is in. This unveiling is done as a situated embodied consciousness. For the individual, to be authentic is to recognize oneself as a situated being-in-the-world and to act as the creator of values that one is. The human being's desire is not to be God, i.e. to be a for-itself–in-itself, rather it is to unveil being. But this cannot happen in isolation. Beauvoir closes the first part of her essay by claiming 'A man alone in the world would be paralyzed by the manifest vision of the vanity of all his goals. He would undoubtedly not be able to stand living. But man is not alone in the world' (Beauvoir 2004a: 115). The second part explains how it is necessary to appeal to the freedom of the Other to ground and justify my unveiling of being. The argument is not Hegelian as such but results in a similar notion of reciprocal recognition of free subjects.

As a free situated embodied consciousness, I unveil being. My intending the world creates the world. I am the being thanks to whom there is a world. However, I would remain trapped in my own subjectivity if there was not an Other who could acknowledge this process. I need the Other so that my unveiling is not lost in the solipsistic trap. 'The Other's freedom alone is capable of necessitating my being. My essential need is therefore to be faced with free men' (Beauvoir 2004a: 129). The Other to whom I will appeal for recognition must be free in order to be in a position to even acknowledge me. She says 'I can concretely appeal only to the men who exist for me, and they exist for me only if I have created ties with them or if I have made them into my peers' (Beauvoir 2004a: 135; translation altered). When I recognize the Other as an impotent object, when I alienate him by oppressing him or when I recognize him as an omnipotent subject that objectifies me through the look for example, there is no mutual recognition of freedom, we are not peers. In such relationships, my project and unveiling of being cannot be grounded and justified by the Other. Either he is made impotent or he does not care, exercising his own potency at my expense. What is needed is for both subjects to retain their freedom, to continue to pursue their projects, all the while recognizing one another as the free beings they are that are engaged in the project of unveiling being. Thus, says Beauvoir, 'Our freedoms support each other like the stones in an arch, but in an arch that no pillars support. Humanity is entirely suspended in a void that it creates itself by its reflection on its plenitude' (Beauvoir 2004a: 140).[9]

We see clearly that the view she presents in 'Pyrrhus and Cinéas' is an artful combination of Hegel's views on the mutual recognition of consciousnesses and Heidegger's understanding of Dasein as the being that unveils being. In *The Ethics of Ambiguity*, Beauvoir continues in the same vein while emphasizing that unveiling is at the heart of authenticity. She puts an emphasis on authenticity that is absent from Heidegger's *Being and Time* for whom, as we discussed in an earlier section, authenticity is merely a mode of being-in-the-world for Dasein. Beauvoir makes more of authenticity. In authenticity, one affirms oneself as an unveiling being and this is the equivalent of affirming oneself as free, for to be free is to unveil being. To be free, to unveil, that is the same movement of existing for the human being, according to Beauvoir. As Gothlin puts it, 'To be authentic for Beauvoir means to unveil the world *with and for others*'.[10] The unveiling, which is the activity of the free being, is done as a *Mitsein* and never in isolation.

What grounds this view in Beauvoir is her acceptance of Merleau-Ponty's phenomenological understanding of the subject in the world. In her review of *The Phenomenology of Perception*, Beauvoir indicates that she embraces the view according to which our body is more than a mere object, it is our 'manner of being in the world, our "anchorage" in this world' (Beauvoir 2004b: 160). However, this anchorage is situated and embodied in a different way than what Sartre was offering: 'my consciousness finds itself "engorged by the sensible." It is not a pure for-itself, or to use Hegel's phrase, later used by Sartre, a hole in being, but rather "a hollow, a fold that has been made and can be unmade"' (Beauvoir 2004b: 163). She thus parts ways from Sartre's ontology. Sartre defines the for-itself as the being that is not what it is and is what it is not. The for-itself is a nothingness of being, a hole that may or may not be filled. As such, it retains its integrity; filled or not, it is a hole. For Beauvoir, however, the for-itself is a fold of being. The fold is truly ambiguous. It does not retain its integrity the same way the hole does. By implication, the fold is constituted by what it encloses in its fold. This is different from the hole that is like a potential container. Ontological authenticity for Beauvoir is to be the fold, that is, to be permeable and constantly shifting in one's own being (which is thus a becoming). This impacts the phenomenological/ethical concept of authenticity which allows for the relation to the Other to be reciprocal.

To be authentic is to be oneself as this being that transcends himself toward a project. The transcending is an unveiling and it is the exercise of freedom. Beauvoir explains that 'This means that in his vain attempt to be god, man makes himself exist as man, and if he is satisfied with this existence, he coincides exactly with himself' (Beauvoir 2004c: 293). Authenticity is defined as this coincidence with oneself which can only be achieved if one exists as the ambiguous being that one is. This means that the individual accepts to always be at a distance from oneself. 'In order to attain his truth, man must not try to dispel the ambiguity of his being but, on the contrary, accept to realize it. He rejoins himself only insofar as he consents to remain at a distance from himself' (ibid.).[11] To coincide with oneself is not to correspond to anything else but a flux, a transcending movement, a being that *is* not but that *exists*. This is very close to Sartre's dictum that one must be what one is not and not be what one is. To correspond to oneself in a static sense is to ossify and let oneself be entangled in the in-itself. Heidegger calls it inauthenticity, Sartre calls it bad faith, Beauvoir agrees that this is the opposite of authenticity. One must transcend oneself toward one's project of being.

However, mere transcendence is not authenticity either. Beauvoir explains that 'To exist authentically is not to deny the spontaneous movement of my transcendence but only to refuse to lose myself in it' (Beauvoir 2004c: 293). Indeed since, for Beauvoir, transcendence is transcendence through immanence. One can transcend only through a plunge into one's own immanence. As an embodied consciousness, the individual may transcend only as immanent. It is a transcendence in immanence, and not a transcendence of one's immanence.

Lundgren-Gothlin brings another perspective to bear on this. As she points out, Beauvoir does not consider the man who transcends himself by oppressing woman as an authentic being. 'One can thus be transcendent and oppress, this is exactly what men have done during history [as shown by Beauvoir in *The Second Sex*], but one is not then really authentic' (Lundgren-Gothlin 1994: 903). Thus, transcendence is a necessary condition for authenticity but not a sufficient one. Transcendence must occur in conjunction with the recognition and valuing of the freedom of the Other. *The Ethics of Ambiguity* reiterates the point about my dependence on the freedom of the Other:

> For a freedom wills itself as authentic only by willing itself as an indefinite movement through the freedom of the Other; as soon as it withdraws into itself, it denies itself on behalf of some object which it prefers to itself [...] the existence of the Other as a freedom defines my situation and is even the condition of my own freedom.
> (Beauvoir 1976: 90–1; translation altered)

As a situated being, I am fundamentally a being with-others as the Other exists in the world and, as a freedom that I recognize, shapes my situation.

The Other's shaping and conditioning of my situation is equivalent to a moulding of my very existence as a transcending being. I transcend myself on the basis of a situation that is made for me by the free Other. To deny the freedom of the Other is to deprive myself of the ground upon which I may transcend myself. To do so would mean a collapse of my transcendence in immanence which she deems to be absolute evil.

In *The Second Sex*, Beauvoir examines how the situation of woman has been affected by man's lack of recognition of her as a free subject. Woman has been relegated to the role of an inessential unfree Other. Beauvoir suggests in the introduction that, to a certain extent, it is the situation that disposes the individual to be authentic or to be in bad faith.[12] One may resist a situation that deprives one of the possibility of existing as free. Not only one may, but one *must*. Indeed, for

> Every time transcendence lapses into immanence, there is degradation of existence into 'in-itself', of freedom into facticity; this fall is a moral fault if the subject consents to it; if this fall is inflicted on the subject, it takes the form of frustration and oppression; in both cases it is an absolute evil.
>
> (Beauvoir 2009: 17)

This is not the first time that Beauvoir mentions absolute evil. In her essay 'An Eye for an Eye' from 1945, she defines absolute evil as the lack of recognition of freedom in an individual. If I oppress another, if I torture him, if I objectify him, I am committing an absolute evil. This idea recurs here in *The Second Sex*. According to Beauvoir, it is the duty of the individual to combat this evil and work toward the liberation of all oppressed individuals. In *The Second Sex*, the case is made for woman. She has been historically oppressed and deprived of her freedom. She has been unable to flourish authentically as a human being. It is necessary to change the situation that is made for woman so that she can flourish as the free unveiling and transcending being that she can be. However, woman is, just as much as man, attracted by the ease of bad faith. She thus often acts as an accomplice of her oppressor. Beauvoir thinks that the outcome for both man and woman continuing to live in what she calls 'the whole hypocritical system' (Beauvoir 2009: 782) is untenable. It leads to hatred of each other as each blames the other for one's own moral failure, what Beauvoir refers to as 'the striking failure of their own bad faith or their own cowardice' (Beauvoir 2009: 772). In any case, both man and woman are committing an absolute evil for 'in *both* cases [inflicted upon oneself or consented upon] it is an absolute evil' (Beauvoir 2009: 17). What Beauvoir calls for is a situation in which both man and woman can affirm themselves as the being they are, a situation in which both acknowledge the other as a free individual in a reciprocal relationship, a situation in which unveiling and transcending is possible for all. The stumbling block here is bad faith. As with Sartre, Beauvoir acknowledges that the temptation of bad faith is great and that the path of authenticity, even if greatly desirable for the flourishing of individuals, is more difficult and anguishing. Further, it is not clear whether the oppressor will give up his privileges in favour of the enjoyment of an authentic situation that will make him feel anguished. To engage in an elucidation of this problem is, however, well beyond the scope of this essay.

Conclusion: Beauvoir's contribution to Sartre's notion of conversion

The explanation for Sartre's conversion to the Other as contained in the *Notebooks for an Ethics* now lies before us. It is thanks to Beauvoir's emphasis on the human being as *Mitsein*, a notion he rejected at the time of *Being and Nothingness*, that Sartre came to understand the positive aspect of the for-itself's dependence on the Other. His take on it was negative in *Being and Nothingness*. It is still negative in *Anti-Semite and Jew*. However, starting with *What Is Literature?* and the *Notebooks for an Ethics*, he envisions positive mutual recognition among human beings. I don't think it is a coincidence that this shift in his thinking happens after the publication by Beauvoir of 'Pyrrhus and Cinéas' and *The Ethics of Ambiguity*. The way she combines Hegel's views on mutual recognition with Heidegger's notion of authentic *Mitsein* allows her to solve the problem of bad faith and to point to the possibility of escaping it. She shows that the ontology of *Being and Nothingness* does not need to be entirely rejected in order for authenticity to be possible. What is required is to rethink the for-itself, to move beyond conflict, convert oneself to freedom, subsume the desire to be God to freedom, and recognize oneself as a being with-others that depends on the freedom of others. All of this is consistent with the way the for-itself and its relation to the in-itself is defined in Sartre's treatise. Beauvoir provides the needed emphasis on the mutual recognition of freedom among being for-itself/with-others, thus allowing Sartre to devise his ethics of authenticity. If Beauvoir has taught Sartre about freedom, as Sonia Kruks has convincingly argued, it seems that she also taught him quite a lot about authenticity.[13]

Notes

1 'We may summarize our characterization of authentic Being-towards-death as we have projected it existentially: *anticipation reveals to Dasein its lostness in the they-self, and brings it face to face with the possibility of being itself, primarily unsupported by concernful solicitude, but of being itself, rather, in an impassioned freedom towards death – a freedom which has been released from the Illusions of the "they", and which is factical, certain of itself, and anxious* (Heidegger 1962: 311).

2 Granted, Heidegger himself and a good number of Heidegger scholars would reject this reading of *Being and Time*. Any reading of the book as entailing an ethics was rejected by Heidegger and his followers. I think, and am not alone in so thinking, that the ethical import of *Being and Time* is clear and that this, ultimately, is what makes of Heidegger also an existentialist and that this is true despite his insistence that he is an ontologist merely concerned with the question of being.

3 Admittedly, using 'good' and 'bad' to refer to the faith of the for-itself is just as bad a strategy.

4 The following studies are well worth considering in this regard: Santoni 1995; Perna 2003; Webber, this volume; in addition I recommend the exchange between Eshleman and Santoni in *Sartre Studies International* (2008).

5 In a note added to the recent French edition, which includes the previously unpublished first notebook, as yet untranslated into English, Arlette Elkaïm-Sartre explains that Sartre's knowledge of Heidegger is only very recent at the time he is writing his diaries (p. 30n1).

6 This is my own translation. The original text reads: 'L'authenticité est un devoir qui nous vient à la fois du dehors et du dedans parce que notre "dedans" est un dehors. Être authentique, c'est réaliser pleinement son être-en-situation, quelle que soit par ailleurs cette situation' (p. 224 in the latest edition). Note the use of 'duty' (*devoir*) in this instance. This suggests that there is some objective value to authenticity. We have to be authentic because there is an exigency to be such that is grounded in our being for-itself which is a being-in-situation.

7 Interestingly, Sartre proposes that being for-others is primordial and being with-others relies on it. This is different from Heidegger's approach which considers them as equiprimordial states for Dasein. As we will see, Beauvoir is closer to Heidegger on this point and emphasizes that our being with-others is as primordial as our being for-others.

8 In her essays on Beauvoir, Lundgren-Gothlin has argued that what distinguishes Beauvoir from Sartre is precisely her fuller understanding and use of the Hegelian master–slave dialectic as well as her appropriation of Heidegger, one that focuses on the *Mitsein* more than on the individual Dasein. See Lundgren-Gothlin 1994 and Gothlin 2002. In the former article, Lundgren-Gothlin explains that Beauvoir's use of the Marxist notion of labour also allows her to better understand the situation of the ethical individual.

9 Beauvoir might be more optimistic than Sartre with regards to interpersonal relations but she is not naïve either. She recognizes that there is a risk that one will be faced with non-reciprocation. If I open myself to the Other and offer my free being in hope of a free acknowledgement of my free being, I might face the objectifying look of the Other as a response, as in the relation of woman to man under patriarchal oppression for example. However, Beauvoir thinks that this is a risk we must take for once met with reciprocal recognition, our appeal can lead to authentic *Mitsein*.

10 My translation of 'L'authenticité pour Beauvoir signifie dévoiler le monde avec et pour les autres' (Gothlin 2002: 74, my emphasis).

11 For a slightly different formulation, see Beauvoir 1976: 13.

12 See the introduction to *The Second Sex*.

13 See her seminal article Kruks 1991, reprinted with some revisions as Kruks 1995.

2

IMAGINATION IN NON-REPRESENTATIONAL PAINTING

Andreas Elpidorou

I do not believe I understand the American 'expressionists' so very well. Many of these paintings ... I feel I do not understand at all. Often they look to me like silly smudges. And if a painting looks like a silly smudge, it is safe to conclude that you do not understand it.

(Jewell 1936; cited in Breslin 1998: 582)

Introduction

Sartre, to be sure, offers us no complete theory of art. For instance, one finds in his writings no set of criteria by which one can demarcate works of art from ordinary, everyday objects. Even though one can speculate about the ontology of the work of art, and perhaps do so in an informed manner, the ontology of the work of art does not seem to have been one of Sartre's priorities. Rather, his contribution to aesthetics lies elsewhere: namely, in his descriptive account of aesthetic experience. To be precise, his contribution is twofold. It is the account itself – the details of his description – but also the themes which unfold in it: freedom, situation, but above all, imagination.

The crux of Sartre's views on painting can be summarized with ease. The object of aesthetic appreciation, he declares, is not the set of material elements of the painting. It is, rather, the irreal content which consciousness forms once the materiality of the work of art is animated by an imagining consciousness. In a word, the awareness of the object of aesthetic appreciation is not perceptual but imaginative. But the ease by which we can summarize the main tenets of Sartre's position should not lead us to believe that Sartre's position is trivial. The truth is very much the opposite. Sartre's views on art are shaped by his phenomenological account of imagination, and the latter is a study of both great complexity and philosophical importance. In it, Sartre undertakes tasks that are perhaps too numerous to be listed here. *Inter alia*, he explicates the structure of imagination; elucidates what takes place when one looks at a painting, photograph, or a caricature and articulates what occurs when one watches a play or an impersonator; shows how imagination is both non-pictorial and distinct from perception; explains imagination's relation to freedom; clarifies the role of belief and feeling in imagination; speaks of pathologies and their relationship to imagination; and, as already announced, explains the role of imagination in aesthetics.

The aim of the essay is to demonstrate that Sartre's descriptive account of aesthetic experience can engage in a meaningful and fruitful conversation with non-representational painting. More specifically, it aims to show that the Sartrean account can bring forth and explain characteristics of non-representational paintings without either reducing or transforming them into works of art which are more adequately classified as belonging to different art movements.

The link between imagination and aesthetics determines the course of this essay, for only in the aftermath of an examination of imagination can one speak of Sartre's views on painting. The structure of the essay is as follows. The second section illustrates why, according to Sartre, imagination is both non-pictorial and distinct from perception. The third is devoted to an examination of painting and focuses primarily on three themes: the role of the canvas, the nature of the aesthetic object, and the relationship between the two. The fourth section, by using the late works of Mark Rothko as an example, demonstrates how the Sartrean account of aesthetics also applies to non-representational paintings. The significance of this application lies in the fact that for Sartre, the painting itself (a real, physical object) is never the object of aesthetic appreciation, a point which holds regardless of the artwork's genre. It is usually thought that non-representational works, in virtue of the fact that they lack recognizable content, refer to nothing, and point to nothing besides themselves. By demonstrating that Sartre's account applies to non-representational as well as to representational painting, the essay contests this conviction and argues that non-recognizability in content is not sufficient to show that the object of aesthetic appreciation must be a real, physical object.

Imagination: some preliminary remarks

Imagination, it is often said, is pictorial: to imagine something is to summon a picture. Many find this view problematic, erroneous, or perhaps even incomprehensible. Yet, even if this matter were somehow to be settled, the relationship between imagination and perception remains undetermined. Do imagination (pictorial or not) and perception involve the same kind of experience as a common element? Sartre's account of imagination speaks to both issues. Once I explicate the reasons why he rejects a pictorial account, I will then show how the structure of imagination is, according to Sartre, unlike that of perception.

In regards to the issue with which we opened this section, Sartre is clear. No pictures reside *in* consciousness, and consciousness is no reservoir of copies or imitations of reality (IPPI: 4–7, 15). When one imagines Pierre, for instance, it is not that one has a 'portrait of Pierre in consciousness' (IPPI: 6); nor is it the case that the object of one's consciousness is this portrait. Rather, to imagine Pierre is to have Pierre – 'the man of flesh and blood' – as the object of one's consciousness (ibid.). Whereas the pictorial account of imagination maintains that when one imagines, the imagined object is reached only indirectly, only due to its resemblance to the summoned picture, Sartre's account holds that 'Pierre is directly reached' (IPPI: 7). What we imagine, Sartre argues, is not a picture but an object. The object appears *as imagined*, and not as the image of something.

Sartre, of course, is not oblivious to the force and appeal of the pictorial account. He is aware both of its unparalleled philosophical backing, and of the fact that this account has become one with 'common sense' (IPPI: 6). Yet despite its pervasiveness, both in the philosophical and everyday realm, Sartre contends that this view ought to be rejected: it is, he deems, the by-product of a fundamental misunderstanding, an illusion in regards to the workings of our minds. Here an interpretative difficulty arises: since the pictorial account comes in many guises, one must conjecture about the exact nature of the account which Sartre is rejecting. Although this task is not one of pure speculation – for one can work backwards and extrapolate from Sartre's objections to the nature of the position criticized – some ambiguities are bound to remain. Minimally, however, the pictorial account must commit to the following three theses: first, mental images or pictures are individual entities; second, these pictures, just like physical portraits, need to be the objects of awareness – if not visual, then mental or inner awareness; third, only inner pictures are the objects of direct and unmediated awareness, external or transcendent objects are not.

Sartre considers and rejects all three theses. The individuality of mental images runs counter both to the 'synthetic structure' and to the transparency of consciousness (ibid.); the assumption that mental images are analogous to pictures or portraits is unjustified, for it assumes and does not demonstrate that 'the world of the mind' is constituted by 'objects very similar to those of the external world' (ibid.); and, finally, the employment of mental images fails to explain the imaginative relation that holds between the object imagined and the object depicted by the corresponding mental image. This final point deserves more attention, for, among other things, it allows us to gain insight into Sartre's account of imagination.

The pictorial account holds that mental pictures are the only objects of direct awareness. Thus, imagination is awareness of pictures and not of objects. Yet, if this is so, it is hard to see how the pictorial account can explain the relationship between the immanent portrait and the transcendent object. To hold, as the pictorial account does, that this relation is established because the picture resembles the object imagined, is deeply unsatisfactory. If nothing else, resemblance is not sufficient for reference (IPPI: 22, 25; see also Goodman 1976; Walton 1990). But how does Sartre circumvent this difficulty? He does so in a twofold manner: he first posits that imagination is always intentional; and, second, he maintains that intentionality, by its very nature, mandates an indissoluble relationship between consciousness and the transcendent object at which consciousness aims.

Taking our bearings from the intentional structure of consciousness, we quickly come to see that an imagined object, a chair, for example, cannot be *in* consciousness, '[n]ot even as an image' (IPPI: 7). Intentionality prohibits this from being the case: 'It is not a matter of an imitation chair that suddenly entered into consciousness and has only an "extrinsic" relation to the existing chair; it is a matter of a certain type of consciousness' (ibid.). An image, Sartre insists, is nothing but a relation. It is the relation of consciousness to its intentional object. The expression 'mental image' is thus interchangeable with 'imaging or imagining consciousness' and not with the expression 'immanent portrait'. Consequently, imagination is 'a certain way in which consciousness presents to itself an object' (ibid.). The imagining consciousness of Pierre, for instance, is not the consciousness of an image of Pierre. It is Pierre himself who one imagines. That is to say, when one imagines, one is attentive to a man and not to a picture. Properly understood then, a mental image is no picture. It is rather a relation to something wholly transcendent.

Imagination, for Sartre, is not pictorial. Yet, it is not akin to perceptual (non-pictorial) experience either. '[T]he image and the perception', he writes, 'far from being two elementary psychic factors of similar quality that simply enter into different combinations, represent the two great irreducible attitudes of consciousness' (IPPI: 120). The two, in fact, 'exclude one another', for where imagination is, perception is not (ibid.; see also 13–15, 126, 180–6; B&N: 282).

The distinguishing mark of imagination is this: in imagination, consciousness is always directed towards what is absent. In perception, by contrast, consciousness is directed towards what is present. This difference is telling, for it makes manifest that the nature of the object-as-perceived is heterogeneous with that of the object-as-imagined: whereas the former is real, the latter is irreal; and, whereas the former is always situated in relation to other perceived objects, the latter is not, for it inhabits an irreal context. The difference between the two is one in kind and not in degree: one is present and real; the other is absent and irreal (IPPI: 180, 125–36).

This absence which marks the object-as-imagined reflects an essential characteristic of imagination. The object-as-imagined stands in opposition to what is real: it exists only insofar as it denies the material world. An act of imagination can take different forms, but essentially it is always marked by negation (IPPI: 12, 181ff.). The irreal 'must always be constituted on the ground of the world that it denies' (IPPI: 186). Imagining consciousness, then, is at once annihilating and constituting: it denies the real and posits the irreal. Thus, to repeat what was earlier stated but left unjustified, imagination and perception exclude one another. To imagine Pierre means that we do not perceive Pierre.

But care must be taken here. We must not conflate the irreal character of the object-as-imagined with the real object at which the imagining consciousness aims. To say that the imagining consciousness presents us with a form of nothingness is not to refute the intentional character of imagination. The imagining consciousness is indeed consciousness of something. Just like perception, its intentional correlate is a real object. Unlike perception, however, 'the object as imagined is an irreality', for imagining consciousness makes present that which is absent (IPPI: 125; see also 18). Consider what goes on when one imagines Pierre. One's attention is directed at Pierre and not at a picture or representation of Pierre. The imagining consciousness aims at the real Pierre, the one 'who really lives in this real room in Paris' (IPPI: 126; see also 7, 18, 21, 125). Yet, Pierre-as-imagined is irreal, since 'in so far as he appears to me as imaged [he] … appears to me as absent' (IPPI: 180; see also 13, 24, 126).

The comparison between perception and imagination yields two further findings. First, the object-as-imagined is made manifest always as a creation: the image is the result of an act of spontaneity. Thus, unlike perception, imagination is always self-determining. It is for this reason that Sartre insists that imagination should not be understood as a secondary or derivative mode of consciousness. Indeed, he goes so far as to say that imagination is a 'transcendental condition of consciousness' (IPPI: 188). The ability to deny the object of perception and to posit in its place an irreality belongs to the essence of consciousness. To deny the object of perception is not to cease to be conscious; rather, it is to posit an irreality which arises out of its negation. This denial, Sartre writes, is constitutive of our freedom; it is essential to who we are. To be free or, what amounts to the same thing, to be a consciousness, is to be able to imagine.

One last characteristic of imagination must be mentioned. In contrast to perceptual observation, imagination is only 'quasi-observation' (IPPI: 10). That is, it is 'an observation that does not teach anything' (ibid.). We can never discover something new in imagination. 'An image', Sartre writes, 'is not learned', but instead, it is 'given whole, for what it is, in its appearance' (IPPI: 9). Contrary to the infinity of profiles that one discovers in a perceptual object, in imagination 'there is a kind of essential poverty' (ibid.; see also 10–11, 57, 84, 140). Imagination, unlike perception, cannot be a source of knowledge. We find in it only that which we have already placed there. Knowledge is a constitutive element of the irreal object: the irreal object is born out of that of which we are already aware. To repeat what we have learned so far: imagination is a conscious and spontaneous act by which the imagining subject quasi-observes an irreal object. With this in mind, we can now turn to Sartre's analysis of the work of art.

The object of aesthetic appreciation

The problem of the work of art, Sartre tells us, 'is strictly dependent on the question of the Imaginary' (IPPI: 188). With this, Sartre declares that it is imagination, and not perception, that reveals to us the object of aesthetic appreciation. The aesthetic object escapes realizing or perceptual consciousness. '[I]t cannot be given to perception', for it differs in kind from the objects of perception (IPPI: 189). Thus, in the case of painting, the painted canvas cannot be the aesthetic object. The canvas is a real object, where the object of aesthetic appreciation is not. But if the canvas is not itself the aesthetic object, then what is its function? According to Sartre, the canvas only has an 'intermediary' role (IPPI: 23). It serves as matter for the imagining consciousness, or, equivalently, as an analogon which enables an 'irreality [the aesthetic object] to be manifested' (IPPI: 189; see also 21).

The canvas exists in the physical world: it is often found in museums, hung on walls, transported from place to place, and occasionally vandalized or burnt. Yet, the canvas is not simply another physical object. It has been intentionally created or painted so as to allow, or even instigate, the awareness of an image. The aim of a painter, according to Sartre, is 'to construct a whole of *real* tones [a material analogon] that would enable [an] irreality to be manifested' (IPPI: 189). A portrait, for instance, acts as an 'invitation', not to perceive the portrait as a real thing, but rather, and through it, to direct our attention at the depicted person (IPPI: 22). '[T]he portrait [of Pierre]', Sartre writes, 'has a tendency to give itself as Pierre in person. The portrait acts upon us – almost – like Pierre in person' (ibid.). Note Sartre's qualification: it is *almost* as if Pierre is there in person. As with any object that appears as imagined, Pierre-as-imagined is an irreality and thus, appears to us as absent. Accordingly, the portrait of Pierre 'is nothing but a way for Pierre to appear to me as absent' (IPPI: 24). The portrait gives us Pierre, although Pierre is not here.

The real elements of any work of art – that is, its physical substratum: the canvas, the sculpture, the installation, etc. – are not themselves the appearing image. The work of art *qua* an object of perception appears to us, for instance, as rectangular, solid, viscous, or coloured. If the work of art appears as the portrait *of* Charles VIII, a depiction *of* haystacks, or the sculpture *of* Venus, it is only because the work of art has ceased to be a perceptual object. It 'is no longer a concrete object that provides me with perception', but instead a physical substratum which stands as the animated matter of an imagining consciousness (IPPI: 21; see also 50). In the case of the portrait of Charles VIII, when one confronts it, one ceases to be aware of the canvas (or better, the wood) and paint. Instead, through an act of imagining, one becomes aware of a human being. But as mentioned before, this does not mean that one is presented with Charles VIII in the flesh. Charles VIII bestows meaning to our imagining attitude: he is the object of our imagining consciousness. Yet, Charles VIII – the man and king – is not present, but only meant. What appears is an irreality, or, to be more precise, Charles-VIII-as-imaged. As Sartre puts it, 'the dead Charles VIII is there, present before us ... and yet we posit him as not being there: we have only reached him "as imaged", "by the intermediary" of the picture' (IPPI: 23).

Hence, phenomenology reveals that our aesthetic experience involves as many as three distinct objects: the physical or real object (for instance, the canvas); the object or subject depicted by the painting (a man, unicorn, field, etc.); and, finally, the irreal object (man-as-imagined, unicorn-as-imagined, etc.). The real object serves as the matter for the animating imagining consciousness or, in Sartre's words, as 'an analogon for the manifestation of the imaged object' (IPPI: 183). The depicted subject or object is the intentional correlate of the imagining consciousness, and it is that which makes a work of art *of* or *about* something. Finally, the irreal object, the imaged or imagined object, is the object of aesthetic appreciation.

The nature of the aesthetic object is thus peculiar: although it depends both on the material analogon and on the depicted object, it is reducible to neither. Furthermore, the aesthetic object appears only when 'consciousness, effecting a radical conversion that requires the nihilation of the world, constitutes itself as imaging' (IPPI: 184). Therefore, the appreciation of the work of art not only requires the distinction between its real and irreal parts, but also the negation or concealment of the real. Yet, this does not rob the materiality of the work of art of its significance. On the one hand, Sartre aligns himself with the commonsensical view that the materiality of a painting, for instance, is precisely that which makes it possible for us to imagine the content of a painting. On the other hand however, and as his discussion of the analogon reveals, the painting is not, as other accounts perhaps would have it, a passive physical object, awaiting to be animated by an imagining consciousness. Although the real elements of a painting are neutral, insofar as they 'can enter into a synthesis of imagination or of perception', they are '*expressive*' (IPPI: 22). It is Sartre's contention then that the matter of the painting solicits the spectator to animate it in order to 'make a *representation* of an absent or nonexistent object', that is, to make present, always as imagined, the depicted object (IPPI: 50). For example, a painting which has been intentionally 'made to resemble a human being, acts on me', says Sartre, 'as would a man' (IPPI: 22). It 'directly moves me', or it 'solicits me gently to take him as a man' (ibid.). The neutrality of the physical matter, therefore, does not mean indifference. 'Spontaneity of consciousness', Sartre writes, 'is strongly solicited' (IPPI: 50).

In light of the aforementioned discussion, one is tempted to interpret the relationship between the real and the irreal – or even between the realizing and the imagining consciousness – as that of cause and effect. That is to say, what effectuates the imagining consciousness, and as a consequence what brings into existence the aesthetic object, is the resemblance between the depiction and the object depicted. But Sartre's analysis precludes this possibility (IPPI: 21–2). Resemblance, he insists, cannot be the *cause* of an imagining consciousness, for it 'is not a force that tends to evoke [a] mental image' (IPPI: 22). He explains:

> Between two consciousnesses, the relation of cause and effect cannot hold. A consciousness is a synthesis through and through, thoroughly intimate with itself: it is at the heart of this synthetic interiority that it can join, by an act of retention or protention, with a preceding or succeeding consciousness. Moreover, for one consciousness to act on another consciousness, it must be retained and recreated by the consciousness on which it is to act … One consciousness is not the cause of another consciousness: it motivates it.
>
> (IPPI: 25–6)

Thus, the relationship between the perceptual and the realizing consciousness is not one of causation, but one of motivation. Strictly speaking then, the perception of the painting does not *cause* the spectator to imagine an object. Rather, once the spectator encounters the painting in the right way, she is motivated to take up an imagining attitude. Or alternatively, the appropriate experience of the work of art should, according to the structure of the imagination *and* of temporality (note Sartre's mention of retention and protention in the above citation), lead to an imagining experience, one in which something that is absent is made present.

The description of our aesthetic experience includes then the clause of encountering or confronting the work of art *in the right way*. But to what does this qualification amount? First, it should be obvious that the clause entails more than the requirement that the conditions of the environment should be such as to allow the (preferably, veridical) perception of the painting. It is undeniable that the work of art can function as an analogon, as matter for the imagining consciousness, only if one is aware of its presence. A painting in the dark solicits, instigates, or motivates no imagining consciousness. Rather, such conditions concern only the materiality of the work of art and not its irreality. As Sartre points out, to direct a spotlight on a painting is only to illuminate the canvas and not the object of aesthetic appreciation. It is, in other words, to light a piece of coloured material and not the '*cheek* of Charles VIII' (IPPI: 183). Yet, in addition to certain real conditions that need to be in place, the spectator must also have certain knowledge or at least certain beliefs about the content of the painting. If one does not know that the portrait of Charles VIII is a depiction of Charles VIII – the king of France and member of the House of Valois – one would then imagine only a man, and not the son of Louis XI who was responsible for invading Italy in 1494. Imagination, as stated above, is quasi-observation and consequently, it 'could not exist without a piece of knowledge that constitutes it' (IPPI: 57).

This is not to say, however, that the imagining synthesis which makes present the aesthetic object is only an intellectual matter – a matter of what we believe or know. One finds in imagination, in addition to beliefs, certain affectivity or feelings. Beliefs and feelings, in fact, constitute two moments and not two parts of the imagining structure (IPPI: 72, 92, 140; see also STE: 49). The imagining experience, in other words, comes with an emotional texture: the picture of a loved one provokes, for instance, a feeling of desire, and if the viewer is motivated to imagine the loved one, the irreality will be marked by this desire. The loved one as imagined appears as desirable. The same occurs, mutatis mutandis, for a painting, or a work of art in general.

Is this emotional texture already present in the analogon, or is it the result of an imagining consciousness? Sartre wants to have it both ways. First, if feelings are indeed constitutive of the aesthetic object, then the manner in which the analogon is constructed must be such that it immediately – namely, without the intervention of imagination – stimulates feelings and affective responses. Only in this way can feelings be constitutive of the imagining consciousness. Sartre concurs. Feelings 'are given with the analogon' and hence, to encounter the analogon is already to be aware of it as affecting (IPPI: 137). Feelings, he further notes, are 'so deeply incorporated with the perceived object that it is impossible to distinguish between what is felt and what is perceived' (IPPI: 139). Thus, part of what it is to be an analogon is to stimulate affective responses, and through these responses to motivate the spectator to effectuate an imagining synthesis. The forms and colours of a portrait of Pierre, for instance, are 'strongly organized' such that they 'almost impose themselves as an image of Pierre' (IPPI: 50). And the image of Pierre is one which already gives us Pierre as lovable, calming, or friendly. Or, consider what Sartre writes when he describes the aesthetic experience of looking at the portrait of Charles VIII: the 'sinuous and sensual lips, that narrow, stubborn forehead, directly provoke in me a certain affective impression' (IPPI: 23; emphasis mine). The canvas provokes affective impressions in the spectator, and it does so directly or immediately (see Kandinsky 1977 for strikingly similar claims). As soon as one looks at the portrait, one is already affected. Charles VIII 'is painted with intelligence, with power, with grace' (IPPI: 189). Thus, there is something in the way Charles VIII is depicted – not only the colours, shapes, or forms, but also the texture of the paint – that allows the spectator to imagine much more than the way Charles VIII looked. The affective impressions also allow the spectator to imagine the type of person he was: hateful, powerful, autarchic, despicable, etc.

But as Sartre writes, we should not fail to see that 'we are capable of a second-order reaction, love, hatred, admiration, etc., of the irreal object that we have constituted' (IPPI: 137). The order of dependence is bidirectional: not only do our feelings influence the irreal content, but also the irreal content may influence us, insofar as we are capable of reacting to it. Hence, the presence of the irreal object is not passive. It makes a difference to the imagining subject. Sartre writes: 'imaging feelings are violent and develop with force. In that case, they are not exhausted in constituting the object, they envelop it, dominate it and carry it along' (IPPI: 138). The feeling of disgust, for instance, might undergo 'a significant modification while passing through the imaging state': it might become 'concentrated', 'more precise', and more intense, to the extent that it can bring about nausea and even vomiting (IPPI: 139). Note that it brings about, but does not *cause* nausea. The two must be kept separate, for conduct in the face of the irreal is *sui generis* and hence entirely distinct from conduct in the face of the real. Sartre is adamant about this: the irreal object can never be a cause, but only an effect. The irreal object lacks any force and thus, 'does not act' (IPPI: 138). Whereas, for example, disgust in the face of the real is provoked by an object, disgust in the face of the irreal is not due to an object. Nausea and vomiting are not the effects of a repugnant irreal object. They are rather, the 'consequences of the free development of the imaging feeling' (IPPI: 138). This possibility of reacting to the already constituted irreality endows the aesthetic object with a second life. True, the way the analogon is constructed stimulates affective responses. This, however, sketches only an incomplete picture. We are also capable of reacting to the irreal object which was in part constituted by the affective responses stimulated by the analogon. In this way, we may bring forth additional responses: ones which could not be foreseen by the artist, but are nonetheless ultimately due to her creation.

Irreality and affectivity in Rothko

To conclude our examination here would run the risk of misleading ourselves, for, hitherto, the essay focused exclusively on works of representational art. To stop at this point would first suggest that resemblance is necessary – if not as a cause, at least as a motivation – for both the imagining consciousness and the aesthetic object; and, second, it would fail to take stock of the central role of affectivity in imagination. In a word, a failure to consider works that are abstract or non-representational would be unjust both to art and to Sartre.[1] In this section, I aim to rectify this. By using the late works of Mark Rothko as an example, I will show

how the Sartrean account of imagination also applies to works of non-representational art. In so doing, I will contest an understanding of non-representational art which maintains that the object of aesthetic appreciation cannot be an irreal object, but must be a real, physical object: the canvas itself.

The late works of Rothko cannot be mistaken. Typically they are described as being 'composed of luminous, soft edged rectangles arranged horizontally on large canvases' (Clearwater 2007: 6). These paintings are the culmination of an artistic path that, prior to reaching a state of pure abstraction, gave birth to expressionistic representational paintings (1920s and 1930s), mythologically inspired paintings (early 1940s), and finally surreal abstractions (end of 1940s). Rothko's later works lack figures, representational content, and images. When we look at these paintings, we see patches and areas of colours, perhaps even coloured columns, but no temples, peasants, objects, faces, or landscapes. One may then object that if a painting by Rothko is a work of art, it is not because the painting functions as an analogon to an irreal content. There is nothing recognizable that motivates our imagination to make present an absent, transcendent object. The work of art, instead, is entirely consumed by, or given in, perception. Thus, contra to the Sartrean analysis, an appreciation of a painting by Rothko does not require an imagining intervention.

This interpretative stance towards the works of Rothko and, at the same time, objection to Sartre's account, embodies the following line of reasoning: if non-representational paintings such as Rothko's lack recognizable content, and recognizable content is a precondition for the spectator to effectuate an imaginative synthesis, then non-representational paintings do not stand as matter that can be animated by an imagining consciousness. Consequently, we are faced with a choice: we can either dogmatically denounce all non-representational paintings as works of art; or, more prudently, we can maintain that imagination does not reveal to us, at least in non-representational works, the object of aesthetic appreciation.

The objection I wish to consider takes the latter path. It declares that the object of aesthetic appreciation is the canvas and not an irreal object which appears once we take up the imagining attitude. Such an outlook, however, relies upon at least three assumptions. The first two are present in the assertion that Rothko's paintings are examples of non-representational art. Rothko's later works are non-representational, this view holds, insofar as they include no recognizable content and insofar as the lack of such content is a sufficient condition for being a non-representational work of art. These assumptions are not without support. They enjoy the backing of many art critics and theorists who both affirm the absence of figures or any recognizable content in the later paintings of Rothko, and who categorize his works as abstract or non-representational (see, for instance, Rothko's interview with Seitz in Rothko and López-Remiro 2006: 75–9; for an exception, however, see Rosenblum 1975: 214). I shall take no issue with these two assumptions. They lie beyond the jurisdiction of this essay. I do, nonetheless, wish to contest a third assumption, one which is often taken to be a corollary of the first two. The assumption can be stated as follows: non-recognizability in content dictates that the object of aesthetic appreciation is a perceptual object. As a consequence, non-recognizability excludes an irreal content and rules imagination to be superfluous. What is expressed in this assumption is the view that works of non-representational art refer and point to nothing beyond themselves, and this feature is enough to preclude an imagining attitude.

Sartre's account, however, rejects this third assumption. The lack of recognizable content is not tantamount to the lack of an irreality. This is not because representation plays no role in art, but rather because the aesthetic object is an irreality born out of the beliefs *and* feelings of the imagining subject. In the case of works of art which are non-representational, it is the latter that take precedence. When the analogon no longer carries the force of resemblance, affectivity is the primary constitutive element of the aesthetic object. When knowledge fails to 'fill the gaps in intuition', affectivity takes control: it 'substitute[s] itself for the intuitive elements peculiar to perception in order to realize the object as imaged' (IPPI: 51, 29; see also 89). Affectivity, thus, does not require representation, and Sartre expresses this quite clearly. 'We are inclined at first to exaggerate the primacy of the representative', he writes. 'One affirms that there must always be a representation to provoke the feeling. Nothing is more false' (IPPI: 70).

Recall that the analogon is immediately affective. There is an affective reaction which needs no mediation, intellectual or imaginative. In the same way that in perception lines are not given to us first 'as lines pure and simple' and only afterwards, 'in the imaged attitude', become elements of representation, the same goes for affectivity (IPPI: 35). The analogon is 'entirely suffused by our affectivity' (IPPI: 141). Shapes, lines, or colours are given to us already 'with this or that affective quality' (ibid.). 'All perception', Sartre writes – and not only the perception of a familiar or recognizable content – 'is accompanied by an affective reaction' (IPPI: 28).

As soon as we realize that affectivity needs no representative content, the interpretative suggestion with which we began this section can be challenged. The painting can always stand as animated matter for an imagining consciousness. Non-representational content neither precludes affectivity, nor prohibits the emergence of irreality. Regardless of what the analogon depicts – or better, regardless of what it fails to depict – it can serve as the animating matter for an imagining consciousness. As Sartre puts it, '[w]hat motivates the appearance of the irreal is not necessarily, nor even most often, *the representative* intuition of the world from this or that point of view. ... [T]he surpassing [of the real] can and should be made at first by affectivity, or action' (IPPI: 185; see also 67).

Note that here, in addition to affectivity, Sartre adds action to the ways by which one can surpass the real. What Sartre means by action is awareness of action or, better, awareness of movement. As such, this addition does not oppose his own principle that the constitutive elements of irreality are knowledge and affectivity. This awareness of bodily movements, which 'can play the role of an analogon for imaging consciousness', is posited as the explanation for a number of phenomena that could not be accounted for either by the affective responses of the subject or by her beliefs (IPPI: 80). Sartre writes: 'This explains why we read so many things in an image whose matter is so poor. Actually, our knowledge is not directly realized on the lines that, by themselves, do not speak: it is realized via the movements' (IPPI: 34). The reason why the role of eye movements tends to be overlooked is because 'visual impressions prevail over the vague and feeble kinaesthetic impressions' (IPPI: 77). However, in pictures which are not perfect depictions, or on surfaces which have not been intentionally designed to depict something, the analogon is constituted by the spectator's awareness of her eye movements. Although one can extend this account to include works of non-representational art – 'action painting' being the obvious candidate – I will refrain from doing so. This extended application faces an obvious objection that demands an answer: the Sartrean account must show that subjects are in fact conscious of their eye movements when perceiving, for example, a Pollock. But most of the time, we are unaware of, and have no (conscious) control over, our eye movements. Be that as it may, the point of this section should be clear: even if a painting lacks representational content, its real elements can still be surpassed – if not by action or knowledge, then by affectivity.

To return to the paintings of Rothko, we need not discover in them figures that resemble objects already found in the world in order to take up an imagining attitude. Simply by perceiving his abstract forms, we are motivated to imagine; if not kings, goddesses, or fields, then objects with indeterminate visual properties but with specific emotional textures. Both imagination and feelings are, according to Sartre, intentional. Hence, if the affective character of a Rothko motivates us to take up the imagining attitude, then what is imagined must be an object beyond the canvas. Imagination always aims at a transcendent object, and if this does not appear in the imagining attitude as a person or a landscape, it will appear *as* something upsetting or calming, *as* something familiar or frightening, *as* something oppressive or liberating. In *No.10* (1950), for instance, the massive yellow coloured area, its position in the canvas, and the contrast between it and the coloured areas beneath it, can strike the spectator as unsettling, distressing, or irksome. One can then be motivated to imagine an unsettling, distressing, or irksome object, which, in virtue of our ability to react to an irreality, can further upset one or put one on edge. On the contrary, in *Untitled (Black on Gray)* (1969/70), not only are the colours much darker, but also the two areas are much closer in colour. This painting can invoke a sense of fatality or serenity, a feeling of fear or tranquillity.

The extent to which a Rothko can emotionally affect the viewer is documented in the visitor's book at the Rothko Chapel, which is replete with entries reporting the ways in which visitors were emotionally moved and, in some cases, even brought to tears by the paintings (for a related discussion, see Elkins 2001). Such descriptions of our aesthetic experience show that the perception of abstract forms, by being affective, gives rise to imagined objects – objects which can, through a second-order reaction, affect us even further. In other words, the painting which envelops the viewer, invokes both images and emotions.[2]

Conclusion: signification in non-representational painting

I will conclude by raising an interpretative suggestion, inspired by Sartre's account, in regards to non-representational painting. The demarcation of non-representational from representational paintings is frequently, but not always, based on the following criterion: non-representational works of art refer or point to nothing beyond themselves. Failure to refer and signify is thus the distinguishing mark of non-representational painting. Consider the following passages, which are indicative of this view:

> When we consider what makes abstract painting different from representational painting, it is clear that abstract painting, precisely by virtue of being non-representational, is exclusively a matter of the placement of paint on a surface. It is abstract precisely because there is no content, it points to nothing beyond or outside itself.
> (Jacquette 2006: 56–7)

> Any work of abstract expressionism will suffice to illustrate painting containing only immanent values of expression ... The abstraction means nothing; the portrait 'means' its subject. What is the ideal entity defining the abstract expressionist painting, which exists only in one copy which refers to nothing beyond itself? Only a theoretician deluded by his own theory will find one.
> (Kaelin 1982: 84; compare Wollheim 1987: Ch. 2;
> Goodman 1978: Ch. 4)

It seems premature, to say the least, to talk of theoretical delusions. How obvious is it that recognizable content is a precondition for reference to a transcendent object? Or better, according to which theory of aesthetic appreciation is non-recognizability in content one and the same with the fact that an abstract creation means or refers to nothing? There are places where Sartre speaks *as if* he shares this view. A non-representational painting, he writes, 'need not *represent* or *imitate* the real', and it can be 'altogether devoid of signification' (IPPI: 190). The same sentiment is repeated elsewhere: Calder's mobiles, he writes, 'signify nothing, refer to nothing other than themselves' (CM: 355). Yet Sartre insists that it would be a 'grave error' to conclude that the work of art is a real object (IPPI: 190). Representational or not, 'painting', Sartre tells us, 'still functions as an *analogon*' (ibid.). But here one feels a tension. How can a painting be devoid of signification and still act as an analogon? Isn't an analogon that which allows consciousness to make present something which is absent?

Sartre's discussion of the differences between a sign and a portrait helps to alleviate the difficulty (IPPI: 21ff.). There, Sartre argues that a portrait is not a sign, since the latter is related to its object only externally. A sign merely points to its object, whereas a portrait makes its object present. A word, for instance, 'awakens a signification, and that signification never returns to it but goes to the thing and drops the word' (IPPI: 23). This, however, does not hold true for a portrait, or, for that matter, for any painting. In the case of a portrait, we continuously observe it, and in so doing our imagining consciousness is 'constantly enriched' (ibid.). 'Intentionality', Sartre writes, 'constantly returns to the image-portrait' (ibid.). Thus, the painting can be devoid of signification, but it is so only in virtue of the fact that it is not a sign: only due to the fact that it does not point to, but rather presents, an object. If this is indeed what Sartre means when he writes that a painting can be 'altogether devoid of signification', then most paintings are devoid of signification (IPPI: 190–1). Regardless of its genre, a painting has been intentionally constructed in such a manner as to motivate us to take up an imagining attitude, and not to direct our perceptual attention to something else. A painting is neither a sign nor an 'identity card' (UP: 552). Instead, it is an instigator of an imagining synthesis.

Consequently, what distinguishes non-representational from representational paintings should not be the fact that only the latter are other-referring. The difference, according to Sartre, lies elsewhere. The distinguishing mark of non-representational painting is that, in contrast to representational painting, it invokes, through the imagination, irreal objects which have never been seen before: 'objects that do not exist *in the painting*, nor anywhere in the world, but that are manifested through the canvas and that have seized it by a kind of possession' (IPPI: 190–1). Here, one should not find recourse to the idea that these new objects are compilations of things already existing in the world, but put together in such a way as to give rise to a new entity. Although such a route might seem tempting, for it is in agreement with Sartre's conviction that imagination is always quasi-observation, conglomerations of existing objects, regardless how novel and creative they are, are unlikely to be the aesthetic objects of non-representational art. As highlighted above, it is affectivity and not knowledge (or belief) which primarily constitutes the aesthetic object in works of non-representational art. As such, there seems to be no difficulty in accepting that a Rothko – or in fact, any non-representational painting – motivates us to give rise to a novel irreal object: an object, which unlike a physical object, has no specific visual determinations, but nonetheless possesses a specific emotional texture. Or, what amounts to the same thing, a Rothko motivates us to give rise to an object which, as Sartre requires, resides neither in the painting nor anywhere in the world.[3]

Notes

1 For present purposes, the terms 'non-representational' and 'abstract' are treated as synonymous. Abstract works of art are taken to be works which are not mimetic representations of reality, and their aesthetic value is not (at least, not solely) a function of their representational ability.

2 Incidentally, the view that the canvas is not merely a perceptual object is also shared by Rothko. 'The most interesting painting is one that expresses more of what one thinks than of what one sees' (cited in Breslin 1998: 261). Or consider what he says when he describes his own intentions as an artist: 'I'm interested only in expressing basic human emotion – tragedy, ecstasy, doom and so on.... And if you, as you say, are moved only by their color relationships, then you miss the point' (cited in Clearwater 2007: 114). For a more detailed description of Rothko's self-interpretation, see Rothko 2004; Rothko and López-Reniro 2006.

3 I am indebted to Jonathan Webber for commenting extensively on a previous instantiation of this essay. His support and comments have been invaluable. I am also grateful to Lauren Freeman, whose numerous suggestions and criticisms have greatly improved this essay.

3

WHAT IS IT LIKE TO BE FREE?

Matthew C. Eshleman

This essay proposes that some of the reasons which render 'What is it like to be X?' kinds of questions recalcitrant to scientific naturalism lie at the heart of widespread vexations over 'free will' but that phenomenology provides a unique method with which to address this matter. Others also share this intuition. In the conclusion to his rightly famous essay 'What Is It Like To Be A Bat?', Thomas Nagel calls for an 'objective phenomenology'. Galen Strawson argues that anyone interested in free will 'must be concerned with the cognitive phenomenology of freedom' (1995: 29). While one frequently finds casual use of the word 'phenomenology' in recent discussions of free will, only a few serious efforts employ the term (Holton 2009; Nahmias et al. 2004), yet these do so in a way hardly recognizable to the tradition established by Edmund Husserl. Of those serious efforts, one of them finds 'surprisingly few' sustained phenomenological treatments in this field of inquiry (Nahmias et al. 2004: 164), only mentioning Alexander Pfänder's *The Phenomenology of Willing and Motivation*, but entirely overlooking the works of Martin Heidegger, Maurice Merleau-Ponty, Paul Ricoeur, Emmanuel Levinas, and Max Scheler in this area. While Jean-Paul Sartre's early phenomenological ontology may seem an implausible candidate to address this perceived lack, I will argue that the spirit of *Being and Nothingness* (but not always its letter) offers largely unappreciated yet helpful phenomenological resources with which to approach the question 'What is it like to be free?'

By 'phenomenology' it will here be meant a first-person reflective method at least recognizable, if not agreeable, to Husserl, who would have recognized and likely agreed with Sartre's method only in his earliest philosophical works, up to but not including *Being and Nothingness* where Sartre employs a hybridized version of phenomenology tied to ontology. Sartre here frequently arrives at ontological claims (that Husserl was at pains to avoid) via transcendental arguments based on phenomenological descriptions (which Husserl would sometimes have endorsed). These arguments begin with a phenomenologically rigorous description of various features of consciousness, like its abilities to imagine (IPPI: 179), raise indeterminate questions (B&N: 47), form negative judgements (B&N: 51), and deceive itself (B&N: 69), and then work in reverse (regressively) to derive the necessary conditions required by the truth of those descriptions. In three important instances Sartre offers variations of this transcendental argument, which concludes that consciousness cannot be wholly determined (by being in the mode of in-itself) and consequently cannot be necessitated by any factual states of affairs. The first and most elaborated instance of this argument occurs in the conclusion of Sartre's most extensive work on imagination (IPPI: 179–88), the second is a rather fragmented version (B&N: 45–58), and the last instance (that I know of) draws out its concrete implications (B&N: 457–8). One finds frequent mention of one or more of these arguments in the secondary literature (e.g. Detmer 1986: 25–6, 2008: 66), but with few extended treatments, which is surprising, since these arguments play a fundamental role in Sartre's early ontology.[1] Unfortunately, this will not change here, for the following three reasons which, along the way, offer a few preliminary remarks on Sartre's analyses of causation, explain why this essay judiciously avoids them, and then sketch the two separate but related problems concerning freedom (randomness and luck) that provide this essay's central focus.

Sartre's argument against determinism

First, all three instances of Sartre's transcendental argument against determinism conclude only what must not be the case in order that consciousness be able to perform some task, namely that consciousness cannot be (wholly) determined by one kind of causation. Hence, these arguments establish only a necessary condition for a positive account of human freedom.[2] Put another way, these arguments deny that determinism (traditionally construed) provides a sufficient set of conditions with which to explain all of human experience. Whether Sartre maintains that all modes of determinism are false turns out to be a complicated question, addressed briefly below. However, even if Sartre's transcendental arguments against (or setting limits to) deterministic causation succeed, this alone does not amount to a coherent view of freedom, as Morriston (1977) notes. Even if some form of indeterminism is true, or if causation involves mixed modes, or something entirely else, the question of whether a coherent account of human freedom can be given remains. Suffice it to say, prominent features of Sartre's positive account of freedom run largely along phenomenological lines. This essay develops several of these features, elaborated below.

Second, although many assume 'that in *Being and Nothingness* Sartre rejected any and all forms of causal determinism' (Morriston 1977: 236), this common assumption stands, minimally, in need of qualification. Sartre's analysis of causation exhibits a great deal of textual ambiguity, and, perhaps, necessarily so, given his ontological commitments. For instance, while Sartre denies that the mode of being-in-itself wholly determines human reality, though such causal forces can and do affect it, he sometimes *seems* to accept 'determinism', but only as applied to inanimate, non-conscious modes of being (B&N: 54–5). He claims that 'mechanistic determinism' can explain certain phenomena (B&N: 136), but he also claims that embodied consciousness (that exists in the mode of being for-itself) experiences 'a permanent rupture in determinism' (B&N: 57). This latter claim *suggests* a commitment to causal determinism that consciousness somehow breaks with. Putting matters this way may seem to hamstring Sartre with something like substance dualism conjoined to a mysterious yet largely unexplained view of causal interaction. On this reading, determinism holds true with regard to material reality but is false when it comes to mental reality. Call this the 'two-realms' reading. Although commentators sometimes read Sartre in this two-realms way, which leads them to interpret his view of freedom as robustly Cartesian (Marcuse 1983; Campbell 1977) and somehow entirely unlimited by anything other than itself (Kruks 1991), this reading misunderstands Sartre's notion of limit (as we will see) and it fails to capture important subtleties in Sartre's ontology.

Sartre almost never talks about different *types* or *kinds* of being but almost always in terms of *modes* of being (see Gardner 2009: 69). Hence, his use of the phrases 'being-for-itself' and 'being-in-itself' or their abbreviated versions 'for-itself' and 'in-itself' should be read as shorthand for the complete phrases 'the mode of being in-itself' (MBII) and 'the mode of being for-itself' (MBFI). In Sartre's considered view, the universe contains only one *kind* of being that can be divided into different modal categories. When understood in this way, Sartre subscribes to a version of substance monism (materialism) conjoined with a modal pluralism (in a way perhaps distantly influenced by Spinoza). Or, to put this matter in terms of contemporary philosophy of mind, Sartre holds something like property dualism, which shares features of the different versions of dualism discussed by David Chalmers (2003), although Sartre's view does not easily fit into any one of Chalmers' alphabetical categories. Consequently, Sartre's modal pluralism could extend to questions concerning causation. Sartre could accept elements from both determinism and indeterminism, or accept various degrees of indeterminism, or his work could motivate an altogether different alternative. In the end, insufficient and ambiguous textual evidence should discourage any quick answer to Sartre's views on causation. Hence, in a limited space, avoiding extended meditation on Sartre's analysis of causation (including modal interaction) proves to be the most cautious and economical route.

Third, while Sartre addresses a central problem in debates over 'free will' that traditionally arises in light of causal considerations, important features of his proposed solution do not make direct reference to causal matters, nor perhaps should they. Sartre, nonetheless, sometimes discusses this problem in causal terms. He argues, on the one hand, that if human experience was strictly causally determined, by which he means that if the sum set of material facts (including the laws of nature) were such that, given those facts, one and only one future were possible, then humans could not be free. Neither would they be able to imagine, ask questions, give reasons, or value things. Sartre, however, also recognizes that at least certain forms of indeterminism render actions random and hence, must also be avoided (B&N: 422–3, 474). Nevertheless, Sartre maintains that one necessary condition for a positive account of freedom requires that an action is free if and only if one could have unconditionally done otherwise (B&N: 476), where by 'unconditional' it shall be meant that an agent's future stands unconditioned by her past, insofar as identical agential pasts can issue different futures.[3] Thus, Sartre self-consciously confronts a long-standing problem traditionally associated with libertarianism (the view that determinism and free will are incompatible, but that humans are free and determinism is false).

The problem of randomness

One well-known version of the problem goes like this: on the assumption that freedom requires choosing amongst unconditional alternative possibilities, and since determinism makes room for only conditional possibilities, determinism is incompatible with genuine freedom. However, any appeal to indeterminism provides no help, for even if it 'makes room' for unconditional alternative possibilities, actions resulting from indeterministic processes must be random. After all, if an identical state of affairs can issue different futures, then nothing about that state of affairs seems to explain why one future rather than any other comes about; such different futures seem random. Indeterministic processes, then, undercut even the most minimal requirements for agent-control, for it looks as if the reported ability to unconditionally do otherwise entails that what one does comes about randomly or as a matter of chance.[4] In short, the commitment to unconditioned, but not chancy, alternative possibilities seems incompatible with both determinism (which rules out unconditional possibilities) and indeterminism (which allows for unconditional possibilities but admits only random ones). Those who believe that these two options (determined and random) 'exhaust the field of options' find this kind of argument decisive (Strawson 1995: 13). This essay argues that Sartre (in spirit) hews a (third) way in between necessity (determinism) and randomness (indeterminism) with a phenomenological account of how unconditional alternative possibilities can be non-random. What follows sketches two primary features that compose Sartre's solution, and indicates why a second problem remains.

First, negatively, problems concerning freedom (in general) and the problem of randomness (in particular) frequently result from methods that employ a third-person viewpoint (adopting or ascertaining the mode of being-for-others) on an *essentially* first-person experience (that exists in the mode of being-for-itself). By an essentially first-person experience, Sartre means an experience (a) necessarily dependent upon our awareness of it, which (b) cannot be directly apprehended (intuited) by other observers. Thus, first-person experience is unlike many *objects* of experience, which exist independently of our awareness of them and can be straightforwardly examined by multiple observers, like material objects large enough to perceive through the senses. For unlike objects that exist independently of our awareness of them, first-person conscious experience depends upon self-awareness. Otherwise put, conscious experience is intrinsically self-conscious (B&N: 6–10). For this reason, first-person experience includes but is not limited to an intrinsic awareness of 'what it is like' to be such-and-such a being (say a 'free-willer') or what it is like to apprehend such-and-such a quality of an object (like colour), but experience itself cannot be parsed off from our awareness of it. If one will allow such a turn of phrase, unlike the (mode of) being of objects like trees and chairs that exist independently of anyone's awareness of them, the (mode of) being of conscious experience is self-awareness. In Sartre's words, consciousness is 'a "phenomenon" in the highly particular sense in which "to be" and "to appear" are one and the same' (TE: 8, see also 36).

Sartre argues that the intrinsic self-awareness of 'what it's like to be … ' built into first-person experience remains tacit and pre-cognitive. Our first-person experience takes as its primary focus the practical world and remains only implicitly aware of itself as related to the world. In a (secondary) reflective act of consciousness, one can redirect (pre-reflective) consciousness from the world and reflect upon conscious experience itself. In this way, one can try to make explicit our implicit awareness of what it is like to be such and such a being or have such and such an experience. Sartre's enterprise in *Being and Nothingness*, which draws on what Husserl called a reflective science, is well understood, then, as an extended effort to make our implicit awareness of what it is like to be free explicit, through a careful reflective phenomenological study. Problematically, Sartre repeatedly insists, when we reflect upon our own first-person experience, we tend to treat it as if it were an *object* independent of our awareness of it and, hence, we tend to treat it in similar fashion to objects that exist in the mode of being-in-itself. Consequently, we sometimes inappropriately attribute qualities to first-person experience itself that apply only to objects independent of experience, a problem that returns below.

This does not mean that the *eidos* of first-person experience cannot be described in objective terms, only that the method employed to arrive at objectivity will not look like that of natural science. The reason for this is, in part, that natural science requires of its objects of inquiry that they exist independently of any particular observer. Hence, they can be observed by

multiple observers, and in a way that allows for straightforward intersubjective correlation. Thus, essentially first-person experience itself cannot
be studied in the same way as objects of natural science, since other people
cannot, as it were, apprehend my experience itself as I experience it.
Perhaps for this reason natural science does very well when it *explains*
objects (or qualities of objects) of sensory perception like colour (in terms
of wavelength and frequency etc.) but it does not do very well when it
comes to *understanding* our experience of colour, which is not, strictly
speaking, experienced as either a wave or a particle. While this puts matters
rather vaguely, suffice it to say that attempts to describe and analyse essentially first-person experience from a third-person viewpoint would not be
problematic, were it not for the proposed hypothesis that such attempts
tend to result in several errors. An instance or two of these errors will be
discussed in the following section on viewpoints.

Second, Sartre's positive solution to the problem of randomness involves
carefully distinguishing between 'possibility' and 'probability' (on the one
hand) and 'randomness' and 'order' (on the other) and parsing off questions
concerning justification from those of randomness. Sartre, in spirit, argues
that randomness does not apply to individual actions, but only to groups of
actions and to life taken as a whole. Randomness, then, equates to patternlessness.[5] Agents, however (at least sane ones), cannot but apprehend
the practical world as ordered (B&N: 333) and they very rarely act in pat-
ternless ways, at least not for any sustained period of time. If correct, to
designate any particular action as 'random' involves a category error. An
individual action may be said to be justified or unjustified, rationally
explicable or not, but a single action cannot be random. Thus, in Sartre's
considered view, actions can be unjustified (in a sense importantly qualified
below) but non-random. So understood, freedom (in part) involves a
perpetual organization of contingent, multiple possible alternatives into a
particular form or way of life. Since different organizational forms are
always possible, and organizational forms themselves admit of variations
in content, freedom exhibits itself as an ever-present possibility of either
rearranging the content in one's form of life or of transforming one's form
of life itself, albeit not without great difficulty (B&N: 476) and, hence,
becoming a significantly different person (B&N: 486). Yet, Sartre argues, we
can find no *ultimate* justification for becoming one person as opposed to
another (B&N: 62).

The problem of luck

This Sartrean solution to the problem of randomness, however, encounters
another more serious and closely related problem that should not be confused with questions concerning randomness. If agents confront multiple
possible ways of organizing life, and if those possible organizations stand

unconditioned by the past, then how can an agent's motives and reasons to act explain or justify why that agent chooses one form of life over any other? If two identical agents (with identical motives and reasons) act differently, then it seems as if those reasons and motives cannot explain different outcomes. Although commentators conclude that such 'choices' would be a matter of 'dumb luck' or chance, a better way to put this (so as not to conflate this issue with randomness) is to say that it seems impossible for Sartre (or anyone, for that matter, committed to robust unconditioned alternative possibilities) to give an 'explanatorily apt connection between the agent's prior reasons and the intentional behaviour to be explained' (Haji 2005: 322). So understood, the problem of action explanation differs in at least one important way from the problem of randomness.[6] Unlike the concept 'randomness' that does not apply to individual actions, the request for an explanation of individual actions seems appropriate. Consequently, the problem of action explanation cannot be so easily sidestepped, as it were, by arguing that it results from a category error. Sartre's approach to action explanation shall be addressed below, after a few schematic remarks on viewpoints and how one especially pervasive kind of thought experiment necessitates a third-person point of view.

Viewpoints

As frequently noted, different subjects give different reports on various features of 'free will' experience like self-control, alternative possibilities, and reason-giving (Nahmias et al. 2004). Consequently, different studies in experimental psychology generate mixed results as to whether experience evidences libertarian or compatibilist theories. While different subjects provide different introspective reports, often framed by an experimental psychologist's questions, phenomenology does not amount to what, during the early rise of experimental psychology, was labelled 'introspection', a form of data-collection initially eliminated from the field as unreliable, though currently making something of a comeback.[7] And traditional phenomenology neither does nor should make *primary* use of reports on 'what ordinary people's experiences are like'. Nahmias et al. turn to the experience of ordinary persons, because they believe that such reports are less theoretically biased than those provided by philosophers (2004: 172). They fail, however, to mention Husserl, who (in my view) correctly argued that certain pre-theoretical biases are built into ordinary perception or what he called 'the natural attitude'. Consequently, the problem of theoretical bias originates in pre-theoretical experience and slips into our theoretical considerations, for which ordinary reports must be approached cautiously.

A complete account of Sartre's efforts to overcome corrupting biases would require a technical explication not only of Husserl's notions of 'the natural attitude' and 'the phenomenological reductions' but also of how

Sartre transposes the natural attitude into bad faith and how he tacitly replaces features of Husserl's phenomenological reductions with purifying reflection. This cannot be done here. Suffice it to say, an acute sensitivity to the different viewpoints one can take upon one's own experience lies at the heart of Sartre's diagnosis for why different people report on 'free will' experiences differently, and why some of these reports generate various theoretical conundrums. The upshot of Sartre's error theory comes down to this. Sometimes when we try to purchase an objective understanding of ourselves, we reflect upon our experience from what amounts to a (pseudo) third-person viewpoint. One attempts to detach and stand back from oneself, as it were, and view oneself as if from the outside, as if from the viewpoint of someone else. Otherwise put, we attempt to view ourselves as others would view us or as we view others. Consequently, we treat our first-person experience as if it were an *object* of inquiry independent of our awareness of it and, in so doing, we sometimes describe features of first-person experience in terms of qualities predicable of only mind-independent objects. Put plainly, we tend to view persons (either ourselves or others) as patients, or more frequently as quasi-patients, instead of as agents (B&N: 66).

To state this matter in an initially rough way, Sartre notes that when reflecting upon oneself as a patient, as a physical thing impacted by other physical things, the future can appear determined, insofar as it can seem completely out of my control, or only conditionally within my control. Whereas, from an *undistorted* agential point of view, the future appears composed of an undetermined and indeterminate (ambiguous) set of non-existent possibilities, out of which one must freely carve an organized form of life. Sartre first sketches these two viewpoints when he describes a man walking along a precipice (B&N: 54–6). The fact that a strong wind could propel him off of the edge, contrary to anything he might intentionally do, motivates a certain form of self-reflection that results in fear. In this case, 'I am given to myself as a thing; I am passive in relationship to these possibilities' (B&N: 54). Since fear results from an inability to prevent (undesirable) events, I can momentarily combat fear by reflecting upon matters within my control. Should I pay closer attention to the twists and turns ahead, or sit down and smoke to calm my nerves, or twist round precariously to pull a map from my satchel? In so viewing myself as an agent, as opposed to a patient, Sartre argues that I escape fear 'by the very fact that I am placing myself on the plane where my own *possibilities* are substituted for the transcendent *probabilities* where human action has no place' (B&N: 54, emphasis added). One's focus on possibilities temporarily eclipses fear, because the agential point of view precludes experiencing oneself passively, as only acted upon, and, hence, probabilistically. To be sure, Sartre's alignment of probability with absence of control and possibility with control, and his supposition that the two stand in some kind of mutually exclusive relationship, initially seems idiosyncratic.

Sartre, however, uses these terms in an importantly qualified sense. While probabilities must be possible in the logical sense of possibility, existential possibilities cannot be equated with or reduced to logical possibilities (B&N: 121). Existential possibilities apply only to phenomena dependent upon conscious experience, insofar as we actively constitute existential possibilities in a way similar to imagination but unlike passive features of sense perception. Put another way, unlike perceptual objects that appear as they do independently of what we 'will', we can freely vary existential possibilities ideationally. Consequently, the active constitution of possibilities necessarily reveals to us their contraries, insofar as our tacit awareness of any possible action reveals the possibility of not doing it or doing something else, though we frequently ignore or distract ourselves from these alternatives (B&N: 65). Thus, for a future action to be existentially possible, I must *be able to* imagine myself as able but not necessarily having to exercise it through a future action. Since I cannot imagine many features of who I am (B&N: 497) or of my situation (B&N: 456–7, 543) as being otherwise than they are, many logically possible actions are (currently) practically impossible and, hence, existentially null.

In sharp contrast, according to Sartre, probabilities apply only to objects that exist independently of our experience, that is, to phenomena grasped in the mode of being-in-itself or the mode of being-for-others (B&N: 219–20). Otherwise put, probabilistic happenings are not, strictly speaking, actively constituted or exercised. Rather, they are passively discovered or disclosed (ibid.). Since they happen outside of our direct control, one does not decide upon probabilities; rather, one calculates and predicts them. For these reasons, events describable as probable are not (strictly speaking) existentially possible and probabilities do not characterize essentially first-person experience of making possible choices, when examined from a first-person viewpoint. According to Sartre, when we speak probabilistically about human behaviours (either our own or those of others) we necessarily adopt something like a third-person perspective. Sartre does not deny that we sometimes think about behaviours in probabilistic terms, or suggest that there is nothing to be gained from so doing, but he adds that our probabilistic considerations require viewing people as patients, passively impacted by various forces, as opposed to agents. Thus, while we can and do talk about human behaviours probabilistically, say, as sociologists, we should not suppose that a viewpoint that regards human behaviours probabilistically can correctly account for free agency.

To begin to appreciate this point, suppose that on Tuesday afternoon I predict my chances of going to a party Saturday night as quite low (say 2 in 7). I have to finish this essay, grade exams and, in the past, I would skip parties under similar circumstances. I end up going to the party all the same. How should this be explained? Is this a mistaken prediction or a change of mind? The answer depends on whether I think about myself from the perspective of an agent or a patient. As a patient, I try to see myself as you see me, as an object independent of myself that can be examined from multiple perspectives. My prediction shares the same status as anyone else's prediction about my behaviour, though I may have different data than external observers. When viewed in this probabilistic way, my logically possible behaviours seem conditional. I could have behaved otherwise had I had different motivations and reasons or had there been different circumstances. If I do not behave as predicted, what can this mean except that new factors arose, that some initial factors escaped consideration, or that a miscalculation occurred. From this third-person viewpoint, my going to the party falsifies my earlier prediction. However, from a first-person agential perspective, I changed my mind about a previous future intention and it frequently seems to me possible to decide otherwise and go against my past predictions, decisions, and intentions. Once more, my uncertainty in making decisions (say early Saturday evening) is essentially different than the kind of uncertainty present when making predictions. My indecision over what to do can arise in different ways but, as argued below, it fundamentally results from a basic failure in justification. I have no ultimate normative grounds upon which to act (B&N: 62, 647). So understood, the uncertainty that arises when predicting behaviour essentially lacks features present during our indecision over what to do. A lack of knowledge and information causes uncertainty when making predictions; whereas uncertainty and, hence, indecision over what to do (sometimes) results from an absence of a basic kind of justificatory grounds.

This discussion has very schematically outlined a dual aspect (as opposed to a two-realms) reading of *Being and Nothingness*. Rather than considering MBII and MBFI as two different kinds of being, we should understand them as two different modes of a single kind of being, where different modes can be viewed from different standpoints. When understood in this way, Sartre's work suggests how some of our vexation over freedom arises from apparently incompatible reports generated by these different points of view. It also suggests how Sartre might account for compatibilist and libertarian reports on 'free-will' experience. The suggestion here, and it is only a suggestion, is that compatibilists *incline* towards third-person views of persons as patients, or quasi-patients, and consequently tend to offer conditional accounts of alternative possibilities; whereas, libertarians *incline* towards first-person views of persons as agents and tend (or used to tend) to offer unconditional accounts of alternative possibilities. These can only be inclinations, since libertarians frequently deploy standard thought experiments that require third-person viewpoints. It will here be suggested that many of our troubles begin with these kinds of thought experiments, since they necessitate third-person viewpoints on experiences that can only be adequately understood from a first-person standpoint.

The temporal rewind thought experiment and randomness

One finds many instances and variations of the following thought experiment in the secondary literature, but they all exhibit the same structural homology. These thought experiments ask us to imagine either identical agents in identical worlds or the exact same agent confronting an identical world numerous times. One challenge, then, is this: if actual agents confront genuinely unconditioned alternative possibilities, then we have to account for how imaginary identical agent-situations can issue different choices and actions. While our account must be both coherent and square with intuitions about making free choices, giving an even plausible account has seemed to many impossible (Caro 2004). To see why, imagine an indeterministic universe in which the following events transpire: Alice struggles with a very difficult decision whether to tell the truth; she tells the truth. Now suppose that God rewinds this world to one minute before her original decision. Everything is identical. What will 'Alice' do the 'second' time? We cannot say for sure what her 'second' action would be. We can only offer probabilistic calculations. Suppose further that God rewinds this scenario 1,000 times over for us to watch and that Alice speaks truly 508 times and lies 493 times. Peter van Inwagen asks, 'Is it not true that as we watch the number of replays increase, we shall become convinced that what will happen in the *next* replay is a matter of chance?' He concludes, 'I do not see why we should not be convinced of this' (2002: 174).

I see no immediately good reasons why we should be so convinced on either phenomenological or conceptual grounds. The phenomenological reply stresses that this thought experiment (and others like it) necessitates a third-person viewpoint, obviously since no one can experience identical choice-situations. Further, that it would be peculiar for Alice to predict what she will do in the process of deciding, or giving a statistical analysis of her possibilities understood probabilistically. If she were to attempt a prediction, she would not be viewing herself as an agent, but as a patient. While Alice's 'actions' may appear random when viewed externally from a third-person viewpoint, from her first-person perspective they appear ordered insofar as whatever choice she makes will have to be woven into a coherent future, where different future orderings always seem possible. The details of the phenomenological case will be given below but, for the moment, the conceptual case begins with the assumption that individual actions cannot be said to be random. Just as we cannot tell whether the single roll of a die results in random data (since maybe the die is fixed), Alice's single action to lie or not cannot be considered random. Only a series of die rolls can reveal randomness, in the sense of patternlessness, and only through patternlessness can we discern (degrees of) randomness (Chaitin 1975). By analogy, we must examine Alice's life taken as a *single* whole. Each particular rewind must be extended to include the same past and the contingently relevant future. When taken as a whole, various contemporary choices can (at least in principle) be woven into differently ordered futures. Consequently, each possible life, when taken as a whole, can exhibit order, regardless of whether Alice lies or not.

Perhaps Inwagen supposes that the experiment generates a series of actions.[8] To the extent that it does, it generates the wrong kind of series. It does not generate a series of actions that compose a *single* life considered as a whole. Rather, it generates different actions that compose different possible lives which, from a third-person perspective, we mistakenly see as random. If correct, the thought experiment (and others like it) does not entail that Alice's action is random; rather it raises a different set of problems. It seems impossible to explain how Alice's reasons, motives, and intentions hook up with her actions. For how can a single set of identical reasons and motives explain different actions? A sketch of a Sartrean answer follows, after a few expository remarks.

Sartre's considered view of freedom and action explanation

The widespread rejection of Sartre's early view of freedom calls for a brief commentary. Sartre's view of freedom is radical, but not for some of the standard reasons supposed. This is not to say that many won't find Sartre's considered view unpalatable. We should not, however, evaluate his view in terms of its unpleasantness but by its plausibility. Sartre understood that his view was not a variety of 'free will' that many would, as it were, find 'worth wanting'. Consequently, Sartre expended considerable energy developing a psychological error theory (bad faith) for why humans pervasively hold poorly justified beliefs that systematically (and intentionally) distort their experience of freedom. One common (but misleading) explanation for the motivation to deceive oneself is that radical, existential freedom provokes anxiety due to its absolute and unlimited nature. The sheer overwhelming sum of possible choices motivates people to widely, but mistakenly, believe themselves to be much less free and responsible than they really are.

Sartre does (initially and implausibly) argue that consciousness finds its limits only in itself (B&N: 11) and, since Sartre equates consciousness with freedom, it follows that 'no limits to my freedom can be found except in my freedom itself' (B&N: 462). This leads many commentators to puzzle over what we might call 'the location problem', namely, in what area of human existence could freedom be limited only by itself and, hence, entirely unlimited in every other way? The considerable implausibility of all of the proposed candidates for such an unlimited realm leads commentators to reject Sartre's view (e.g. Føllesdal 1981; Busch 1990). A second problem follows from the location problem. The purported unlimited nature of freedom makes it impossible to judge individual agents or groups to be more or less free than any other. Call this the problem of degrees.[9] Aside from the fact that these two problems stand in sharp conflict with our basic intuitions, they also undercut the above commonly held assumption that Sartre himself supposes that humans generally believe themselves to be much less free than they really are.

Of course the location and degrees problems would entail overwhelmingly good reasons to reject Sartre's view of freedom as wildly implausible, were it not for the fact that both problems rest upon serious misinterpretations of the text. Sartre employs a Cartesian method that progresses analytically from extremely abstract and simple concepts to a complex and concrete whole. As Sartre's analysis becomes increasingly concrete, Sartre significantly revises abstract claims made early in the text and, consequently, Sartre abandons all claims to the unlimited (and unconditioned) nature of freedom in the second half of *Being and Nothingness*. In Sartre's considered view, Others limit my freedom (B&N: 285–6, 310–11, 546) not only factually (say by refusing someone admittance into a country club on the basis of phenotype), but also ontologically, insofar as the objectifying gaze of Others modifies one's very structure (B&N: 284). Consequently, whereas, in the early portions of *Being and Nothingness*, being-for-itself was initially considered pure possibility (B&N: 119–29), and the ego to be solely self-constituted, Sartre now offers a new definition of the psychological self, as 'the limit between two consciousnesses as it is *produced* by the limiting consciousness [i.e. the Other] and assumed by the limited consciousness' (B&N: 310). This social constitution of our psychological make up introduces antecedent (historical) meanings (B&N: 531–2) that condition how we interpret and evaluate our situation (B&N: 351–2).

Sartre eventually calls this socially introduced modification my being-for-others and, he argues, in light of this, that the 'very stuff of my being is the unpredictable freedom of another' (B&N: 286). Consequently, 'I am a slave to the degree that my being is dependent at the very center of a freedom which is not mine and which is the very condition of my being' (B&N: 291). This limitation to freedom should not be understood as a 'head-on obstacle which freedom encounters, but a sort of centrifugal force which *causes* everything which it undertakes to have one face which freedom will not have chosen' (B&N: 547, emphasis added). Elsewhere Sartre claims freedom can only be conceived as 'an aberrant synthesis of the in-itself [MBII] and nothingness [MBFI]' (B&N: 507). So understood, in Sartre's considered view, our free choices exhibit an intrinsic ambiguity or admixture of passive, socially-given elements and our free internalization (*intériorisation*) of them (B&N: 531–52). Freedom, then, describes the ambiguous processes by which we make ourselves out of what we have been made to be, a point Sartre makes more explicit later in his career. So understood, actions cannot be understood in exclusion of or reducible to the (causal) contribution of any single mode of being. Otherwise put, 'free will … turns out to be a marshy notion' (Kidd 2009: 10), one that plausibly involves mixed modes of causation.

If correct, the radical nature of Sartre's view of freedom does not concern its being somehow absolute in any sense of being unlimited by social forces or unconditioned by antecedent historical meanings. Rather, the radical nature of freedom involves how, on the one hand, our actions link up with justification and, on the other, the necessity with which Sartre finds it almost always possible, although frequently very difficult (B&N: 476), to make choices that alter one's form of life in some significant way. Sartre infamously argues, 'freedom is the unique foundation of values', such that 'nothing, absolutely nothing, justifies me in adopting this or that particular value, this or that particular scale of values. As a being by whom values exist, I am unjustified' (B&N: 62). So understood, the overwhelming experience of freely choosing results simultaneously from the ever-present confrontation with a limited set of alternative possibilities, in combination with our all-too-human failure to ultimately justify which of the many possible actions we should perform, which person we should become: 'hence my anguish … [over the possibility] of becoming radically other [than who I currently am]' (B&N: 475, see also 486). For those who fancy a melodic turn of phrase, call this 'the problem of my existence'.

Even though Sartre argues that humans pervasively and mistakenly believe in various kinds of ultimate justification (like Categorical Imperatives, Christianity, Marxist Ideals, or Neurobiology) as a kind of existential prophylactic to our fundamental normative uncertainty that encompasses all of our choices, this does not mean that we do not frequently justify our actions in non-ultimate senses.[10] Sartre also argues that the lion's share of our non-ultimate justifications are, on the one hand, in some sense *ex post facto* (B&N: 473). And, on the other, that I am unable to make justificatory sense out of at least some of my present choices, until some indeterminate point in the future (B&N: 558–60). Strangely, then, in Sartre's considered view, our non-ultimate justifications for action arrive both too early and too late. What follows takes each temporal facet in turn.

Non-ultimate justification for action frequently comes too late. According to Sartre, most of the time we already intend to do something and then offer what amounts to (anterior) rationalizations. More specifically, our reflective deliberations over what to do mostly take place within in a series of lived (pre-reflective) projects that frame our decisions in advance. Sartre employs the term 'project' vaguely and rather overly broadly to include any organizational form that conditions how one makes sense out of and organizes the world into practical possibilities. Projects include specific goal-oriented activities like going to the store for materials to make protest signs, but they also include general forms (like being a Revolutionary Marxist) that frame larger groups of particular actions. These more general forms (being Marxist) are themselves embedded in even more general projects, like an inferiority complex. Sartre argues that one can trace projects of increasing breadth, until one eventually arrives at the fundamental project and, hence, to one kind of explanatory end. So understood, our most basic projects provide the conditions for the possibility of deliberation about particular actions and sub-projects, but we normally do not deliberate about those pre-cognitive conditions (B&N: 483–6). Thus, our reflective deliberations form a kind of epiphenomenal surface over our lived projects out of which actions emerge. For reasons like this, Sartre says, the chips are already down (B&N: 473), by which he means that most of what we call justification or reason giving comes after what we have already (pre-reflectively) set to do.

In some important cases, attempted justification (or the demand for justification) comes too early. These cases typically occur when possible actions create conflicts between one or more of my projects, or require significant revisions to old projects or the creation of new ones, what Kane (1999) sometimes means by 'self-forming' actions. These self-forming, or self-transforming, actions differ from the above cases of actions consistent with already established projects and they sometimes lead to a kind of anxious indecision. Sartre argues that reasons, motives, and actions (ends) form an indissoluble whole, insofar as they occur simultaneously (B&N: 471).[11] Consequently, our actions constitute our reasons and motives in the action itself. They do not come before. We cannot, however, currently understand our reasons for these kinds of actions until some point in the future, after we have accumulated a new series of relevant experiences. In this way, our reasons and motives exhibit a fundamental indeterminacy, insofar as we can weave actions into different possible futures that make sense out of our contemporary actions in different ways.

Conclusions

So understood, my future appears hazy and composed of unfixed possibilities that will constitute the meaning of my present actions differently and create differently ordered existences. While pre-existing projects frame my future, they do not determine it, and they cannot prevent choices that abandon, transform, or revise them. Of course, were I to fundamentally change myself, who I become always stands as someone who used to be who I was (Wang 2006). A religious person self-transformed into an atheist is, nonetheless, an atheist who was once religious. Otherwise put, the same present action can be constituted differently by weaving it into different futures but it remains non-arbitrarily tied to a fixed past. So in these kinds of cases, I cannot fully understand my present choices, until sometime after the fact. Thus, from Alice's first-person perspective, her present struggle over whether to lie or not may stand on a horizon that appears like the fuzzy picture on an old UHF, poorly tuned, black-and-white television, rather than a garden of forking paths. Life only looks like a (well-groomed) garden of forking paths, to take an understandable but misleading metaphor employed by Kane (2007: 5–6), when viewed from above, that is, from a third-person perspective. From within the fog of life, one modulates the 'control knobs' and tinkers with life's possibilities, which bring a hazy picture into focus, but without ever achieving complete clarity. In this way, Alice's lying forms her life in one way, it frames one series of possible future actions that retrospectively explain what she did, while truth-telling composes another possible ordering. However, even if, or just because, her choice lacks some ultimate sense of normative justification, it must, nonetheless, be non-randomly woven into an ambiguous future. It just so happens that life can be non-randomly ordered in many different ways. But which way?

Perhaps three and only three general forms of choice present themselves to our first-person experience. First, in cases of continuity, our past reasons and motives seamlessly hook up with present actions and propel us, generally without hesitation, into the future. Rewind this world but always with the same results. Alice tells the truth every time. Second, in cases of indifference, where none of our future possibilities outweigh one another and, importantly, where the cost of action is low, say, whether to eat at the local Thai or Vietnamese restaurant, we would willingly flip a coin. In the last and most important case of existential indecision, perhaps due to a conflict between projects or from external pressures or simply when one stands back in the effort to purchase an objective standpoint on one's life, one sometimes experiences an anxious mood. One recognizes the acute fact that life makes no ultimate sense, and that no ultimate justification warrants one action over another. These cases differ from cases of indifference in at least two essential ways. The cost to the actions is high and one would be unwilling to flip a coin. 'No other animal suffers this condition.'[12]

In this latter case, in Sartre's view, or something quite like it, freedom describes the experience of our ultimately unjustified carving of contingent possibilities into various non-random, constantly evolving wholes. If correct, these ultimately unjustified but non-random actions present a case somewhere in between necessity (determinism) and randomness (indeterminism). In this way, I hope to have merely taken a short Sartrean step towards a plausible account of how identical agent-situations can issue different non-random but ultimately unjustified futures, even though I have not shown that we are in fact free. Whatever the case may be, to say that 'Sartrean freedom is not ultimately distinguishable from chance' (Morriston 1977: 237) is to conflate the problem of justification with that of randomness.[13]

Notes

1 Wesley Morriston (1977) discusses the third version of this argument in some detail, but finds it lacking.

2 Sebastian Gardner helped me to see this point.

3 Gardner (2009: 157) argues that alternative possibilities remain a secondary conceptual consideration for Sartre. Gardner does not discuss whether, according to Sartre, an action could be free if one could not have done otherwise. This option may seem odd but it should not be dismissed out of hand. On this reading, Sartre maintains something like source libertarianism (see Fischer et al. 2007) with secondary leeway considerations. This interesting suggestion shall not be pursued in this essay.

4 For versions of this argument, see Ayer 1954 and Strawson 1995.

5 For an information theoretic definition of randomness that cannot apply to single units of data, see Chaitin 1975 and 2001. Space constraints prevent this essay from showing precisely why single actions cannot be said to be random.

6 For two noteworthy and helpful discussions of Sartre on questions concerning randomness and action explanation that, however, tend to conflate these two matters, see Morriston 1977 and Wang 2006.

7 For an interesting account of how introspection lost its footing as a valid source of data for psychological research, see Lyon 1986.

8 In an earlier work, Inwagen himself argued that the concept 'randomness' does not properly apply to individual actions (1983: 128–9). However, in light of Alice, Inwagen 'no longer regard[s] this argument as having any merit' (2002: 171).

9 For examples of this kind of criticism, see Merleau-Ponty 1962 [1945], McGill 1949, and Kruks 1991.

10 With some hesitation, I take (the early) Sartre to mean that non-ultimate normative justification always boils down to a kind of hypothetical imperative. If I wish to be such and such a kind of person, I must conduct my life in such and such a way. But there is no ultimate justification to choose between various lives.

11 What I call a reason, Sartre generally calls a 'motive' (*motif*), as in the motive to commit a crime. And what I call a motive, Sartre calls a 'motivation' (*mobile*). For Sartre, motives are objective: 'Why did you steal a loaf of bread?' 'Because I was hungry'. And motivations (what I here call motives) are subjective: 'Because I have no qualms stealing from the bourgeois'. Hazel Barnes misleadingly translates '*motif*' as 'cause' and '*mobile*' as 'motive' (see B&N: 457n1).

12 C. Huggins turned this marvellous phrase.

13 I want thank to Jonathan Webber for a magisterial job orchestrating several workshops and editing this collection, Sarah Richmond for help and feedback that made this essay possible, my colleagues Tom Schmid and Heath White for their critical insights along the way, and also Herbert Berg for his patience with my mad ramblings.

4

THE TRANSCENDENTAL DIMENSION OF SARTRE'S PHILOSOPHY

Sebastian Gardner

The thought that I will explore in this paper is that the Sartre of *Being and Nothingness* and the earlier writings is in certain fundamental respects a *transcendental* thinker, and that viewing him in this light makes a positive, favourable difference to how we understand and assess his ideas, arguments, and position as a whole.

The use of such plastic and open-textured categories in the history of philosophy is, of course, notoriously treacherous, and 'transcendental philosophy' is probably in no better shape than most. Consequently there will be some interpretations of the claim that Sartre is a transcendental thinker which make it (pretty much) trivially true, and others that make it (pretty much) plainly false. If transcendental means simply lying in an open-ended line of descent from Kant, then of course Sartre is a transcendentalist, along with almost every other modern European philosopher. If, on the other hand, a philosophical position qualifies as transcendental only if it pursues the very same agenda as that of Kant's first *Critique*, then drastic reconstructive surgery would be required to show Sartre to be a transcendental philosopher.

The task, therefore, is to come up with an interpretation of the claim for Sartre's transcendentalism that is sufficiently strong to be interesting, but not so strong as to lack plausibility. Rather than attempt to fix the meaning of 'transcendental' at the outset – which would lead off into thickets from which it would be hard to find an exit – I am going to work through half a dozen headings which will, I think, be accepted as denoting characteristic features of transcendental philosophy. These include transcendental argumentation and transcendental idealism, the hallmarks of transcendentalism. So if under each of the headings enough of a case can be made for their centrality to Sartre's concerns – if it can be shown not merely that Sartre says certain things which can be squeezed under those headings, but that he is deeply engaged with the relevant issue – then the cumulative effect, I hope, will be to vindicate the historical claim and, much more importantly, to give an idea of why it matters.

Sartre's anti-naturalist strategy

Sartre uses the term 'transcendental' fairly freely in *Being and Nothingness*, but that on its own does not count for much, and the Sartre who emerges from much of the analytic commentary on *Being and Nothingness*, or who has been touted as a post-structuralist *avant la lettre*, does not look to be transcendental in any important sense. And it is true that many things seem to pull Sartre away from the transcendental paradigm, including his rejection of idealism and criticism of the transcendental subject of Kant's theoretical philosophy; his rejection of Husserl's transcendental ego and the *epoché* of transcendental phenomenology; and his dismissal (as it may seem) of epistemology in favour of a purely descriptive version of phenomenology. If Sartre is pictured as third in the phenomenological line, after Husserl and Heidegger, and as having stripped the transcendental reduction out of Husserl and anthropologized *Being and Time*, then he will seem to have shed precisely those elements in Husserl and Heidegger which are residually transcendental.

We begin, however, to get an idea of why Sartre may be counted a transcendental philosopher, if we reflect on the underlying motivation for his construction of a position which departs from Kant, Husserl, and Heidegger. Any account of Sartre's philosophical motivation must give a central place to Sartre's opposition, on libertarian and axiological grounds, to philosophical naturalism. This itself is a thoroughly and famously Kantian matter, and so, more specifically, I want to suggest, is the anti-naturalist strategy that Sartre pursues, even as it brings him into conflict with Kant.

Kant's solution to the problem of human freedom, in so far as it rests on the conditions of transcendental idealism and the pure practical reason of Kant's metaphysics of morals, is rejected by Sartre, but Sartre takes over one key feature of Kant's solution, while regarding Kant's construal of the problem as in one basic respect misguided.

What Sartre *accepts* from Kant is the notion that we differ ontologically from natural objects; what he *rejects* is Kant's conception of us as enmeshed *ab initio* in the web of empirical causality, from which we need to extricate ourselves, our relation to our freedom being thereafter epistemically *indirect*. Instead, Sartre tries to show that we can regard our freedom as *primary* – rather than restricting knowledge of freedom to the context of morality, Sartre holds that freedom is implied by every aspect of cognition and self-consciousness, so that it is unnecessary, and a mistake, to think that we need to enter a special plea for exemption from empirical causality in order to lay claim to freedom.

Put like this, it may seem doubtful that Sartre's libertarianism can avoid being merely dogmatic. But there is a sense in which, far from irresponsibly *ignoring* the intuition in favour of naturalistic determinism and merely counter-asserting the reality of freedom, Sartre acknowledges the truth in naturalism, as he takes it to be, and allows the whole of his philosophy be shaped by it. The naturalist's conception of the independent reality of nature is expressed in Sartre's conception of being-in-itself, and Sartre considers that naturalism is correct in so far as the *paradigm* of an entity with full, genuine being is indeed a material object, or, put differently, that whatever falls outside the bounds of material nature cannot have (full, genuine) being and so must be 'nothing'.

Thus far Sartre's thought parallels eliminative materialism, but Sartre takes the following further step. Having made a clean sweep – having disposed of the idea that there is a unified ontological realm, an order of nature within which we find ourselves located – we are positioned to reaffirm our own existence and grasp correctly its ontological character: since it is true, as the naturalist says, that only material nature meets the conditions for full and genuine being, and because we must nonetheless think of ourselves as existing in *some* manner – eliminative materialism is, from the relevant subjective angle, literally unthinkable – we are required to think of our existence as exemplifying a different *mode of being* from that of material nature, *antithetical* to nature's mode of being; hence Sartre's identification of the human subject's mode of being with 'nothingness'.

Sartre's strategy, therefore, is to offer an interpretation of the philosophical intuition which underlies naturalism, grant its authority, and then, turning the tables, to *use* this intuition to *reveal freedom* – in a way analogous to that in which Descartes uses scepticism to reveal the true grounds of knowledge.

The immediate advantages of Sartre's strategy over Kant's, as I indicated, are that it avoids resting freedom on precarious moral conditions, and that (if it works) it secures freedom while leaving external reality intact, rather than reduced to a transcendental representation.

This second point is of particular importance to Sartre. Sartre objects to the manner in which the Kantian transcendental subject encompasses or *contains* the world, and sees it as his task to secure freedom without recourse to idealism. In Sartre's view, while realism makes freedom impossible, idealism makes it too easy – and thus gives a false account of freedom – by virtue of its failure to appreciate the nature and quality of our immersion in the world. Sartre thinks that idealism removes from things their hard existential edge. For Sartre, the objects which surround and *bear* on us, and in relation to which our freedom needs to be sustained philosophically, are not – as he supposes they are for Kant – mere functions of our knowledge of them, things subject to the legislation of our understanding; the reality of freedom, Sartre thinks, requires that we be related to objects *qua* their being, and that objects be known to be *irreducible* to our knowledge of them. Sartre wants to think of the human subject not as containing the world, but as encountering it, so to speak, on an equal footing. Navigating between and beyond realism and idealism is thus necessary, on Sartre's view, for the vindication of freedom.

Sartre's rejection of the idea, accepted by Kant, that the mind instantiates empirical causal relations, is supported by his theory in *Being and Nothingness* of the theoretical and practical sources of the error which underpins the common-sense conception of human subjects as natural objects. Thus although Sartre's position is more revisionary than Kant's, the revision is defended.[2]

Sartre's transcendental argumentation

Sartre's anti-naturalist strategy would not qualify as transcendental, however, if the *grounds* given by Sartre for drawing the relevant anti-naturalist conclusions were not of the right kind, and as I noted earlier, it may be thought that Sartre's project is wholly descriptive and eschews questions of grounding, his indifference to foundational matters being most overt in the context of epistemology.

A recent study of Sartre claims, in his defence, that we should not always be looking for *arguments* in Sartre's texts, since if the phenomenological descriptions he gives are convincing, then arguments are not needed (Morris 2008: 55). Now if this were so – if Sartre's achievement were to merely *re-present* the manifest image of the world in primary colours, and if he were merely *insisting on* this image, reminding us of our immersion in it – then Sartre would have broken with the transcendental tradition in a crucial respect. On such a reading, phenomenological description is what does the real work in *Being and Nothingness*, Sartre's implicit claim being that the manifest image is ultimately self-sustaining. The ontological talk in *Being and Nothingness* would then be either a rhetorical shadow cast by Sartre's map of human phenomenology, or the result of a simple, non-transcendental inference from the appearances. In other words, if the authority of phenomenology flows directly from its actuality, then either Sartre has a phenomenology but no metaphysics, or he has a metaphysics but this is grounded non-transcendentally.[3]

Sartre's apparently negative attitude towards epistemology may seem to be evidenced in his rejection of what he calls the 'primacy of knowledge'. According to Sartre, this mistaken assumption underpins swathes of modern philosophy, including Kant and Hegel. Sartre does not state in a single definition exactly what the assumption of the primacy of knowledge amounts to, but it is clear from the contexts in which Sartre uses the notion that it encompasses all philosophical methodologies which give *priority* to questions of knowledge or justification of belief, the result of which, Sartre supposes, is an implicit reduction of being to a function of thought or representation.

Sartre's objections to the primacy of knowledge include accordingly the objection which Jacobi makes to Kant and Fichte, and Schelling to Hegel, that being is irreducible to thought, and a correlative objection to the effect that philosophy which gives priority to questions of knowledge cannot overcome the logical separation of being from representation, and so cannot take us out of our subjectivity.[4]

Sartre may accordingly appear to be saying that, since epistemology is necessarily futile, we can rightfully ignore problems associated with knowledge and belief. (Sartre's self-association with and borrowing from Heidegger can also be taken as a ground for thinking this to be his view.)

I think, however, that it is a mistake to read Sartre as *substituting* phenomenological description for argument, or as simply turning his back on epistemology. The passages in Sartre which may seem to have purely and merely descriptive import are correctly viewed as instances of transcendental argumentation of the complex type analysed by Mark Sacks in his discussion of Sartre's account of other minds (2005a; see also Sacks 2005b and 2005c). The basic idea, stated in the roughest terms, is that (certain) transcendental necessities – for example, in the case that Sacks discusses: our judging our experience to be of a world which presents others to us – allow themselves to be grounded by thoughts as *indexed* to situations or situated thinkers. The non-inferential immediacy of a type of experience – in Sartre's other-minds case, the experience of concrete shame – is not itself the proof: the transcendental proof consists in *reflection* on the pre-reflective phenomenology which discloses the thought embedded in it, not with respect to its bare conceptual content, but as informed by the subject's perspectival situation. This type of transcendental argumentation contrasts with the type found paradigmatically in Strawson, where the motor of argument is supplied by conceptual analysis and the discovery of relations of presupposition between (unsituated) propositions.

If this is correct, then Sartre is not in fact disengaged from the modern epistemological tradition in the manner of Heidegger. While it is true that Sartre does not aim to answer the sceptic directly and on his own terms, it is not true that Sartre follows Heidegger in *repudiating* epistemology on the grounds that an existential error is involved in the very posing of epistemological questions or entertaining of sceptical possibilities. Sartre's response to scepticism is more oblique than a traditional empiricist or rationalist response, but it incorporates a recognition that sceptical doubts are *meaningful*. The sceptic's and traditional epistemologist's shared mistake, Sartre believes, is to look to *reflective* consciousness for *answers* to epistemological questions,[5] but no mistake is involved, *contra* Heidegger, in the posing of the questions themselves, which indeed have their answers, at the *pre*-reflective level. So, whereas Heidegger urges us to de-conceive ourselves altogether as Cartesian–Kantian subjects, Sartre holds fast to the idea that there are apodictic cognitions and that self-conscious subjectivity provides a terminus to demands for epistemic justification.

The transcendental mould is clearly visible in Part II of *Being and Nothingness*, which specifies on the one hand the structures of the human subject, and on the other, the formal features of empirical reality.

The most abstract and fundamental structures of subjectivity, on Sartre's account, are selfhood, temporality, and transcendence, and he aims to show that these are necessary for our conscious being. In place of any attempt to deduce for example the temporal form of experience from the *concept* of consciousness of objects, Sartre's transcendental method is to bring us to realize – at the phenomenological, situated level – that *our* consciousness could not fail to be temporal, by giving us insight into the ways in which our consciousness is connected *internally* with our temporality, in other words, to show how *what it is* for us to be conscious, and *what it is* for there to be time (for us), make one another intelligible. In place of Strawsonian chains of deduction, Sartre's transcendental argumentation offers lateral, horizontal interconnections revealing the mutual cross-conditioning of the immediate structures of the for-itself.

It follows that in tracing back the basic features of empirical reality – spatiality and temporality, determinacy, quality and quantity, causality and so on – to the structures of the human subject, Sartre is concerned not to demonstrate the necessity of those features in the strong sense of showing the *conceptual impossibility* of alternatives (e.g. non-spatio-temporal awareness of the in-itself) but to indicate the way in which the formal features of empirical reality and the structures of the subject interlock, the latter making the former intelligible by supplying their *a priori* conditions. This is enough to support at least some weak claims regarding the necessary conditions of experience. For example, to the extent that Sartre shows how *spatialization* of the in-itself is what *for us* plays the role of allowing the subject to make itself co-present with being-in-itself, and how the principle of causality coheres with the temporality of the human subject, Sartre can be said to establish the necessity of space and causality for empirical reality, albeit in a weaker sense than Kant, or Strawson, claims to be able to establish. Sartre leaves it thinkable that the experience of some logically possible conscious subject might be e.g. non-temporal, but if Sartre is right, then we should be indifferent to this possibility, since it cannot intersect with anything recognizable as *our* mode of being. (I will say more about this restriction of philosophical scope in a later section.)

Of particular importance is the way in which the *teleology* of the human subject provides the final foundation of Sartre's transcendental proofs. Teleology is involved, for instance, in the transcendental proof of other minds, in negative form: the Other is given to me *contra-purposively*, as a negation of my freedom. Without this, the ontological transformation of my being effected by the Other's Look could not be registered, and the Other could not be given as subject.

That knowledge as such and in general must be regarded as embedded in the subject's teleology comes out explicitly in Sartre's treatment of the concept of knowledge in Chapter 3 of Part II, where the question addressed is not *whether* we have knowledge, *contra* the sceptic, nor of the conditions under which it is *rational* to form beliefs with whatever degree of confidence, but of *what* knowledge *is*. The result is what one might call a *metaphysics of cognition* as distinct from a theory of knowledge in the more usual sense. As Sartre puts it, 'knowledge is reabsorbed in being' (B&N: 239), where the being in question is the teleological being of the human subject; cognition is analysed as an essential moment in the subject's structure of transcendence.[6]

There is much more to be said about the distinctive features of Sartre's transcendental argumentation.[7] But the point most important for present purposes is that Sartre, though evincing none of the worry about objectivity, relativity, and rational belief-warrants that sets in motion much epistemology, is not excluded from the transcendental tradition by an indifference to epistemological concerns, and is very much in the business of pinning down transcendental necessities by means of a situated form of transcendental argumentation.

Perennial issues of transcendental philosophy

So far I hope to have shown that the driving force and overall shape of Sartre's philosophy has a Kantian character – an obvious point – and, perhaps less obviously, that the method Sartre uses in pursuing his anti-naturalist strategy is, at least in substantial part, transcendental. Now I move onto other, more intricate aspects of Sartre's transcendental profile.

The following four issues are ones with respect to which any philosophical position which lays claim to be able to show the existence of transcendental conditions – and which in addition seeks to comprehensively rationalize (explain and justify) its use of transcendental argumentation, which is to say to explicate itself metaphilosophically – must take a stand:

A The (metaphysical) question of the *reality* or *ideality* of the *objects of cognition*.
B The (metaphysical) question of the *ontological status* of transcendental conditions themselves.
C The (metaphilosophical) question of the relation of the *theoretical* and the *practical*.
D The (metaphilosophical) question of the *standpoint* of transcendental philosophy and the correspondingly defined *perspectival* or *extra-perspectival* status of transcendental claims.

I will take these in turn and consider the answers that Sartre may be thought to give to these questions.

Sartre and realism/idealism

The first issue, then, is Sartre's position regarding the reality or ideality of objects of knowledge, and as I have already noted, Sartre describes himself (consistently and emphatically) as neither a realist nor an idealist. The puzzle is *why* Sartre should declare himself beyond *idealism* – given that, as I have said, demonstrating that empirical reality presupposes an *a priori* contribution of subjectivity appears to be a central part of the enquiry in *Being and Nothingness*.

Supporting the construal of Sartre as a kind of idealist is the observation that, when Sartre talks of avoiding realism and of its incoherence, what he has in mind is a position which construes (i) objects as existing independently of consciousness just *as we are conscious of them as being*, and (ii) our cognition of those objects as due to their exercising some *causality* which is accidental to their intrinsic nature (see B&N: 173–4, 247, and the definition of realism at 609; see also IHP: 4). This corresponds to the position which Kant describes as treating objects of experience as things in themselves and calls transcendental realism. So it may seem reasonable to interpret Sartre as rejecting *transcendental realism* – as well as of course the merely empirical idealism of Berkeley – and as affirming a combination of *transcendental* idealism with *empirical* realism, all on the familiar pattern of Kant. This would cohere with the fact that Sartre quite clearly takes the term 'idealism' on some occasions to mean phenomenalism, and on others, to involve a commitment to the primacy of knowledge – in short, he tends to equate idealism with Berkeley's idealism or with Kant's particular version of transcendental idealism (as he understands it).

If this were all, then there would be little reason for us not to override Sartre's self-description and re-categorize his position as a form of transcendental idealism, one which avoids reducing the *being* of objects to a function of cognition in the way that Sartre thinks Kant does. This proposal runs up, however, against Sartre's explicit anti-idealist statements.

Sartre wants to combine three claims: (1) That, *pace* realism, the 'problem of the connection of consciousness with existents independent of it' is 'insoluble' (B&N: 15), in so far as 'transcendent being could not act on consciousness' (B&N: 194). (2) That, *pace* idealism, 'subjectivity is powerless to constitute the objective' (B&N: 18), and that 'consciousness could not "construct" the transcendent by objectivizing elements borrowed from its subjectivity' (B&N: 194); the for-itself 'adds nothing to being' (B&N: 232). In addition, I have said, (3) Sartre envisages a *correlation* – at the very least – of the intelligibly differentiated object-world with the fundamental structures of the human subject.

The problem is that, on the transcendental idealist interpretation of Sartre, it seems that this correlation will need to be understood as a relation of *constitution* (or 'construction') – in other words, (3) appears to conflict head-on with (2).

Is there any way of squaring (2) and (3)? The following possibilities suggest themselves: first, that the correlation of the object-world with human subjectivity is due to the structures of subjectivity, but is secured by some means *other* than a relation of object-constitution; second, that it is an instance of some sort of pre-established harmony; and, third, that the correlation does not need to be regarded as 'due to' anything at all, because it does not stand in need of explanation.

The first possibility still carries an echo of idealism, but it would be understandable if, in the absence of object-*constituting* activity, Sartre considered it sufficiently remote from Kant and Husserl for the label to be dropped. It requires, nonetheless, a positive account of the manner in which the subject determines-without-constituting its objects. The second possibility similarly needs amplification, since if a harmony has been established between subject and world, then surely an explanation is owed for its having been established.

Attention to the following elements in Sartre's philosophy allows us to make some progress:

(1) There is a suggestion of a combination of the first two possibilities in Sartre's doctrine of the subject's 'responsibility for the (my) world'. What this may be interpreted as claiming is that the correlation is established, not by God, but by my *freedom*, in my 'original choice of self'. On this account, the accord between the for-itself and its world of objects is established in a way analogous to that in which the author of a fictional work engineers coherence within the fiction between (a) the characters, and (b) the scenes and plot which compose the world which the characters inhabit: the harmony is established not *within* the (fictional) world – as realism and idealism, by analogy, mistakenly suppose – but from a point *outside* it, by my pre-mundane choice of self.

(2) A metaphysical position which attributes the constitution of the objects of cognition to the structure of the subject, and which, like Kant, *stops* the story at that point, counts straightforwardly as a subjective idealism. But if the structures are traced back in turn to a *pre*-subjective source – such that, when the subject posits objects, its positing of objects derives ultimately, albeit indirectly, from *being itself* – then it is not so obvious that we have an idealism, or at any rate, that we have an idealism of Kant's *subjective* sort. And on Sartre's full metaphysical account, as I will explain later, this is exactly the picture – when the subject bestows structure on being-in-itself, yielding an intelligibly differentiated world of objects, it follows an imperative which derives in the last resort from being itself. (This sort of position, it may be argued, is both Hegel's and Heidegger's.)

(3) Consideration of Sartre's conception of being-in-itself helps us to understand why Sartre does not regard his account of the subject-relatedness of the object-world as leading him to reproduce Kant's transcendental idealism. For Sartre, an object O may be considered in two respects: (i) *qua* its mode of being, namely its being-in-itself (= the ground of its determinacy), (ii) *qua* its belonging to the differentiated object-world (= the respect in which the form of O interlocks with the structures of our subjectivity). This distinction is neither a distinction of individuals, nor of different sets of properties of one and the same individual. Instead, existing-in-the-mode-of-being-in-itself pervades, in adverbial fashion, O *qua* item in the object-world.[8] The distinction of reality and appearance thereby gains no purchase, and things in themselves are not invoked, for while it is true that O considered *qua* the object-world is considered *in relation to* the subject, and that O considered *qua* being-in-itself is *not* considered in relation to the subject, the latter does not count as consideration of O 'as it really is': because being-in-itself is categorially property-less – rather, it is the *ground* of things' having properties – we cannot talk of 'how', or 'the way that', being-in-itself is. Hence there is no sense in which Being-in-Itself can be thought to comprise Reality.

In combination, these points provide Sartre with a metaphysical position which we may justifiably describe as a form of transcendental idealism, but which we can understand Sartre's declining to describe as idealistic, and which allows us to see beyond the apparently gross contradiction comprised by (1)–(3). If determination of the object-world in accordance with the structures of the for-itself is the joint result of the individual's original choice of self and an imperative deriving from being, then it proceeds at a different, higher level from that at which intra-subjective, object-constituting Kantian transcendental psychology operates. It is also important to recall that Sartre's account of this determination is not designed to answer the question that Kant's idealism addresses, namely the establishing of an anti-sceptical relation of knowledge, since scepticism, on Sartre's account, is put out of business at an earlier point, namely by the ontological proof in the Introduction. The transcendental argumentation in Part II of *Being and Nothingness* is therefore uncoupled from an idealism which, like Kant's, secures the 'matching' of self and world on the basis of form-giving processes occurring within the subject, and renders objects knowable only in so far as they possess an inferior degree of reality. By contrast, Sartre's conception of being-in-itself provides for the irreducibility of the being of O, allowing Sartre to deny that O is constituted, in the Kantian sense, by subjectivity.

Sartre and the ontological status of transcendental conditions

The issue of the ontological status of transcendental conditions – that is, of whether truths which express transcendental necessities imply directly the existence of realities which make them true, or which are directly required for the truth of the conclusions of transcendental arguments[9] – is broached by Sartre on the very first page of his very first philosophical publication, *The Transcendence of the Ego*, a fact which is surely of significance for the claim that Sartre is attuned to the preoccupations of transcendental philosophy:

> We have to agree with Kant when he says that 'it *must be possible* for the "I think" to accompany all my representations'. But should we thereby conclude that an I inhabits de facto all our states of consciousness ... ? It seems that this would be to distort Kant's philosophy. The problem of critique is a *de jure* problem: thus Kant affirms nothing about the de facto existence of the 'I think' ... The real issue is rather that of determining the conditions of possibility of experience ... But there is a dangerous tendency in contemporary philosophy ... which consists of turning the conditions of possibility determined by critique into a *reality*. This is a tendency that leads some authors, for instance, to wonder what 'transcendental consciousness' may actually *be* ... Transcendental consciousness is, for him [Kant], merely the set of [*de jure*] conditions necessary for the existence of an empirical consciousness. In consequence, to make the transcendental I into a *real* entity ... is to make a de facto and not a *de jure* judgement, and that means we adopt a point of view radically different from Kant's.
>
> (TE: 2–3)

Sartre's concern here is with the transposition of Kant's thesis concerning the 'I think', into Husserl's thesis of the existence of a transcendental ego, which provides Sartre's target in this early work. Borrowing Kant's terminology, Sartre distinguishes *de jure* from *de facto* philosophical claims, and regards each as belonging to strictly different species of philosophical project, committed to a different philosophical method. Kant's thesis of the 'transcendental unity of apperception' must be accepted, Sartre affirms, but such a thesis concerns, he says, 'conditions of possibility of experience', 'logical conditions' which as such can have no (direct, unconditional) existential presuppositions or implications: the transcendental unity of apperception has a purely *de jure*, and no *de facto*, character; it specifies, Sartre says, 'merely the set of conditions necessary for the existence of an empirical consciousness', not something that *itself* exists (TE: 3).

Husserl's *phenomenology*, by contrast, is supposed to be a scientific and *descriptive*, not a 'critical', study of consciousness: it proceeds via intuition and aims at determining (fundamental, absolute) facts of consciousness, which are real existences. Husserl's thesis of the existence of a transcendental ego – which, Sartre assumes implicitly, rightly or wrongly, Husserl wishes to base on considerations borrowed from Kant – rests therefore on a confusion of phenomenology with Critical philosophy. The mistake of deriving a *de facto* conclusion from a *de jure* consideration, and of identifying statements of conditions of possibility of experience with ontological assertions, is according to Sartre not peculiar to Husserl: it afflicts also, he claims, various other schools of contemporary philosophy, and shows itself in gross form in the conception (of Boutroux) of transcendental subjectivity as 'an unconscious' which 'floats between real and ideal realms' (TE: 4).

This early work shows Sartre's lucid awareness of the issue of the relation between transcendental conditions and ontological commitment, and Sartre's early position, we have just seen, is that (1) there are sound arguments for necessary conditions of possible experience, (2) the conclusions of which are necessarily ontologically *uncommitted*. In so far as philosophical investigation results in either positive or negative ontological assertions – as does Sartre's own account of the self in *The Transcendence of the Ego* – it is on Sartre's view doing something different from what Kant, properly understood, is doing.

Sartre never revisits the *de jure/de facto* distinction explicitly – these terms do not appear at all in *Being and Nothingness* – but it is clear that in *Being and Nothingness* he continues to think of Kant as engaged in a different species of philosophical project from his own 'phenomenological ontology', as he now calls his philosophical method, and what additionally becomes clear is that Sartre now thinks that Kant's project incorporates a mistake. Whereas in the earlier work Sartre leaves us guessing as to what attitude he wants to adopt towards Kant's *de jure* transcendental conditions, in *Being and Nothingness* the very concept of such a condition is rejected, on the grounds that it reflects the assumption of the primacy of knowledge, which is the assumption of conceiving being as a function of idea or representation: Critical idealism is, Sartre says, 'a system which reduces the ensemble of objects to a connected grouping of representations and which measures all existence by the knowledge which I have of it' (B&N: 249).

Sartre's claim in *Being and Nothingness* is, therefore, that although the reasoning of Kant's transcendental argumentation may be valid, the *description* under which Kant brings the conclusions of those arguments – the interpretation Kant gives of them – incorporates a mistake, which can be avoided only by giving those conclusions an ontological, *de facto* interpretation.

We may now be wondering how much leverage Sartre has got against Kant, in other words, how effective Sartre's rather sweeping charge of 'assuming the primacy of knowledge' really is.

At this point I want to draw attention to a highly important passage in the chapter on transcendence (B&N: 198–9). Here Sartre gives a different and independent argument against Kant's Critical project, one which, if Sartre is correct, shows that transcendental conditions *must* be construed ontologically. (The passage also offers, incidentally, an explicitly Kantian characterisation of the enquiry in the present section of *Being and Nothingness* as directed to what 'must render all experience possible and ... establishing how in general an object can exist for consciousness' (B&N: 199).)

The argument is, in summary, the following. The most basic transcendental condition of knowledge of any object is knowledge of the non-identity of the object known and oneself as knowing subject. This knowledge cannot, for obvious reasons, be empirical. But if transcendental conditions were *themselves* matters of knowledge – principles which are contents or objects of the intellect – then an intellectual operation of giving *application* to the relevant transcendental principle would be required, and this would presuppose the object's being *already* given in some way, in order for the transcendental principle to be applied to it by the intellect. But if the object were already given, then it would need to be given as either (i) belonging to my subjectivity, (ii) external to my subjectivity, or (iii) neither belonging nor external to my subjectivity, i.e. undetermined. The first and the second options entail that the work which the principle is supposed to do has already been done. The third leaves room for the transcendental principle to be applied, but entails that objects are only ever grasped as distinct from my subjectivity *by virtue of* some feature which is *not* incorporated in what is originally given to me. And this is unacceptable, for not only is it phenomenologically false, but it reduces the sphere of the not-I to a theoretical extrapolation.[10]

In other words, if there are to be *a priori*, transcendental conditions of cognition – as there must – then these must *precede* cognition, and so (in the absence of any alternative) must be deemed identical with the *being* of the subject, an aspect of its 'upsurge' (namely, the internal negation of being which the upsurge incorporates) rather than its stock of knowledge or representations; so they cannot be merely *de jure*.

In sum, although Sartre regards his philosophy as divided sharply from that of Kant – 'phenomenological ontology' as opposed to 'critique' – we can re-characterize their relation in terms of a difference of view as regards the ontological status of transcendental conditions.

The next point that needs to be made explicit is that, on Sartre's account, there is fundamentally but one transcendental condition, and this, of course, is simply *consciousness* – consciousness holds the place, in Sartre's ontological order, of the principle of apperceptive unity which stands at the summit of Kant's non-ontological order of transcendental principles. This point can be elaborated in several ways.

First, in order to appreciate the full strength of Sartre's claim, we should note its difference from the claims of Kant and Husserl. To say that consciousness is *itself* a transcendental condition is something different from, and stronger than, saying either (i) that consciousness is *subject to* transcendental conditions, or (ii) that investigation of consciousness *discloses* a transcendental field. The former, Kantian claim does not attribute trans-cendentality to consciousness *per se* but to certain representations that consciousness must deploy *in so far as* it attains objective cognition, while the latter, Husserlian claim reserves the attribute of transcendentality for that which is attained *via* consciousness. Both make consciousness a trans-cendental functionary, but they do not *identify* its mode of being, as I am suggesting Sartre does, with transcendentality.[11]

Second, making explicit the identification of consciousness with trans-cendentality casts in a new light the extremely bold claims concerning the nature of consciousness made in the Introduction to *Being and Noth-ingness*. If consciousness were something merely come across *a posteriori* in empiricist-introspective fashion, or even in some more sophisticated phenomenological manner, then claims about the nature of consciousness would need to be constrained accordingly, and in such a light Sartre's foundational claims about consciousness are bound to appear dogmatic or at least under-argued (as many have found them to be). If, *per contra*, con-sciousness simply *is* transcendentality – if consciousness is equivalent to *that-which-enables* a world of objects – then consciousness cannot be likened to any other item and must be regarded as inherently *non-objectual*, meaning not just that consciousness should be accorded some or other feature(s) not possessed by objects at large, but that it must not be burdened with any feature whatsoever borrowed and carried over from the object-world. Any such feature would interfere with its transcendental role. In order for con-sciousness to have the requisite purity, it must be conceived in a way which implies positively that it *could not have* object-derived features.[12] The trans-cendental conception of consciousness is connected directly, therefore, with its specific ontological characterisation as nothingness: whatever is held to be transcendental cannot have anything of the character of an object – not even its being – and so, if it has existential status, must *be* 'nothing(ness)'.

Third, we should note that the ground-floor question of why Sartre commits himself *ab initio* to a Cartesian method in philosophy hereby receives its answer. The justification for starting with consciousness or the *cogito* is discussed in some detail in a paper written after *Being and Noth-ingness*, where Sartre's defence of his Cartesianism consists of a rebuttal of the usual objections that it entails solipsism and idealism, and an argument that every alternative epistemology reduces knowledge to mere probability, destroying certainty and thereby knowledge (CSKS: 113–14, 119).[13] This account allows us to relate Sartre's Cartesianism to the standard reasons found in modern philosophy for adopting a first-person, subjective starting point. However, these epistemologically orientated reasons are not rehearsed anywhere in *Being and Nothingness*, where the question of Carte-sianism's justification is not even raised, and a concern with the possibility of knowledge can hardly be adduced as a sufficient explanation of Sartre's adoption of Cartesianism in that work. More plausibly, the fact that no specific and explicit reason is articulated in *Being and Nothingness* for starting with consciousness is due to Sartre's axiomatic conviction that consciousness is a transcendental condition.

Sartre and the relation of the theoretical and the practical

The next issue concerns Sartre's relation to the thesis or principle of the primacy of practical reason, a notion which plays an important and complex role in post-Kantian thought. Because the rational integration of theoretical reason with practical consciousness and axiological interests is integral to the transcendental tradition, the question presents itself for all forms of transcendental philosophy, of the conditions under which the agreement of the practical and theoretical images of reality can be secured. The question is, therefore: does Sartre think that the rationality of beliefs about theoretical matters is properly *determined*, at least in some contexts or at some levels, by our practical interests, or does he regard theoretical enquiry as wholly *autonomous* in relation to the practical?

On the one hand, it can seem that Sartre leans heavily on the primacy of practical reason, and that he attempts to show how we must conceive things *in order that* we may consider ourselves free. On this view, *Being and Nothingness* should be regarded as showing what results when a libertarian conception of freedom is assumed and our theoretical image of the world is recast in its light.[14] A suggestion of this emerged earlier, with the point that the teleology of the for-itself provides the bottom line of Sartre's transcendental argumentation.

This reading of *Being and Nothingness* as practically grounded underlies the suggestion that the book results in a species of fiction which has regulative force for the practical point of view (see Bürger 2007), and it is assumed also by critics of Sartre who claim that *Being and Nothingness* provides a *reductio* of the libertarian conception of freedom, or alternatively, that it discredits the principle of the primacy of practical reason by showing how its employment (at any rate, in Sartre's unrestricted form) licenses metaphysical absurdities.

On the other hand, the very structure of *Being and Nothingness*, by virtue of its beginning with questions of ontology and pursuing these on a basis which makes no explicit reference to values or practical interests, moving slowly towards an ethics, seems to imply firmly the autonomy of theoretical reason.

Remarks made by Sartre in a late interview support this interpretation (IRPG: 45). Sartre repudiates the definition of ontology as 'an interpretation of things that enables us to see at a distance the conditions necessary for human fulfilment', and affirms that ontology is instead the study of being 'for the purpose of reconstituting the edifice of knowledge' and 'nothing else', declaring that our practice and evaluative beliefs must give way to whatever ontology dictates. Sartre's intended revision of our values – his attempt in *Being and Nothingness* to get us to stop treating value as a feature of the in-itself and ourselves as substantial entities, by persuading us of certain theoretical propositions concerning the ontology of value and the self – seems to follow exactly this pattern.

The text of *Being and Nothingness* gives every suggestion that once again, as with the choice between realism and idealism, Sartre considers that he does not need to choose between the two options, and I think that we can understand why he should think this.

Because consciousness for Sartre is from the outset *already* practical and value-orientated – consciousness is an expression of being-for-itself, and the for-itself, as the term implies, is constituted by a teleology – practical and theoretical reason are fundamentally united at a subjective level, in the being of the subject. Sartre's idea, which has an important historical pre-cedent in Fichte, is that an 'ought', or 'having-to', or 'obligation' – a fact or structure describable only in a practical, imperatival idiom – belongs to the fabric of reality, and that theoretical cognition, though differentiated in specific ways from practical consciousness, is a necessary aspect of the practical necessity in which human subjectivity consists. This gives us a *subjective* unity of the functions of theoretical and practical reasoning, a unity within the subject.

Exactly such points of unity are employed in Sartre's transcendental argumentation, as the following illustrates. In the chapter on temporality (B&N: 165ff.), Sartre seeks to show, as I said earlier, that our consciousness is necessarily temporal, and that its temporality has a 'dynamic' character, meaning that the for-itself necessarily apprehends itself as having '*become* Past' and as arising 'to become the Present of this Past' (B&N: 165). Sartre argues that this dynamic cannot be grasped in terms of concepts of perma-nence and change and that it requires us to conceive the subject as 'a spontaneity of which we can say: it *is*. Or simply: *This* spontaneity should be allowed to define itself' (B&N: 171). The crucial point for present pur-poses is Sartre's use of the normative-deontological expression 'should be allowed to … ', *devrait se laisser définir par elle-même*, and his equation of this with '*is*': Sartre is suggesting that in thinking this spontaneity, we do not think of ourselves as objects of theoretical judgement alone; the judgement 'I am a spontaneity' is *both* a theoretical assertion *and* an expression of practical consciousness, and so manifests a point of indifference between theoretical and practical thought. This is confirmed shortly afterwards when Sartre explains that the thesis which he has just presented 'by using the concept of spontaneity which seemed to me more familiar to my read-ers', can be restated in his own terminology as a matter of the for-itself's 'having to be', *ayant à l'être* (B&N: 172).

In the terms I used earlier, the situation, or perspective, of having-to-determine-oneself, provides the necessary frame for Sartre's transcendental argumentation.

As regards the *objective* unity of practical and theoretical reason, the agreement of their respective images of the world: on Sartre's account, the correct ontology is necessarily one that is extrapolated from consciousness – this is his explicit commitment to Cartesianism as a philosophical methodology – and the only ontology which *can* be derived from consciousness, so *Being and Nothingness* argues, is one that underwrites our practical orientation, in a revised, purified and corrected form. The agreement of the theoretical and the practical images of the world, the objective unity of practical and theoretical reason, is therefore no mere fortunate accident – it is guaranteed by Sartre's Cartesian method in theoretical philosophy in conjunction with his conception of consciousness as an expression of freedom.

The axiological motivation of Sartre's philosophy referred to earlier is therefore taken up and fulfilled directly within his system, meaning that Sartre has no need to formulate and invoke (as Kant does) the primacy of practical reason as a *distinct principle* within his system, appeal to which is required in order to direct theoretical reasoning from the outside in directions favourable to our practical interests.

Sartre and the standpoint of transcendental claims

With respect to the first three perennial issues in transcendental philosophy, I have argued that Sartre's position is both consistent and in important ways original. The situation changes – as regards not originality, but consistency – when we come to the final issue, concerning the standpoint from which Sartre's philosophy is made out. This involves a difficulty which, I will argue, takes us to the outer limit of Sartre's project.

There can be little doubt that Sartre regards the philosophical outlook which he articulates in *Being and Nothingness* as encompassing and making transparent reality in its entirety.[15] Sartre of course regards some matters as ultimate brute 'facts', to be accepted without further explanation: for instance, at the very highest level, the existence and nature (or non-nature) of the in-itself. But the ultimacy of these 'contingencies' is *not* due, for Sartre, to any failure or our conceptual, linguistic or other abilities to keep pace with the projected objects of our knowledge. Nowhere does Sartre acknowledge limits to human or philosophical cognition: when we reach a terminus in our attempt to grasp matters philosophically, it is not because we have run out of cognitive resources, but because that is where the end of things lies in reality. It is not, therefore, that the in-itself has a concealed constitution which God or perhaps some future physical science could grasp but which we are unable to make out – according to Sartre there *is nothing more* to the in-itself than what we know of it. As he puts it, 'all is there, luminous' in the broad daylight of consciousness (B&N: 591).

There are reasons, moreover, why it may be thought of paramount importance for Sartre that the claims of *Being and Nothingness* should be comprehensive, complete, and unqualified. For one thing, Sartre's thesis of absolute freedom needs to be able to withstand sceptical doubt, and (arguably) any concession that his philosophy offers only a limited view of our situation will fail to rule out the possibility that the freedom which he claims for us is absent from reality and merely belongs to a great, systematic illusion. More generally, the contingencies which Sartre describes need to be interpreted as metaphysically ultimate in order that Sartre can claim for them the crucial significance of exposing the metaphysical *loneliness* of the human situation, the humanly restricted scope of the principle of sufficient reason, an unclouded appreciation of which Sartre regards as essential for our assumption of self-responsibility. Anything less than metaphysical ultimacy would, in Sartre's view, open the door to speculative possibilities – which Sartre associates with theology and Hegel, and wants to exclude at all costs – to the effect that there is after all a rational structure in reality at large which transcends the being of the for-itself, and which may be regarded as grounding and rationalizing human existence; the effect of which, Sartre believes, would be to relieve us of the task of self-determination at the most fundamental level. This is enough to explain why, at an early point in *Being and Nothingness* – at the end of the Introduction – Sartre emphasizes that the work aims to locate man's place in relation to being as a whole.

Now the idea that philosophical enquiry can achieve unrestricted compass is naturally associated with the idea of a 'view from nowhere', a philosophical standpoint above all mere particular, conditioned points of view. However, it is also undeniable that a great deal of Sartre's discussion is emphatically *perspectival*: much of Sartre's philosophical labour is directed towards taking us inside the correct angle of philosophical vision, in order to induce in us a heightened awareness of the *perspectival character* of the phenomenon under discussion. Indeed this point – that Sartre's accounts of how things should be conceived are conditional upon our grasping them from such-and-such an angle – came out in connection with Sartre's 'situated' form of transcendental argumentation.

By way of illustration, consider Sartre's statement, in the context of his theory of freedom, that 'there is no question here of a freedom which could be undetermined and which would pre-exist its choice. We shall never apprehend ourselves except as a choice in the making' (B&N: 501). This is naturally read as demanding that we shift from attempting to conceive freedom as an aperspectival metaphysical fact, to a perspectival appreciation of freedom. Numerous examples of this kind of argumentation in *Being and Nothingness* could be given. In a late interview Sartre said that in *Being and Nothingness* he 'wished to define [consciousness] as it presents itself to us, for you, for me' (IRPG: 40).

There is therefore a puzzle. Sartre appears to offer at one and the same time both a view from nowhere or *extra-perspectival* conception of reality, and a view from somewhere or *perspectival* conception. These two standpoints are not distributed across different sets of phenomena or relativized to different topics of discussion; characteristically Sartre combines both within the breadth of a single paragraph or even sentence.

With regard to the historical affiliations of each, the perspectival standpoint suggests an 'immodest', absolutist, Fichtean version of Kant's strategy of a Copernican revolution in philosophical method, a conception of the task of philosophy as an elucidation *of* the human point of view, *from* and *for* the human point of view, fortified by the claim that this is the *only* point of view, that all would-be 'God's eye' conceptions are null and void. The extra-perspectival standpoint, by contrast, is associated with the metaphysical ambition and theocentric orientation of early modern rationalism, or of Hegel. Which, then, represents Sartre's true metaphilosophical view?

I suggest that Sartre regards the two standpoints as equally necessary, and yet again not as excluding one another but as *coincident* and *complementary.* The coincidence of the two standpoints consists in the idea that it is only by pushing the perspectival standpoint to its limit that we can come to grasp aperspectival reality. The phenomenological ontology of *Being and Nothingness* does not merely and modestly describe how we should *suppose* things to *be* in the light of how they *appear* to us, rather it expresses Sartre's metaphilosophical conviction that it is only when things are exhibited in their fully perspectival character that we can know them as they *are in themselves,* as they would be if apprehended 'from nowhere'. This fits well with Sartre's claim to have dissolved the very opposition of realism and idealism.

The complementarity of the perspectival and extra-perspectival standpoints is expressed in Sartre's intention to offer two, interlocking views of the for-itself, one interior and one exterior. The former shows us how the human subject is related to itself and how the object-world arises in the context of that self-relation. In entertaining the interior view, we *occupy* the perspective of the for-itself, *participating* in its upsurge. Sartre's transcendental argumentation serves this end. The latter involves an apprehension of the for-itself in relation to what is not itself, unmediated by its self-relation. In entertaining the exterior view, we *contemplate* the perspective of the for-itself, *beholding* its upsurge.

We are led then to ask whether this position, as Sartre himself works it out, is coherent and defensible, that is, whether Sartre succeeds in harmonizing the two standpoints. For although there is no contradiction in the idea of conjoining the (external) description *of* a perspective with a (internal) description of what is revealed *from* that perspective, a question is raised unavoidably when this schema is taken, not in its ordinary empirical application, but to define a philosophical project: What standpoint do we occupy in so far as we entertain the conjoined description? What provides for the coherent integration of the conjoined standpoints?

Here I need to be brief.[16] There are several contexts where, I think, a tension between the perspectival and extra-perspectival standpoints is visible,[17] but there is one in which it becomes especially salient and acute.

This is Sartre's anthropogenetic story. Sartre makes a claim regarding the genesis of being-for-itself, namely that being-for-itself is being-in-itself which has undergone a nihilation:

> The For-Itself is like a tiny nihilation which has its origin at the heart of Being; and this nihilation is sufficient to cause a total upheaval to *happen* to the In-itself. This upheaval is the world ...
> As a nihilation it *is made-to-be* by the in-itself.
>
> (B&N: 637–8)

What is the importance for Sartre of this idea? One might perhaps suppose it to be a mere speculative aside, a bit of picture-thinking, but it proves essential to *Being and Nothingness*, in two ways. First, Sartre thinks that the anthropogenetic story is necessary in order for him to be able to claim that he has a conception of being *as such* and in general – it is needed, he says, if we are to think of the two realms of being-in-itself and being-for-itself as linked to form being as a whole. Second, the anthropogenetic story is essential for many of the key claims in Part II of *Being and Nothingness*. It is presupposed by Sartre's accounts of self-consciousness (B&N: 103), of 'lack' as a structure of the for-itself (B&N: 110ff.), of the metaphysics of human motivation, and of the 'facticity' of the for-itself (B&N: 108), without which Sartre would have no theory of freedom to speak of. It also plays an important role, I suggested earlier, in resolving the puzzle regarding Sartre's professed non-idealism.

The difficulty comes with the fact that the anthropogenetic story gives rise, as Sartre notes, to a 'metaphysical problem which could be formulated thus: Why does the for-itself arise from being [à *partir de l'être*]?' (B&N: 639). Sartre establishes that there is only one candidate for an answer to this question: namely that being-in-itself gives rise to being-for-itself in order to rid itself of contingency, to 'found itself', to become God or cause-of-itself.

This would mean, however, that the in-itself's generation of the for-itself has been conceived as a *purposive project*, and the attribution of a project to the in-itself contradicts, of course, Sartre's conception of being-in-itself. Sartre recognizes all of this:

> [O]ntology here comes up against a profound contradiction since ... [i]n order to be a project of founding itself, the in-itself

would of necessity have to be originally a presence to itself, i.e., it would have to be already consciousness.

(B&N: 640)

The contradiction suggests that at this point, if not at others, Sartre's two standpoints are not in harmony: the perspectival standpoint instructs Sartre to restrict himself to the human standpoint, the interior view of the for-itself, and so to declare the question regarding the origin of the for-itself gratuitous or empty; while the extra-perspectival standpoint, the exterior view of the for-itself, demands that we find a way of thinking being-for-itself and its genesis in relation to being as a whole.

In Section 1 of the Conclusion (B&N: 641ff.) Sartre leans towards the first option, though not without considerable ambiguity, and perhaps without realizing that if his anthropogenetic story is empty or a mere fiction, then the danger presents itself that so too are the theories – of self-consciousness, facticity, and so on – which presuppose it.

Fichte or Schelling

Light can be shed on this problem in Sartre by drawing comparison with an earlier point in the history of post-Kantian philosophy.

I have referred several times to the similarity of Sartre's views with Fichte's, and there is much more to be said on that topic. The philosopher whom Sartre recalls with his anthropogenetic story, however, is undoubtedly Schelling, Fichte's critic and successor. Schelling does not tell the same story as Sartre, but the accounts that Schelling gives of the genesis of self-consciousness in writings of the period from roughly 1800 to 1813 are unmistakeably of the same order as Sartre's anthropogenetic theory, and directed to the same *explanandum*, namely, to grasping how individual self-conscious subjectivity can arise out of pre-self-conscious being.[18]

The contradiction which we saw emerge in Sartre's anthropogenetic story, I now want to suggest, mirrors and reproduces the differences and disagreement between Fichte and Schelling. While Fichte asserts, in orthodox transcendental fashion, the priority and sufficiency for all legitimate philosophical purposes of the perspective of self-consciousness from which his *Wissenschaftslehre* is developed, Schelling counter-asserts the need for this idealistic perspective to be supplemented and completed by a 'realistic' philosophy which starts from *being* rather than self-consciousness, alleging, in criticism of Fichte, that a philosophy of self-consciousness which shirks this task is deficient and ultimately ungrounded.

The relation of the straightforwardly transcendental, subjectivity-based elements in *Being and Nothingness* to Sartre's anthropogenetic story parallels, I am therefore suggesting, the relation of Fichte's *Wissenschaftslehre* to

Schelling's idealist–realist speculative philosophy. And the contradiction which surfaces in Sartre's account may be regarded as the result of his having as it were, on the one hand, adhered to Fichte's metaphilosophy, which says that the perspective of the I suffices to give us an absolute picture of reality and, on the other hand, accepted Schelling's position that taking the absolute view requires us to think of self-consciousness from the standpoint of being as a whole.

If Sartre were to succeed in defusing the contradiction – and, as I noted at the end of the previous section, he at any rate makes an attempt to do this – then it could be claimed on Sartre's behalf that he shows a way of mediating the opposition of Fichte and Schelling and that his position provides an alternative, arguably superior, to each of theirs. If, on the other hand, the contradiction abides, then it is fair to say that Sartre's position can be made consistent only by resolving itself in the direction of either Fichte or Schelling, where each of these resolutions will entail, in different ways, a profound alteration to Sartre's conception of the in-itself.[19]

Sartre and the transcendental tradition

It is surely remarkable that Sartre – whose knowledge of Fichte and Schelling in the period of composition of *Being and Nothingness* was either negligible or non-existent, though he had enough knowledge of Hegel to recognize that Hegel's system should be regarded as at least putting a question mark over the reality of individual freedom – should have come so close to reproducing the early German idealist positions, and that the Fichte-to-Schelling development from 1794 to 1813 should be (so to speak) rerun, in the way I have tried to indicate, in Sartre's philosophical development from 1936 to 1943, in the course of which Sartre is carried far from his original mid-1930s conception of himself as a phenomenologist who has said goodbye to metaphysics and returned to the purely concrete.

Why should this be? What most deeply distinguishes Sartre from Husserl and Heidegger at the level of philosophical motivation is the concern with human freedom, and it is this Kantian motive which, it seems correct to suppose, causes Sartre not only to remodel phenomenology on a more orthodox Kantian pattern, but also to modify Kant's position in profound ways, leading Sartre into Fichtean and Schellingian territory. I began my discussion by suggesting – in a reconstructive spirit – that Sartre is helpfully viewed in direct relation to Kant, but Sartre did not of course regard himself as setting out from and attempting to get beyond Kant. Rather, to the extent that Sartre took his orientation from classical German philosophy, his aim was to get away from Hegel. These two paths may be thought to converge, however: if Kantian idealism is insufficient to realize its own philosophical ends, and if Hegel's transformation of Kantianism sacrifices too much of what originally animates the project of Critical philosophy, then we are directed towards the non-Hegelian forms of German idealism represented by Fichte and Schelling.

Two things are thereby signalled for transcendental philosophy in general. First, the case of Sartre contradicts a widely accepted narrative of the development of transcendental philosophy, according to which the overall historical trajectory of transcendentalism consists in a progressive thinning of its metaphysical commitments, and in its finally coming down to earth at a point where it is able to unite with a rich naturalism. Second, consideration of Sartre indicates the likelihood that, in so far as the transcendental project is committed to a *strong* conception of human freedom, a system of freedom along the lines of either Fichte or Schelling is hard to avoid. Whether that commitment is to be retained or shaken off, and whether in its absence the transcendental project is sufficiently well motivated to hold our interest, are questions which – to the extent that our interest lies in Sartre's philosophy as a systematic whole – there is compelling reason to pursue.

Notes

1 Nature and being-in-itself are not the same, of course, but the differences are not presently relevant.

2 The view I have ascribed to Sartre – that Kant's position is insufficiently anti-naturalistic and ends up compromised, a halfway house – reproduces an attitude to Kantianism prominent in the early post-Kantian period.

3 The way is then open to the comparison, pursued by Katherine Morris (2008), of Sartre with the late Wittgenstein, as offering philosophical therapy.

4 A point which echoes the famous objection of Barry Stroud (1968) to transcendental arguments.

5 Answers of the type that a Strawson-type transcendental argument could supply.

6 The teleology of the for-itself demands its transcendence, one aspect of which is the *knowing* of the object: knowledge is an immediate presence of consciousness to the thing (B&N: 195–6), necessitated by the for-itself's having to constitute itself as *not being* the thing' (B&N: 197). Space does not allow me to pursue the point, but Sartre's approach to epistemology has an important similarity with that of Fichte: see Horstmann (forthcoming) on 'grounding-oriented' as opposed to 'justification-oriented' anti-sceptical positions.

7 Two brief observations, which for want of space I will have to leave unexplored. (1) In consequence of Sartre's ontologization of the transcendental, the distinction is elided between the two tasks of giving (a) a proof of a transcendental necessity, and (b) a metaphysical explanation of why the necessity obtains. For example, Sartre merges the question, 'How can we *explain* this dynamic character of temporality', with the task of 'show[ing] that its dynamic is an essential structure of the For-itself' (B&N: 170). (2) Sartre is not always clear about the necessity he wants to attach to the formal features of empirical reality: see e.g. his statements at B&N: 227 and 231–2 regarding the possibility of a world without motion or change. There is also considerable variation by topic in the modality of what Sartre holds to be shown by his enquiry. For example,

Sartre seems to argue that there must be motion (B&N: 236), while with respect to the principle of causality (B&N: 230–1), his claims seem to be restricted to only a *correlation* of formal features of empirical reality with structures of the for-itself.

8 Note that 'consideration' here has ontological, not merely methodological, significance: the qualification in-itself attaches not to the mode in which we do our considering, but to what is under consideration, namely O itself.

9 See the formulation and analysis of this issue in Sacks 2000: Ch. 6.

10 The question of the conditions of the absolutely primitive distinction of I and not-I figures in Fichte too as an important reason for going beyond Kant, in sections 1–5 of the Second Introduction to the 1797 *Wissenschaftslehre*, but Fichte does not draw an ontological conclusion.

11 An alternative formulation of the contrast I want to draw: Kant and Husserl allow a distinction to be drawn between transcendental *roles*, and that which *occupies* them, while Sartre denies, with respect to consciousness, that this distinction can be drawn.

12 This shows the remarkable similarity between the concept of consciousness in Sartre, and Fichte's conception of the 'I' as a *Tathandlung*, a non-objectual self-reverting Act which furnishes a transcendental foundation.

13 Sartre also addresses here an objection he finds in Heidegger: that the *cogito* cannot escape instantaneity. The only alternative to the *cogito* in the theory of knowledge, Sartre claims, is (Hegel's) coherentism.

14 In *Existentialism Is a Humanism*, Sartre says that human dignity leads to postulating subjectivity 'as a standard of truth' (EH: 41).

15 Merleau-Ponty criticizes Sartre on this exact count (e.g. 1964: 74, 77, 91).

16 For more detailed discussion, see Gardner 2006.

17 These include Sartre's accounts of intersubjectivity, transcendence, and value. Compare Sartre's affirmation that lack is an objective ontological structure of the for-itself (B&N: 110) with his claim that the teleology of the for-itself 'exists only for the For-itself' and 'disappears with it' (B&N: 240). The point can be made also with reference to assertions such as: 'For the indifference of being is *nothing*: we can not think it or even perceive it' (B&N: 214). In such characteristically Sartrean movements of thought, perspectival and extra-perspectival elements are juxtaposed forcibly: we step outside our perspective, or seem to do so, when we judge that being is indifferent to us, only to realize that this judgement is empty because it requires us to escape our perspective, which is impossible. At time Sartre wrestles quite explicitly with this doubling and superimposition of standpoints. For example: 'The For-Itself is God in that it it decides that Being has a meaning, Being will have a meaning *for the for-itself*. But since the For-itself is an absolute/subject, it is absolutely certain that Being will have a meaning ... if the In-itself has a meaning for the Absolute/subject, this meaning, absolutely experienced, is absolute' (NE: 485–6). In this instance, the tension is located in Sartre's simultaneous (i) extra-perspectival elevation and installation of the for-itself in God's vacant place, making it appear that the for-itself receives metaphysical certification, and that its claims are sanctioned, from an external standpoint, and (ii) absolutization of the perspective of the for-itself; making it difficult to determine what 'absolute experience' of the In-itself's 'absolute' meaningfulness might consist in. The case can be made that the contradiction resurfaces in the *Critique of Dialectical Reason*: see Sartre's fascinating discussion of 'matter' (CDR1: 180–2) and acceptance of 'the following two true but [*primâ facie*] contradictory propositions: all existence in the universe is material; everything in the world of man is human' (CDR1: 181);

Sartre's claim is that his newly avowed, non-theological 'monism' transcends the contradiction.

18 See e.g. Schelling 2001 [1813]: 123–4, 136; discussed in Gardner 2006.

19 Suggesting that Sartre has an inkling of the option represented by Schelling, note the (somewhat obscure) remarks on the possibility of a 'metaphysics of nature' at B&N: 644–5.

5

BEING COLONIZED

Azzedine Haddour

[handwritten: Being is experienced on the outside. consciousness is a nothing new.]

Introduction

'It is not in some hiding-place', Sartre writes, 'that we will discover our-selves; it is on the road, in the town, in the midst of the crowd, a thing among things, a man among men' (IHP: 5). Here Sartre is closer to Baudelaire than Proust, in that he strives to rid existentialism of Proustian infatuations with psychoanalysis. According to Sartre, we discover ourselves not through introspection but by looking outside; 'everything is finally outside', he asserts, 'everything, even including ourselves. Outside, in the world, among others' (IHP: 5). The self does not inhabit consciousness; the latter can neither be reduced to an inner process of cogitation nor confused with a nebulous substance called the psyche. Consciousness is a *nothingness*; being is experienced on the outside. The self is constructed in its interaction with others, in the outside world, or to put it in Heideggerian terms, as being-in-the-world.

Sartre situates the consciousness of self at the nexus of a relation of reciprocity between one 'seeing-the-Other' and 'being-seen-by-another' (B&N: 281). Through the look, there is an upsurge of being, or as he puts it, an 'irruption of the self' – 'I see *myself* because *somebody* sees me' (B&N: 284). One becomes conscious of oneself by becoming conscious of Others. Objectness is one of the characteristics of this being-for-others (B&N: 277–8).[1] The look is crucial in establishing intersubjective relations; relations which are hostile and conflictual (B&N: 451). Sartre conceives of these relations in terms of a master/slave Hegelian dialectic which oppo-ses the master of the gaze to an objectified Other.[2] The first moment of this dialectical schema is the realization of being objectified by the look; the second moment is when, in returning the look, the Other is objectified. My project in this article is to elaborate on the workings of this dialectical operation in *Anti-Semite and Jew* and *Black Orpheus*. How does Sartre apprehend the being-of-the-colonized in a schema where he appropriates the trope of the slave to hypostatize the alienation of the 'being-seen' at the end of the Other's objectifying look? As they offer themselves to the

73

Other's appraisal, both the Jew and Negro experience their Being-for-Others as a source of anguish and alienation. Could they return the look? Could they possibly discover themselves in the crowd, by interacting with other people, as men in the midst of other men? Could they ever overcome the determinants of facticity without falling into the pitfalls of inauthenticity? Is their consciousness to be apprehended just from the outside? In the first section of this article, my intention is to assess what Albert Memmi calls the 'philosophy of points of view' in *Anti-Semite and Jew*. In the second, my focus will be on *Black Orpheus*, and on Frantz Fanon's critical review of Sartrean existential phenomenology.

Philosophy of view points

According to Sartre, the Jew's identity is an '*identity of situation*' constructed through the objectifying gaze of the anti-Semite (A&J: 72). If the Jew did not exist, he contends, the anti-Semite would invent him (A&J: 13). How does the Jew view himself 'in the midst of a society that takes him for a Jew' (A&J: 72)? Deep down, Sartre writes,

> the Jew considers himself the same as others. He speaks the same language; he has the same class interests, the same national interests ... Yet they give him to understand that he does not belong, that he has a 'Jewish way' of speaking, of reading, of voting. ... the root of Jewish disquietude is the necessity imposed upon the Jew of subjecting himself to endless self-examination and finally of assuming a phantom personality, at once strange and familiar, that haunts him and which is nothing but himself – himself as others see him. You may say that this is the lot of all, that each of us has a character familiar to those close to us which we ourselves do not see. No doubt: this is the expression of our fundamental relation to the Other. But the Jew has a personality like the rest of us, and on the top of that he is Jewish. It amounts in a sense to a doubling of the fundamental relationship with the Other. The Jew is over-determined.

> (A&J: 78–9)

In *Being and Nothingness*, Sartre describes 'the transfiguration of the Other' as an ambivalent dialectical operation that oscillates between objectification and subjection, a constant movement from transfiguration to degradation, from the Other-as-subject to the Other-as-object, and vice versa. This movement must not be confused with what Sartre dubs as the 'doubling of the fundamental relationship with the Other'. In this relation, the Other assumes a productive and yet contradictory function: at one level, the Other represents the speculum through which the process of individuation

74

and differentiation takes place; a process which crucially subjects individuals by making them distinct and yet belonging to the group. The Other is that which engenders difference within the same group. At a second level, the Other is that which conversely brings about the exclusion of those who are perceived by this group as different and not belonging. This perception removes in fact individuality from the subject and ostracizes difference. Like the Negro, the Jew has got a distinct personality and *in addition* to that the Jew is a Jew, which sets him apart from the rest of the group. Like the Negro, the Jew is *over*determined by his ethnic difference. In fact, ethnic difference becomes a supplementary characteristic which comes to define the Jew as a Jew. The Otherness of the Jew becomes an absolute difference which as a supplement attaches itself to the body of the Jew. It is a sort of (to use the language of Jacques Derrida) 'supplementary double', or (to use Fanon's) a 'mask' which comes to superimpose itself on the character of the Jew determining the Jew as an inassimilable other (A&J: 83), kept at the very heart of society only to serve an economic function, that which 'a Christian could not undertake without defiling himself' (A&J: 66–8). Such difference is doubly alienating; this alienation is of a different order to that described by Sartre in 'normal' intersubjective relations. The stereotypical views of the anti-Semite, he argues, poison the life of the Jew; in order not to conform to these views, the Jew overdetermines his conduct from the inside (A&J: 95). Overdetermination is the consciousness of oppression and alienation; it is the opposite of ideology which, as a stratagem, gives rise to false consciousness by hiding the objective conditions of its subjects as oppressed subjects. The Jew is not the subject of an ideology insidiously working to exploit him but he is the object of the anti-Semite's views that patently alienate him from himself and from others. The Jew is made to perceive himself through the prism of the anti-Semitic discourse as an outsider. In Sartre's phraseology:

> The Jew, because he knows he is under observation, takes the initiative and attempts to look at himself through the eyes of others. This objectivity toward himself is still another ruse of inauthenticity: while he contemplates himself with the 'detachment' of another, he feels himself in effect *detached* from himself; he becomes another person, a pure witness.
>
> (A&J: 97)

Sartre represents both the anti-Semite and Jew as partners implicated in the discourse of anti-Semitism, but this partnership never implies reciprocity.

One of the most contentious and problematic aspects of *Anti-Semite and Jew* (arousing the acrimony of its Jewish readers) is its jargon of authenticity and inauthenticity that Sartre employs to delineate the ambivalent character of the Jew. According to Sartre, '[the inauthentic Jew] looks at his coreligionist with the eyes of an anti-Semite' (A&J: 103) or 'look[s] at [his] own personalit[y] with the eyes of the democrat' (A&J: 117). The inauthentic Jew is one who seeks *avenues of flight* from an insufferable situation. In his quest 'to be recognized as a man by other men', he is tempted 'to lose himself in the crowd of Christians' – i.e. to obliterate his difference in a universe of 'anonymity' and efface the traces of his ethnicity in a 'humanity without race' (A&J: 98). The inauthentic Jew embraces a universalistic and universalizing conception of the world that excludes the very idea of race. Sartre characterizes the inauthentic Jew as a 'disembodied' Jew whose 'passion for the universal' necessitates the loss of 'individual traits' (A&J: 111). The inauthentic Jew espouses the critical rationalism of the democrat that demands the same rights for Jews as other men, 'not as concrete and individual products of history' (A&J: 117). Sartre bemoans 'the impossible dream of universal brotherhood in a world that rejects [the Jew]'.

> It is our eyes that reflect to him the unacceptable image that he wishes to dissimulate. It is our words and our gestures – *all* our words and *all* our gestures – our anti-Semitism, but equally our condescending liberalism – that have poisoned him. It is we who constrain him to choose to be a Jew whether through flight from himself or through self-assertion; it is we who force him into the dilemma of Jewish authenticity or inauthenticity. We have created this variety of men who have no meaning except as artificial products of a capitalist (or feudal) society, whose only reason for existing is to serve as scapegoat for a still prelogical community.
>
> (A&J: 135–6)

Sartre seems to remove the possibilities of choice from the Jew, as he asserts that it is us who fix him by defining him. How could he be in bad faith if the possibilities of choices were denied to him? How could he ever be inauthentic or authentic, if it were us 'who constrain him to choose to be a Jew whether through flight from himself or through self-assertion'? However, and in spite of this contradiction, Sartre maintains that the authentic Jew is one who realizes one's condition as a Jew and assumes it despite adversity (A&J: 90). Authenticity can lead to two conflicting political decisions: (i) the Jew can choose to be authentic by asserting his place in the French community as a *French Jew*; (ii) he may also decide to create an autonomous Jewish nation possessing its own soil and autonomy. In Sartre's view, these two choices are not mutually exclusive and 'might be reconciled and made complementary as two aspects of Jewish reality' (A&J: 139–40).

In *Portrait of a Jew*, ten years after the publication of *Black Skin, White Masks*, Memmi echoes Fanon's criticism of Sartre. I will have occasion to return to Fanon's criticism below. With one stroke Memmi brushes to one side what he calls 'the philosophy of points of view', that is the Sartrean representation of Jewishness. 'Whatever the corrosive acuity of that point of view', Memmi writes, 'the Jew is not merely the product of other men's views. He is not only the man who is looked upon as a Jew. If he were only that, he would be nothing more than pure negativity, anxieties and confusions, wounds and sores' (1962: 80). Memmi characterizes Sartre as the non-Jew of *good will* who has failed to understand truly the plight of the Jew. Given another opportunity, Memmi argues, Sartre would offer a more positive representation of the Jew; and 'it is in that perspective, generous but mutilated, that we must place Sartre's concept of the Jew as the pure expression of a non-Jew, a view so popular at the end of WWII. It is a friendly concept, eager to help, to save the Jew, but not enough to take account of the reality of Jewish existence' (1962: 262). Memmi refutes Sartre's assumption that the Jew is nothing but a reflection of the gaze of the anti-Semite. He is adamant that 'if Jewishness is only a tissue of lies and misunderstanding, with that defamatory placard removed from his back, the Jew, in short, no longer exists' (1962: 264).

Taking his cue from Memmi, Lawrence Kritzman dismisses Sartre's view of Jewishness. 'In spite of Sartre's goal to defend Jewish "plight"', he remarks, 'his focusing on Jewish characteristics, and on Jewishness as a socially constructed way of being, led him to formulate a negatively conceived essentialism on what he termed the "Jewish question"' (1995: 99). Kritzman intimates that the Sartrean model, which is predicated upon a dialectical relation between anti-Semite and Jew, between self and Other, between sameness and difference, constructs Jewishness as 'the result of the gaze of the anti-Semite' (ibid.). The Sartrean situation, according to Kritzman, 'produces a sense of difference derived from the petrifying order of the same' (1995: 101). He levels the charge against Sartre of constructing 'the "Jew" [as] both the sight (the vision) and the site (the *locus*) of the anti-Semite's existence. Within this framework, the "Jew" becomes the repository of absolute hatred'. Kritzman conflates Sartre's critique of anti-Semitism with the gaze of the anti-Semite which objectifies, scapegoats and excludes the Jew. It is misleading to suggest, as does Kritzman, that Sartre (or at least his model of analysis) 'overdetermines Jewish subjectivity and makes it the effect of the anti-Semite's visual prowess' (1995: 100).

Like Kritzman, Susan Suleiman (1995, 1999) takes Sartre to task for reproducing the discourse of the anti-Semite. Michael Walzer (1995) also takes a similar line of criticism accusing Sartre for voiding Jewishness of its historical and cultural content. Whilst Walzer draws on Memmi, in fact he reiterates Fanon's critique of Sartre in *Black Skin, White Masks*, excoriating Sartre for his Marxist eschatology which announces the disappearance of the Jew at the end of history with the advent of a classless society. Denis Hollier takes issue with Suleiman; his reading of the solution Sartre proposes to the 'Jewish question' is at odds with Walzer's. According to Hollier, Sartre's intervention must not be interpreted as part of a Marxist eschatology subsuming the Jewish question into a project of a future class-less society. His approach to the question, Hollier writes, 'doesn't fit the Marxist perspective of the end of history ... it is not mankind's triumphant exodus out of history, but Israel's negotiating the end of its exile from history' (1999: 155). Hollier defines the concept of assimilation in his work decon-structively: it does not exact from the Jew conformity and submission in the name of universalism. It announces post-Hegelian enlightenment, i.e. 'the pure openness of historical synchronicity', the advent of a society that has more than one history but shares the same time, a society risking '[its] past in the other's language, in the other's time' (1999: 159). This sort of assimila-tion is predicated on an ethical imperative that respects the other's difference.

White gaze, black face

In *Black Orpheus*, Sartre contends, the gaze reveals the secret of being and hypostatizes its essence. He inscribes colour, as well as vision, within a colonialist economy that perpetrated the dominance of the white. He per-ceptively points out that the poets of negritude are now returning the look, as they fix their 'steady and corrosive gaze' on the white man who 'has enjoyed for three thousand years the privilege of seeing without being seen' (BO: 10, 7). Through their poetic expression, they become consciousness of themselves, but this coming-into-consciousness is different from class consciousness. As Sartre explains:

> The Negro, like the white worker, is a victim of the capitalistic structure of our society, and he discovers a solidarity of interests beyond the nuances of skin colour with certain classes of Europeans oppressed as he. Such a solidarity incites him to plan a society without privilege where the pigmentation of the skin will be treated as a simple accident. But, if the oppression is a common one, it is patterned after historical and geographical conditions. The black man is a victim of it, inasmuch as he is black, in his role as colonized native or as a deported African. And since he is oppressed in his race and because of it, it is first of his race that it is necessary for him to take conscience. He must compel those who, during the centuries, have vainly attempted, because he was a Negro, to reduce him to the status of the beast to recognize him as a man. Now here, it is not escape, nor trickery, nor 'crossing the line' that he can consider. A Jew, white among white men, can deny that he is a Jew, can declare himself a man among men. The Negro cannot deny that he is Negro nor claim for himself this abstract uncoloured humanity. He is black. Thus he is held to authenticity.

> (BO: 14–15)

Negritude as a coming-into-consciousness 'differs in nature from that which Marxism attempts to waken in the white worker' (BO: 16). The proletariat becomes conscious of itself as a class, determined by the capitalistic motions of profit and loss and conditioned by its objective situation. This coming-to-consciousness is objective, it is in accordance with the Sartrean theory that we discover ourselves in the world as people amongst other people and not by retreating into the inner recesses of the self through the process of introspection. It is, Sartre argues, 'exactly the opposite of a redescent into one's self; it has to do here with a recognition in and by action of the objective situation of the proletariat, a situation determined by the varying circumstances of production and distribution' (BO: 13). Class consciousness is at the antipodes of the consciousness of race; and according to Sartre 'the Negro who vindicates his negritude in a revolutionary movement places himself, then and there, upon the terrain of Reflection, where he wishes to rediscover in himself certain objective traits growing out of African civilizations, or hopes to find the black Essence in the wells of his soul' (BO: 17). This retreat into subjectivity, argues Sartre, gives rise to poetry.

Sartre opposes white to black, class-consciousness to negritude, subjectivity to objectivity: the language of the white European worker as objective and devoid of poetry to that of the Negro as subjective, a source from whence springs poetry. The white worker, though exploited in his labour and oppressed in his body, is treated by the bourgeoisie as a human being.[3] Oppressed in his body and soul, the Negro is, on the other hand, alienated 'in the midst of the cold buildings of the white culture and the white techniques'; to remove the shackles of its oppression, he returns to African culture, which Sartre describes as a 'redescent into the burning Hell of the black soul' (BO: 19, 21).

The specificities of a given society are captured by what Sartre calls 'the untranslatable locutions of its language'; because they do not have a common language, the black poets of the diaspora are henceforward forced to appropriate the language of the white colonizer to express their views (BO: 22). Elaborating upon the ways in which they adopted language, Sartre writes:

> Dispersed by the slave trade to the four corners of the earth, the blacks have no language common to them all; to incite the oppressed to unite they must have recourse to the words of the oppresser. It is the French language which will furnish the black singer the largest audience amongst the blacks, at least within the limits of French colonization. It is in this language, pale like the flesh of the chicken, pale and cold as our gods, and of which Mallarmé said, 'it it is the neutral language "par excellence", since its genius requires an attenuation of all colours too vibrant or variegated'; it is in this

language, for them half dead, that Damas, Diop, Laleau, Rabear-ivelo pour the fire of their skies and of their hearts. Only through it can they communicate; like the scholars of the sixteenth century who understood each other only in Latin, the blacks rediscover themselves only on the terrain full of the traps which white men have set for them ... And since words derived from ideas, when the Negro declares in French that he rejects French culture, he takes in one hand that which he has pushed aside with the other.

(BO: 22–3)

Sartre establishes a correlation between language and existence or in his parlance 'a pre-established harmony [that] rules the correspondence of the Word and of Being' (BO: 25). Words are, Sartre writes, 'like sensory organs, like the mouth and the hands, open windows to the world'. Language provides for the poets of negritude access to a white world in which they were hitherto denigrated; 'since the oppresser is present even in the language they speak, they will speak this language to destroy it' (BO: 26). Their use of French idiom is *deconstructive*, affecting 'the holocaust of words' and the 'auto-destruction of the language' (BO: 25) which maintained the hierarchical coupling of white and black, the domination of the former over the latter. By subverting the 'language which consecrate[s] the priority of white over black' (BO: 27), the poets of negritude poetize the French language. In this respect, the poets of negritude are the most radical and revolutionary of the *avant-garde*. By reaching to the depths of being, they project 'a certain form of humanity concrete and well determined' (BO: 37). Sartre describes their descent into these depths as an attempt 'to plunge under the superficial crust of reality, of common sense, of reasonableness, in order to touch the bottom of the soul to awaken the immemorial powers of desire' (BO: 33, 34). This introspective turn to self concurs with the surrealist project to 'recover beyond race and ... class ... the silent dazzling shadows which no more oppose themselves to anything' (BO: 36). Negritude deconstructs the hierarchical coupling of binary opposites: 'It is not a question of meeting in a calm unity of opposites but rather a forced coupling, into a single sex, of black in its opposition to white' (BO: 36). Negritude sets itself against Europe's colonial white culture which denigrates the Negro and perpetrates his oppression. Negritude announces the death of the denigrated Negro and the birth of the black soul; this 'dialectic law of successive transformations' empowers the Negro to coincide with himself in his negritude (BO: 31). Simply put: it is the 'being-in-the-world of the Negro' (BO: 41).

Sartre describes negritude as 'a sort of poetic psycho-analysis' (BO: 58) which helps men of colour discover who and what they are. It is at one and the same time necessity and freedom; a 'datum of fact' and a 'value'; an object of 'empirical intuition' and a 'moral concept'; facticity of blackness

and will to be (BO: 58). He characterizes negritude as a 'moment of separation or of negativity' that heralds the ultimate unity of the oppressed people
against colonial oppression. It is a moment of negativity and separation
because it smacks of racism, but this sort of 'anti-racist racism' paves the
way to the abolition of racial and ultimately class differences (BO: 15, 59).
Negritude is, at one and the same time, the colour of being (BO: 59) and
'nudity without colour' (BO: 62); it is a celebration and disavowal of colour;
it is love, the coming together of differences. Despite warning against the
confusion of the specificity of class with the facticity of race (BO: 59), Sartre
could not help but reproduce the binary language which opposes white to
black: the former representing Capital, the latter Labour; the one employs
intellection, the other comprehension. For Sartre, the notion of class is
abstract and universal and that of race is concrete and particular; class is 'a
methodical construction emerging from experience', race is 'the product of
a psycho-biological syncretism' (BO: 59).

Men of colour have to renounce their negritude in order to join the
workmen's march towards universal history. Negritude must be dialectical;
it must surpass itself in order to fulfil its ambition of acceding to universality: a project which coincides with Marxist teleology. Put in Sartre's
words: 'At a blow the subjective, existential, ethnic notion of negritude
"passes" as Hegel would say, into the objective, positive, exact notion of
the *proletariat*' (BO: 59). Furthermore:

> Negritude appears as the weak stage of a dialectical progression: the
> theoretical and practical affirmation of white supremacy is the
> thesis; the position of Negritude as antithetical value is the moment
> of the negativity. But this negative moment is not sufficient in itself
> and the blacks who employ it well know it; they know that it serves
> to prepare the way for the synthesis or the realization of the human
> society without racism. Thus Negritude is dedicated to its own
> destruction, it is passage and not objective, means and not the
> ultimate goal.
>
> (BO: 59–60)

Ultimately the Negro must lose his negritude, i.e. the particularities of race,
in the same way as 'the white worker also takes conscience of his class to
deny it, since he wishes the advent of a society without class' (BO: 62).
'It is', writes Sartre, 'at the moment that it renounces itself that it finds
itself' (BO: 62). To attain universality, the specific must obliterate itself; to
become universal, men of colour have to overcome their facticity. Here we
confront a major contradiction in Sartre's position: the poets of negritude
must ultimately renounce that which they ought to celebrate: their negritude. In addition, how could these men renounce their facticity which holds
them to authenticity and not act in bad faith? Indeed, oppressed people

must take responsibility to rid themselves of oppression, but how could the black man overcome the facticity of blackness? '[I]t is', says Sartre, 'at the bottom of his heart that he finds race and it is his heart which he must tear' (BO: 63).

Contra to his earlier view that consciousness is nothingness and being is experienced outside, in the case of the Negro Sartre admits that the latter finds himself not outside in the crowd but in the inner depth of the heart. The existential phenomenology Sartre situates at the interface of inside/ outside, subjective/objective, black/white, is problematic in Fanon's *Black Skin, White Masks*. It is in a white crowd, as we are going to see in Fanon's case, that the Negro discovers his difference but can never lose the determinants of his facticity, the markers of ethnicity which have made him victim of racism and colonial oppression.

With a touch of irony, Fanon suggests that philosophy and more specifically ontology cannot deal with the being-of-the-black. He attempts to rationalize the world but it is the world that rejects him because of his colour. 'Since no agreement was possible on the level of reason', he writes, 'I threw myself back toward unreason' (1986: 123). The reference to Senghor is explicit; it refers us to his deconstructive attempt to reverse the binary couplets of black/white, nature/culture, irrationality/rationality which perpetrated the inferiority of the former and the superiority of the latter. Like Senghor, he 'wade[s] in the irrational' and finds himself at home in negritude. 'From the opposite end of the white world', Fanon maintains, 'a magical Negro culture was hailing me' (1986: 123). For a moment, he is convinced by Senghor's rejection of Cartesian logic which governed the white world, as he asserts that 'the body is not something opposed to what you call the mind. We are in the world. And long live the couple, Man and Earth!' Taking his cue from men of letters, like Senghor and Sartre, Fanon is adamant that 'white civilization overlooks subtle riches and sensitivity' (1986: 126–7). With negritude, he writes, 'here we have the Negro rehabilitated, "standing before the bar", ruling the world with intuition' (1986: 127). In the sodality of the disciples of negritude, he discovers a relation of coexistence with the world. Is this relation defined in Sartrean terms?

As he accuses the white man of attempting to colonize and enslave the world by deploying reason as an instrument of oppression, Fanon parodies the views of those who conceive of negritude as 'an insurance policy on humanness' in a world that has become prosaic and soulless. Those who 'feel that they have become too mechanized', Fanon ironically notes, are now turning to ask men of colour for 'a little human substance' (1986: 129). Fanon's ironical criticism seems to target the author of *Black Orpheus* who presents negritude as a source of poetry. How can the Negro provide 'a little human substance' when he is dehumanized? Sartre can only gloss over, as he poetizes, the material suffering of the Negro.

As has been suggested, the creolization of French language is for Sartre a revolutionary act that disrupts the conceptual bond the signifier has with the signified: a deconstructive operation which produces poetry. There is nothing revolutionary and poetic about the appropriation of pidgin French. Creole does not have the same revolutionary impetus for Fanon. The phenomenon of language is very important for him, as it provides the key to 'the dimension of *the other*'. Like Sartre, he contends that language provides access for man to be-in-the-world: it puts him face-to-face with Being. Simply put: 'to speak is to exist absolutely for the other' (1986: 17). Language is not a neutral structure: to speak a given language, Fanon argues, is to assume the whole weight of a culture, and the black Antillean who relinquishes creole and learns how to speak French properly is in fact donning a white mask (1986: 36). He espouses rather than turns against the French language.[4] He adopts French language so as to lose himself – the facticity of his blackness – in a white world. To address him in pidgin is to talk down to him, or as Fanon puts it: 'to fasten him to the effigy of himself, to snare him, to imprison him, the eternal victim of an essence, of an *appearance* for which he is not responsible' (1986: 35).

Relations of identity are problematic for the Negro who is made to situate himself in relation to two systems of cultural reference. Intersubjective relations double on racial difference. Being-for-others is doubly a source of alienation and anguish. Elaborating on the ontology of the Negro, his being-black-in-the-world-of-the-white, Fanon writes:

> As long as the black man is among his own, he will have no occasion, except in minor internal conflicts, to experience his being through others. There is of course the moment of 'being for others', of which Hegel speaks, but every ontology is made unattainable in a colonized and civilized society … In the *Weltanschauung* of a colonized people there is an impurity, a flaw that outlaws any ontological explanation. Someone may object that this is the case with every individual, but such an objection merely conceals a basic problem. Ontology – once it is finally admitted as leaving existence by the wayside – does not permit us to understand the being of the black man. For not only must the black man be black; he must be black in relation to the white man. Some critics will take it on themselves to remind us that this proposition has a converse. I say that this is false. The black has no ontological resistance in the eyes of the white man. Overnight the Negro has been given two frames of reference within which he has had to place himself. His metaphysics, or, less pretentiously, his customs and the sources on which they were based, were wiped out because they were in conflict with a civilization that he did not know and that imposed itself on him.
>
> (1986: 109–10)

Racism has perverse effects on the ontological constitution of Negro. In a white society, he encounters an objectifying gaze that denies his subjectivity. This gaze disrupts the harmonious relationship the black subject has with his body and self. By internalizing the views of the white, the Negro starts to perceive himself through the prism of a racist discourse which contests his own identity. He is made to adopt the posture of a third person that views himself with the critical 'detachment' of a 'pure witness'.

The Negro is one who others regard as a Negro. He cannot experience his being through others, Fanon argues, since he has 'no ontological resistance' to the white man's objectifying gaze (1986: 109–10). The encounter with this gaze gives rise to the fragmentation of the black man's self. In a phraseology which summons up Sartre's *Anti-Semite and Jew*, he writes: 'And then the occasion arose when I had to meet the white man's eyes. An unfamiliar weight burdened me. The real world challenged my claims. In the white world the man of colour encounters difficulties in the development of his bodily schema. Consciousness of the body is solely a negating activity. It is a third-person consciousness' (1986: 110–11).

Constructed by the Other – the white man – through an arsenal of racist stereotypes, the corporeal schema of the Negro is a historico-racial one. Fanon describes it as '[a] slow composition of [the] *self* as a body in the middle of a spatial and temporal world', better still, as 'a definitive structuring of the self and of the world – definitive because it creates a real dialectic between [the] body and the world' (1986: 111). His encounter with the interpellating gaze of the white child – 'Look, a Negro!', then 'Mama, see the Negro! I am frightened!' (1986: 112) – shatters his corporeal schema in terms which invoke Sartre: 'it was no longer a question of being aware of my body in the third person but in a triple person'. The look subjects Fanon to an objective self-examination; he is made to occupy not 'one but two, three places'; he is made to perceive himself not only from an 'I' or a 'third-person' vantage point, but to see himself through the critical eye of the Other, a speculum which refracts a distorted view of his body. In encountering the look of the Other, Fanon loses *mastery* and experiences alienation, the decentring of his world and the decomposition of the self. He apprehends himself as seen in the crowd from the point of view of a world marked by racism. The feeling of nausea and shame reveals to Fanon a view of himself at the end of the Other's look, the feeling of being exposed, his nakedness; it is the consciousness of being the object of the Other's judgement and appraisal.

What the Negro strives for is 'to be a man among other men' (1986: 112); he wants to lose himself in the anonymity of the crowd, to pass unnoticed but his facticity – 'being dissected under white eyes, the only real eyes' (1986: 116) – betrays him. This facticity, i.e. his blackness, is, Fanon writes, 'dark and unarguable' (1986: 117). Referring to Sartre's discussion of the Jew's overdetermination in *Anti-Semite and Jew*, Fanon writes:

In *Anti-Semite and Jew*, Sartre says: 'They [the Jews] have allowed themselves to be poisoned by the stereotype that others have of them, and they live in fear that their acts will correspond to this stereotype. ... We may say that their conduct is perpetually overdetermined from the inside'.

All the same, the Jew can be unknown in his Jewishness. He is not wholly what is. One hopes, one waits. His actions, his behaviour are the final determinant. He is a white man, and, apart from some other debatable characteristics, he can sometimes go unnoticed. He belongs to the race of those who since the beginning of time have never known cannibalism. What an idea, to eat one's father! Simple enough, one has only not to be a nigger. Granted, the Jews are harassed – what am I thinking of? They are hunted down, exterminated, cremated. But these are little family quarrels. The Jew is disliked from the moment he is tracked down. But in my case everything takes on a *new* guise. I am given no chance. I am overdetermined from without. I am the slave not of the 'idea' that others have of me but of my own appearance.

(1986: 115–16)

Fanon laments that both the Jew and Negro are oppressed in their body. Like the Jew, the Negro lives in a diasporic state. Nevertheless, there is a difference between the two: '*wherever he goes, the Negro remains a Negro*' (1986: 173). Unlike the white Jew, Fanon contends, the Negro does not have the choice to be *authentic* or *inauthentic*. No avenues of escape are available to him: overdetermined from without, the Negro is trapped in a corporeal schema.

The Negro might aspire to the ideals of universality proclaiming the inalienable rights of a human sameness, but as soon as he encounters the racist language of the white he is imprisoned in his blackness, a characteristic of which he cannot divest himself. Fanon bemoans that 'the first encounter with a white man oppresses him with the whole weight of his blackness' (1986: 150). He is keen to stress that the Negro is not a prisoner of an insidious ideology but of his own appearance: his blackness. The racial drama is not ideological, the symptom of false-consciousness internalized but repressed by the Negro. This drama is manifestly 'played out in the open'. The Negro does not experience racism at the level of the unconscious. The Negro suffers in his body. 'In terms of consciousness', writes Fanon, 'the black consciousness is held out as an absolute density, as filled with itself' (1986: 134). What keeps this consciousness self-enclosed is the fact that the white master does not recognize its existence. The absolute other for the white is and remains the Negro, and the reverse is true (1986: 138). The black is the visual representation of that which negates the ego: the non-self that can be neither identified nor assimilated. This assumption was upheld by colonialism in reality and racism at the level of the imaginary.[5]

Relations of identity are experienced as an encounter with the Other. Self-validation is realized through the gaze of the white man, a speculum which projects a negative image of the Negro. Commenting on inter-personal relations in his native Martinique, Fanon observes that

> The Martinicans are greedy for security. They want to compel the acceptance of their fiction. They want to be recognized in their quest for manhood. They want to make an appearance. Each one of them is an isolated, sterile, salient atom with sharply defined rights of passage, each one of them *is*. Each one of them wants to *be*, to *emerge*. Everything that an Antillean does is done for The Other. Not because The Other is the ultimate objective of his action in the sense of communication between people that Adler describes, but, more primitively, because it is The Other who corroborates him in his search for self-validation.
>
> (1986: 212–13)

Fanon describes the Martinican society as a 'society of comparison', a neurotic society suffering from an inferiority complex. The problem with the Negro 'soul' does not reside in the unfathomable depth of the indivi-dual self but at the heart of society. Fanon holds society responsible for the myths which objectify the Negro; colonial myths which denigrate and inculcate in the Negro 'white attitudes'.

Taking his cue from Sartre, Fanon contends that man realizes himself as a being-in-the-world, either fulfilling the possibilities of freedom or thwart-ing them by aggression and enslavement.[6] 'The self', he argues, 'takes its place by opposing itself' (1986: 222). It is at one and the same time affirma-tion and negation; it is the will to be free, but it is also the will to power that negates the realization of human freedom. Like Sartre, he is adamant that every consciousness, in its attempt to realize the project of its ethical dimen-sion, is 'a movement of love' and 'a gift of self'. 'The person that I love', Fanon writes, 'will strengthen me by endorsing my assumption of my manhood, while the need to earn the admiration or the love of others will erect a value-making structure on my whole vision of the world' (1986: 41). In a colonial situation, interpersonal relations are impossible; this gift of self and movement of love become sources of frustration, dishonesty, self-contempt and inauthenticity.

In *Black Skin, White Masks*, Fanon examines the black and white rela-tionship which is determined by a dual narcissism, a narcissism which seals the white in his whiteness and the black in his blackness. According to him, only psychoanalysis can interpret the structure of this dual complex. His psychoanalytical approach is at variance with Sartreanism. Fanon contends that the black man suffers from an inferiority complex: an economic inferiority which is subsequently internalized, better still, epidermalized (1986: 13). However, by arguing for sociogeny, Fanon goes counter to Freud's autogenetic perspective which only considers individual factors. Fanon is of the view that 'Man is what brings society into being' (1986: 13); the alienation of the Negro is not just an ontological question. To comprehend it, Fanon situates it on the level of *subjectivity* and *objectivity*, taking into account the Negro's individuality as well as the overriding determining social factors.

Unable to assimilate and pass unnoticed, the Negro is an anxious man who cannot escape his own body – the facticity of his blackness (1986: 65–6). Although he could overcome the social determinants of class, through hard work and intelligence, and improve his social status, the Negro 'is incapable of escaping his race' (1986: 67). The black man who is culturally shaped into the image of the white man 'struggle[s] to free himself from a purely subjective conflict' (1986: 70). The Negro who undergoes a process of *lactification* but finds himself repudiated and rejected in a white world leads a neurotic existence and '[i]t is this tripod – the *anguish* created by every abandonment, the *aggression* to which it gives rise, and the *devaluation of self* that flows out of it – that supports the whole symptomatology of this neurosis' (1986: 73). This neurotic subject does not discover himself in the crowd, a man among men, as Sartre intimates; but he retreats into himself to lead an introvert existence. Rejected by others, he suffers from a lack of self-esteem and looks for approval in the white man's eyes. After reading *Being and Nothingness*, Fanon 'came into the world imbued with the will to find a meaning in things, [his] spirit filled with the desire to attain to the source of the world, and then [he] found that [he] was an object in the midst of other objects' (1986: 109). The gaze sealed him into a 'crashing objecthood'; 'the glances of the other fixed [him] there, in the sense in which a chemical solution is fixed by a dye' (1986: 109).

Conclusion

If the Jew is overdetermined from the inside, as Sartre argues, it is because he is alienated in a world where he cannot interact with others. Sartre calls for an ethics which would promote social pluralism that empowers the Jew to be in the world and discover himself in the crowd through inter-subjective relations. In *Anti-Semite and Jew*, Sartre rebukes the 'inauthentic Jew' for both denying his facticity and retreating into the refuge of inner self away from the tormenting gaze of the anti-Semite. As has been argued, for Sartre, the consciousness of self is an intersubjective activity discovered objectively outside the self; the consciousness of race, an activity which he situates at the level of reflection, as a re-descent into the depths of the soul. In *Black Orpheus*, he paradoxically maintains that the Negro's retreat into the inner recesses of the self, to discover himself, is a source of poetry.

Taking his cue from Fanon, Memmi dismisses Sartre's 'philosophy of points of view' which conceives of Jewishness as the product of other men's views. Fanon contends that ontology cannot comprehend the being of the colonized black. His metaphor 'black skin/white mask' establishes a tangled relation between inside/outside, between self/facticity, between consciousness/world, for-itself/in-itself, putting Sartrean existential phenomenology on its head: consciousness is not nothingness; being for the Negro is not experienced on the outside. Fanon is adamant that the Negro is over-determined not just from the inside but from the outside. The being colonized is a for-itself–in-itself occupying an ambiguous position between being and nothingness. In his discussion of conflictual relations of inter-subjectivity, Sartre uses the trope of the slave to describe the alienation of self at the end of the look of the Other. Nonetheless, he seems to be oblivious to the historical signification of the trope, what Fanon calls historico-racial bodily schema of the Negro. Fanon reminds Sartre that the Negro is the ultimate other. The conflict is not just an existential phenom-enology of intersubjective relations but it is historical, affecting the Negro's body and un/conscious.

Despite the criticism levelled by Memmi and Fanon, Sartre determined the work of the latter two postcolonial thinkers. The influence of *Being and Nothingness*, *Anti-Semite and Jew* and *Black Orpheus* is perceptible in their theorizing; the ethical dimension of his existential phenomenology is funda-mental to their anti-colonial project. In *Existentialism Is a Humanism*, Sartre writes, 'my intimate discovery of myself is at the same time the revelation of the other as a freedom that confronts my own and that cannot think or will without doing so for or against me. We are thus immediately thrust into a world that we may call "intersubjectivity". It is in this world that man decides what he is and what others are' (EH: 45). Sartre's existential ethics is predicated on the assumption that we discover the dimension of our exis-tence in the outside world as we interact with others. To ensure our free-dom we must respect the freedom of others; the values which inform our choices to realize our freedom must be therefore universal. Simply put: these choices must be ethical in that they impact on others.

Notes

1 Upon this relation of objectness, Sartre elaborates: 'if the Other-as-object is defined in connection with the world as the object which *sees* what I see, then my fundamental connection with the Other-as-subject must be able to be referred back to my permanent possibility of *being seen* by the Other. It is in and through the revelation of my being-as-object for the other that I must be able to appre-hend the presence of his being-as-subject. For just as the Other is a probable object for me-as-subject, so I can discover myself in the process of becoming a

probable object for only a certain subject. This revelation cannot derive from the fact that *my universe is an object for the Other-as-object, as if* the Other's look ... came following a definite path to place it on me. I have observed that I cannot be an object for an object. A radical conversion of the Other is necessary if he is to escape objectivity. Therefore I cannot consider the look which the Other directs on me as one of the possible manifestations of his objective being; the Other cannot look at *me* as he looks at [an object]. Furthermore objectivity cannot itself derived *for me* from the objectivity of the world since I am precisely the one by whom *there is* a world; that is, the one who on principle cannot be an object for himself' (B&N: 280–1).

2 In Sartre's parlance: 'While I attempt to free myself from the hold of the Other, the Other is trying to free himself from mine; while I seek to enslave the Other, the Other seeks to enslave me' (B&N: 386). In this dialectical schema, 'being-seen constitutes me as a defenceless being for freedom which is not my freedom. It is in the sense that we can consider ourselves as "slaves" in so far as we appear to the Other. But this slavery is not a historical result – capable of being surmounted – of a life in the abstract form of consciousness. I am a slave to the degree that my being is dependent at the centre of a freedom which is not mine and which is the very condition of my being' (B&N 291).

3 Sartre bemoans that the colonized Negro, by contrast, was treated like a beast of burden: 'Our soldiers overseas reject metropolitan universalism, and apply a *numerus clausus* to human kind: since no one can rob, enslave or kill their fellow human beings without committing a crime, they establish the principle that the colonized are not fellow human beings' (WE: 142).

4 Like Michel Leiris, Fanon is adamant that 'Creole seems already predestined to become a relic eventually, once public education ... has become common enough among their disinherited classes of the population' (1986: 27).

5 For further elaboration on the intersection of the 'symbolic' and 'imaginary', and the impact which Sartre's phenomenology of the look and Jacques Lacan's 'mirror stage' had on Fanon, see Haddour 2006.

6 This is what Fanon meant by saying that man is a *yes* and a *no*: 'Yes to life. Yes to love. Yes to generosity. But man is also a no. No to degradation of man. No to exploitation of man. No to the butchery of what is most human in man: freedom' (1986: 222).

6

A SARTREAN CRITIQUE OF INTROSPECTION

Anthony Hatzimoysis

I

Sartre draws a sharp distinction between *consciousness*, on the one hand, and *inner sense* or *knowledge of (it)self*, on the other: 'La conscience n'est pas un mode de connaisance particullier, appelé sens intime ou connaisance de soi' (B&N: 7). I would like to explore the meaning of the terms involved in that distinction with a view to highlight its significance. My analysis 'departs' from Sartre's argumentation, in both senses of that verb: it takes Sartre's own thesis as the guiding principle of the ensuing analysis, yet it employs that analysis on a set of views that are not addressed in Sartre's own corpus. What makes those views relevant to our discussion is that they model consciousness on knowledge of (it)self, and they think of the latter as delivered by the exercise of inner sense. My discussion will be brief and, I hope, to the point. I will argue that contemporary attempts to revive an inner sense approach to knowledge of (it)self encounter serious difficulties; they thus fail to articulate a viable alternative to the Sartrean approach to consciousness. But first, let me clarify a few terminological issues.

II

The two notions contrasted with consciousness are *sens intime* and *conscience de soi*. Hazel Barnes renders those terms correspondingly as 'inner meaning' and 'self-knowledge' (B&N: 7). The translation of *sens* as 'meaning' is erroneous because the context of Sartre's discussion is not semantic but epistemic. In the particular section where the phrase occurs, Sartre is at pains to distinguish *conscience* from inward directed *connaissance*, whether it is called '*sens intime ou connaissance de soi*'. *Sens intime*, therefore, identifies not a type of meaning but a mode of 'particular knowledge' (*connaisance particulier*). Other renderings of *sens intime* may include 'intimate sense' or 'innermost sense'. However, given that Sartre's turn of phrase indicates that

90

his main target is how *sens intime* has been employed in the philosophical tradition for modelling *conscience* onto *connaissance*, and that the relevant term for that kind of modelling in the English philosophical tradition is 'inner sense,' I have opted for that translation of *sens intime*. 'Inner sense,' along with 'internal sense,' and 'internal observation,' is a term widely employed in defence of introspectionist accounts of one's awareness of oneself, and our discussion will accordingly be placed under the heading of a general critique of the introspectionist view of self-awareness.[1]

Regarding *connaissance de soi*, it is advisable to adopt a translation that retains the ambiguity of the original construction of the French phrase, which may denote either (i) a cognitive state's knowledge of itself, or (ii) knowledge of a thing called 'the self'.[2] 'Knowledge of (it)self' is probably the right candidate, but I shall also be employing the more common 'self-knowledge' when the context of our discussion makes clear whether it refers to consciousness's cognition of its activity or to one's knowledge of one's self.

Finally: *conscience*. The term means 'consciousness' but it is worth noting that in Sartre's own system of thinking, as well as in that of some of his opponents, consciousness comes with a dimension of self-consciousness. The issue that divides them is primarily how, if at all, self-consciousness is involved in the ordinary consciousness of the world. Sartre's opponents (as presented by Sartre) affirm that consciousness' awareness of itself is necessarily governed by a subject–object duality characteristic of the perceiving/perceived or of the knowing/known relations. For Sartre, on the other hand, the attribution of such duality misrepresents the character of consciousness' awareness of itself, since, in the vast majority of conscious activities in our ordinary engagement with reality, consciousness is simply (non-positionally) conscious of itself being (positionally) consciousness of its intentional object.

For Sartre, the question of self-consciousness is never far removed from the discussion over the nature of consciousness as such; and given that a prominent account of self-consciousness treats it as an instance of self-knowledge, and that the latter is considered as supplied by the exercise of some kind of introspective faculty, a defence of the Sartrean approach goes hand in hand with a critique of the 'inner sense' or 'self-knowledge' model of consciousness. And that critique is what we shall pursue in the following three sections.

III

Introspectionism can be introduced through a simple line of reasoning: if we are to be aware of ourselves, there has to exist some way in which we are able to somehow look at, tune in to, or be acquainted with what goes on inside us; let's call that, whatever it happens to be, 'introspection'.

That line of reasoning might sound reasonable, but its apparent cogency owes a lot to its lack of specificity: so generally put, 'introspection' is not the answer to a philosophical call for the analysis of self-awareness, but a convenient name for the phenomenon we try to understand.

We might make some progress by invoking etymology: coming from the Latin word *introspicere*, 'introspecting' denotes the activity of 'looking inside'. According to the perceptual (mainly, visual) model of introspection, our access to our own current mental states is to be conceived on the model of sense-perception, differing from other perceptual activities only by its purported destination, i.e. by the fact that it is directed inwards rather than outwards. Contemporary accounts of introspection present it as a highly-reliable perceptual faculty that delivers reports on current mental states, which can exist independently of being noted by, or reported to their owner. By employing introspection, the subject receives direct information about his present mental states and correctly identifies the occurrence and character of those states on the basis of how they appear to him from the inside.

Along with the standard accounts come the standard criticisms, which focus mostly on the implausibility of the introspectionist idea of having sense-experience of our current mental states. If introspection were exactly like perception then our awareness of ourselves would be in some important respects exactly like sense-experience of perceptible objects. Yet, the criticism goes, no one can take seriously the view that we are aware of our own thoughts by having sensations or quasi-sense-experiences of them, or that in being aware of a sensation, such as a tickle or a pain, we have yet another sensation or experience that is 'of' the first one, and constitutes its appearing perceptually to us in a particular way.[3]

Those criticisms against introspectionism appear to me cogent, not only in the case of our awareness of belief states, where postulating sense-experiences of them sounds rather far-fetched,[4] but also in the case of our awareness of our sensations. Assuming that pain is essentially a sensation, we do not experience pain by having a sensation of a pain sensation: we just have a pain sensation. And when we suffer a headache we do not have a sense-experience of our experience of headache. Denying that claim would commit one to a choice between two doubtful claims: either that the headache and its perceptual awareness belong to different kinds of sensation, and we therefore become aware of our headache by the seeing, hearing, listening, touching, or tasting of it; or that the headache and its awareness are of the same kind, and therefore that we become aware of it by having a headache *of* our headache (a toothache *of* our toothache, etc.). Given the implausibility of those claims, it is, I believe, reasonable to conclude that the notion of 'inner sense' gives us the wrong picture of ordinary self-awareness.

However, those criticisms appear to me to leave themselves open to a simple counter-argument on behalf of the introspectionist. Showing that sense experience, of any sort, is not involved in awareness of our mental states does not amount to a rebuttal of introspectionism, unless it is independently established that perceiving something requires having a sense-experience of it. If the alleged sensation-intermediaries between the perceiver and the perceived are but an obsolete commitment of a problematic theory of perception, the introspectionist may hold on to the perceptual model of inner awareness without having to articulate convincing responses to the above mentioned criticisms.

It is at this point, I think, that the Sartrean approach can move the dialectic forward by explaining why the introspectionist account is misguided, whatever view about the role of sensation in perception one happens to uphold. Sartre's analysis of perception provides adequate material for blocking the inner-sense theory of self-awareness. In particular, Sartre's phenomenological account of perceiving an object, *in contrast to* merely thinking of it or imagining it, identifies certain characteristics of the relevant experience that are not applicable to our awareness of current mental states. In the next section I give a *précis* of the Sartrean account of seeing an object, followed by a list of reasons as to why the perceptual model of introspection cannot succeed in the case of self-awareness of our own belief-states. In section V, we shall explore how these considerations bear upon the introspectionist account of sensation-states.

IV

Can we refute the introspectionist model without appealing to sense-impressions? Is it actually possible to establish that perception is not the way we become aware of our mental states, whatever theory about the *nature* of perception one happens to hold? The answer I think is yes. I shall attempt to justify my thesis by drawing on the minimal requirements for visual perceptual experience – requirements extrapolated by attending to some basic facts about the *phenomenology* of perception. The level at which my argument moves is descriptive not explanatory. The facts to which I appeal, as articulated by Sartre in *The Imaginary* (IPPI: 8–11, 112–22), are quite basic and hardly controversial. Yet, they highlight some crucial disanalogies between perceiving on the one hand, and being aware of occurrent belief states, on the other.

The contrast to be drawn here concerns a perceptible object, such as a cube, and a mental occurrence with propositional content of the form expressed in (what the defenders of introspectionism take as an uncontroversial case) the avowal of one's own belief.

Perception is a conscious act that intends its object always in a specific way: the object appears from a particular angle and at a certain distance, showing itself in this or that particular manner. Although, in the multitude of our perceptual experiences of some object, what is revealed to us in profiles is the selfsame object, the particular way the object appears to us at each moment might differ according to the standpoint we occupy relative to that object. The difference here can be identified as a difference in the content of the various experiences of the same object. My perception of an object is partial: only one part of the object is directly given to me at any moment. The other sides are given as non-currently-visible, yet they are part of what I experience: what I experience is the object. Each *side* is given under different perspectives: the side is given differently to me if I hold the cube straight before me at eye level or if it is three yards away at the left hand side of my visual field. An *aspect* signifies the way in which the sides are given in each *profile*, i.e. in the temporary individuated presentation of an object. The object is given to me in a manifold of profiles. The identity of the object is given through these manifolds, but it is not another side, or aspect of the object: the cube is not another aspect of itself. Perception is directedness beyond what is strictly registered in sensation. Although only one aspect of the cube is exhibited in my sense-experience, I take myself to perceive a three-dimensional thing with hidden sides because of the *empty intentions* directed at them. Perception is always ad-perception. Perceiving something involves appreciating various matters about that thing that go beyond what is directly registered in the sense-experience (see B&N: 2–4).

For those reasons, Sartre insists, one cannot immediately capture an object in perception (as one does in thinking or in conceiving something): one has to *learn* an object, and to achieve that, one has to make (sometimes literally) a tour of it (IPPI: 8). Furthermore every perception is a particular view of one segment of the world. It is not the case that I see e.g. a pen and then add other things next to it or under it so as to give it a context. What I immediately see is a complex of objects out of which I focus on one of them. Perceiving is, in that sense, the seizing of something from out of a set of objects that are co-given. I do not see a pen and then think: 'let's put a desk under it, and add a wall behind the desk, and put a book next to the pen'. Instead I take in the scene as a whole and my perceiving of the pen is made in the light of the background of those other objects. Finally – and rather crucially for our discussion – the awareness of those other objects is not *mediated by* or *inferred from* facts about the object on which I focus.

I submit that none of the above features characterizes belief-states, or any other (propositionally) contentful mental occurrence, expressed in (or as the introspectionist would have it: reported by) an avowal. My *belief* that I see a pen on my desk (as opposed to the perceptible pen, or the desk) is not adumbrated.[5] The belief itself does not present itself to me in one side: there is no back and front to it, no hidden sides that will come to view if I turn it around, or if I change position so as to make a mental tour of it. Furthermore, awareness of *my belief that* 'I see a pen on my desk' does not spring to appearance surrounded by other beliefs of mine, lying behind or next to it. Note that this fact does not commit us to an atomism or individualism about the content of our beliefs – it is not, in other words a semantic or conceptual claim to the effect that each belief may stand on its own. The claim is of phenomenological nature: while focusing on *my belief that I see a pen on my desk*, there are no other beliefs surrounding it. If, in trying to explore my belief, I start drawing connections, thinking of various others of my beliefs – such as my belief about fovea movements, or my belief about the rules that govern human communication, or my belief about the changing fashion in office furniture, or my belief about the mechanics of ink-flow, or my belief about the laws of gravity, etc., *my belief that I see a pen on my desk* is no longer present – if it becomes so, it is because I just brought it back to the centre of my attention. All that is in sharp contrast, phenomenologically, with the perceiving of the pen which implicates directly (and non-inferentially) not only the facing side of the pen, but also its underside, the desk-surface on which the pen lies, the book adjacent to it, etc.

The above considerations provide some solid phenomenological support for the claim that the awareness of an occurrent belief state cannot be cast on the perceptual model of introspection. But this does not mark an end to the debate. Even if the introspectionist admits to the phenomenological incongruence of conceiving of the awareness of propositionally contentful mental states, as an instance of perceiving inwards, he may wish to apply his 'inner-sense' theory to the domain of phenomenal states, such as pains, thrills, aches, tickles, or other sensations. In the following section I consider a subtle way of pursuing this introspectionist line, and I explicate why, in my view, it encounters some formidable phenomenological problems.

V

We saw in section III that an important criticism directed against intro-spectionism is that it entails the implausible claim that we are aware of our sensation or sensory experience by having yet another sensation or sensory experience that is of the first one. The introspectionist may attempt to respond to that criticism by maintaining that we can introspect our phenomenal states without having a sensation of them.

According to an important recent proposal, a subject introspects her sensations or, in general, any of her phenomenal states by demonstrative attention to the content of the relevant experience (Gertler 2001).[6] Intro-spection of a phenomenal state involves referring to it with a *pure* demon-strative, which, in contrast to a *perceptual* demonstrative, requires neither a descriptive content nor a causal link with its referent. This new introspec-tionist account is happy to admit that we do not, literally speaking, perceive our own sensations; but this admission does not mar the account, since (its defenders may argue) demonstrative reference, achieved through attention alone, is *not* perceptual.

What the new account offers is an analysis of introspection in terms of attention. Its main claim is that we come to know, or at least, that we become aware of our phenomenal states by employing the faculty of attention. But is attention the right candidate for explicating introspection? The answer according to some introspectionists is 'yes, by default': all explanations must come to an end somewhere; the demonstrative attention account's explanatory bedrock is the notion of pure attention; and – according to that line of reasoning – the notion of attention itself is unanalysable.[7]

What the account offers is an analysis of introspection in terms of attention. Employing attention is a pervasive feature of our life; attending to someone or something is a more or less constant element of our conscious engagement with the world; it is not only reasonable to expect that attention is available when we turn our mental eye inwards; it would perhaps be unreasonable to think that our inner world is off limits to attentive observation.

And yet I think that this account is incorrect. It is incorrect because it is based on an incorrect view of attention. It assumes that attention is another source of information at our disposal, next to seeing, touching, smelling, or thinking. But attention is not some kind of faculty alongside those others – rather it is a *modality* of sensory, perceptual, or intellectual faculties.

Attention is what makes observing different from merely seeing, what turns hearing into listening. We do not have the perceptual faculty of hearing sound and another faculty of attention, such that when we put the two together we get another faculty – that of listening to sound. We do not switch sources of information about anything when, from hearing someone talking, we begin listening to him. In my opinion, attention concerns the active involvement on the part of the subject in the processing of information. Attention is not a separate source of becoming knowledgeable, informed, or aware of anything, next to seeing, touching, remembering, or thinking (all of these can be done attentively or non-attentively); rather, attention denotes the subject's being able to draw on information in a specific way.

To make clear how exactly the above points bear upon my critique of the demonstrative attention account, it might help to retrace, for a moment, the main steps of my argumentation. Introspection is thought to be a quasi-perceptual mechanism for gaining knowledge of our sensations or other phenomenal states. A classic objection to the perceptual model of introspection is that we have no sense impressions of our phenomenal states. The response comes from the introspectionist that sense impressions are not required for introspecting phenomenal states – attention does not involve sense impressions, and attention is all that it takes for acquiring information, or becoming aware of, or getting knowledge about our phenomenal states. I argued that this response is not credible because it takes attention to be a source of information, whereas attention is rather the way in which a source of information is acted out: it signifies a modality of perceptual or intellectual activities not an activity in its own right.

To see this point in a bit more detail, consider one of the major accounts of attention as a kind of *faculty* or *resource*, an account that has been very influential in recent discussions over the nature of self-knowledge, and to which my Sartrean approach is opposed. Here is a telling paragraph:

> there is a single, general kind of attention of which perceptual and sensational attention and conscious thought and imagination are all subspecies ... It is a familiar truth about attention that any one of these kinds of attention can interrupt any one of the others. Perceptual attention can be interrupted by conscious thought; conscious thought can be interrupted by external events which capture the thinker's attention; either of these two subspecies of the occupation of attention can be interrupted by imagination; and so on. What we have here is ... apparently some form of competition for the exclusive use of a limited single *faculty* of attention ... The familiar facts about attention are explained if there is a single, suitably high-level *resource*, drawn upon by either perception, conscious thought, or imagination.
>
> (Peacocke 1998: 66, emphasis added)[8]

What we get in the above extract is a picture of our mental terrain, according to which there is a faculty or resource of attention, and the other faculties are competing with each other so as to get its – *attention*. Taken literally, the above theory maintains that our usual (sensual, perceptual, cogitative, etc.) faculties are trying to draw the attention of the faculty of attention.

I submit that this is a counter-intuitive result; it sounds strange, to my ears, to claim that certain faculties or activities try to win the attention of attention. And the best way to avoid that strangeness is to think simply of the relevant (sensual, perceptual, cogitative, etc.) activities as done *attentively* or *non-attentively*. Take the case of visual perception. Seeing done attentively involves foveating a particular object, 'zooming in on' the object, as we say. This is usually done not by physically bringing the object forward, but by excluding from our seeing other portions of our visual field. To attend to an object is to reduce what we may call the perceptual noise surrounding it; but this reduction of distraction is always necessarily relative to the (sensual, perceptual, cogitative) activity through which one is conscious of the object. We can only attend in sight, or in hearing, or in tasting, or in touching; we can never just *attend*.

The bearing of the above for our discussion is that attention is the wrong candidate for substituting the perceptual model of introspection of the phenomenal states – not because the perceptual model of introspection is the correct answer, but because there is no attention as such, independently of the activity or exercise of the faculty, which the term 'attentively' qualifies.

VI

Sartre claimed that neither 'inner sense' nor 'knowledge of (it)self' gives us the right measure for conscious awareness. Introspectionist accounts of how we become aware of our mental states run counter to Sartre's claim. I attempted to substantiate the Sartrean approach to that issue, partly by invoking Sartre's phenomenology of perceptual experience (sections III and IV) and partly by elaborating on his critique of faculty psychology so as to achieve a more accurate and conceptually less muddled view of attention (section V). Pointing to the serious inadequacies of the introspectionist model should facilitate the reading of the relevant sections of Sartre's work. My critique of some currently popular 'inner-sense' accounts of self-awareness aimed, *inter alia*, to clear the way for an unprejudiced interpretation of Sartre's text. However, it is worth noting again that the text we examined is near the beginning of *Being and Nothingness*; a proper understanding and appreciation of Sartre's rich theory of consciousness begins, rather than ends, with the issues we explored in this paper.

Notes

1 On 'inner sense' see Russell 1912: 51, 1921: 5; Armstrong 1968: 95, 337; and more recently, Byrne 2005, 2010. The term 'internal sense' is employed from the heyday of British empiricism to the present: see Locke 2008 [1690]: Bk 2, ch. 1, §4; Mellor 1978: 55. See finally John Stuart Mill's important defence of introspection through a discussion of 'internal observation' in 1961 [1865].

2 To be exact, both of those interpretations should be distinguished from yet another, which refers to (iii) one's knowledge of oneself *as* oneself; for further discussion see Hatzimoysis (2010).

3 See Shoemaker 1994 for a classic statement of that critique and Moran 2001 for an important development; see also Bar-On 2004 for a critical exposition of the relevant debate.

4 Yet, see Goldman 1993 for the claim that we come to know of what we believe by the sensory or phenomenal qualities of our belief states, and Robinson 2005 for a detailed – and, to my mind, convincing – response.

5 For Sartre's use of the notion of *Abschattung* as applied to perceptual awareness of things in the world, see B&N: 3. Regarding my choice of example for illustrating the contrast between an object perceived and a mental state avowed, it could be objected that statements which involve the expression 'I see ... ' may not count as avowals, since they are not statements about facts to which we have privileged access, while they are subject to various epistemic errors from which proper avowals are supposedly immune. Thus, it would be better to state 'It visually appears to me that ... '. However, that objection is not relevant at this

point: what matters for our discussion is 'my *belief that* I see … ', to which, according to introspectionists, we do enjoy privileged access. On the notion of 'privileged access' see Ram Neta's careful discussion in his 2010 article.

6 See also Gertler 2010 for a critique of some alternative introspectionist, as well as rationalist, accounts of self-knowledge. It should be noted that I refer to Gertler's insightful work as a source on which the introspectionist would do well to draw in order to respond to the Sartrean criticism; this does not entail that Gertler herself would wish to commit her position to the broader introspectionist cause, or that her overall position on phenomenal self-knowledge should be construed as a move in the dialectic I am describing.

7 Gertler puts the point very nicely: 'Every account rests on some unanalyzed notions … The demonstrative attention account gains support from the claim that "attention" is unanalyzable. For surely it is a virtue of a theory … that its explanatory bedrock is actually unanalyzable' (2001: 318–19).

8 For a recent employment of Peacocke's approach, see insightful discussion of deliberation in Owens 2010.

7

IMAGINATION AND AFFECTIVE RESPONSE

Robert Hopkins

> ... the question arises what it is to imagine someone feeling
> something or other and how this is related to feeling that
> thing ... Strange and awkward as it is, [the question] has,
> I feel – and here, of course, I only echo traditional opinion –
> many consequences for the theory of morals, for the theory of
> art, let alone for the theory of the person.
>
> (Wollheim 1973: 60)

Our question won't quite be Wollheim's, but it is very close. Many exercises
of imagination are in some way bound up with affective states or (as I shall
also call them) feelings. How, exactly, does feeling enter into imagining? Is
the feeling merely imagined, along with whatever objects for it we conjure?
Or is the feeling real, a genuine response on our part to a merely imaginary
scene? Perhaps there are other possibilities. And perhaps imagining exhibits
them all, different possibilities obtaining on different occasions.

In *The Imaginary* Sartre offers a wonderfully rich discussion of these
matters. In answering our question, we will take him as our guide. But first
let's see why the issue mattered to him. Whatever the question's wider
significance, Sartre had quite specific reasons for investigating it.

Sartre's stake in the matter

One of the central ambitions of *The Imaginary* is to distinguish imagining
from perceiving. For Sartre, even when imagining is at its most perceptual,
as for instance in visualizing, it has features quite different from those
perception involves. One of the key differences he identifies concerns
learning. While perceiving is the paradigm state that teaches us how things
are, imagining is the reverse (IPPI: Pt 1, ch. 1, §3). It is uninformative
through-and-through.

Despite the occasional unguarded claim to the contrary (e.g. IPPI: 9),
Sartre does not mean that nothing can be learned from imagining. At the
very least, imaginings can teach us about our ability to imagine things. If

I want to know whether I can imagine a fugue in four parts, the obvious way to find out is to try. Equally, imaginings can indicate one's wider state of mind. Finding myself recurring to images of suffering might teach me that I'm anxious, or depressed. Such commonplaces are not, I think, Sartre's target. Now, in cases such as these we learn one thing (that we're capable of a certain imaginative task, or that we're depressed) by imagining another (a fugue, disasters, etc.). In perception, in contrast, we generally learn that things are a certain way by perceiving them to be that way. Sartre might hope to use this as the contrast between imagining and perceiving: only perception teaches us that things are as it represents them to be. However, this claim too faces difficulties. Suppose I try to work out whether the sofa will fit through the door by rotating it in imagination. Could this be a way to learn whether it will go? If so, the case involves learning that the sofa will fit by imagining that it does.

Perhaps Sartre would simply deny that imagining the sofa going through the door really can tell us whether it will fit. He doesn't say much about objections like this, and seems not to feel under pressure to counter them. However that may be, I think he is best read as making a claim that evades these challenges. The examples so far have focused on whether imagining can teach us about *the world*. Whether it can or not, a further question remains. This is whether we can ever learn *how we have imagined things as being*. It is clear that Sartre thought not. The content of our imaginings is something to which we have immediate and infallible access: 'the object of an image is never anything more than the consciousness one has of it' (IPPI: 10). I suggest we take Sartre's claims about imagining's incompatibility with learning as expressing this thought. Imagining leaves no room for learning what we have imagined. So read, Sartre need not deny that imagining can inform us about the world in all sorts of ways (*contra* e.g. P. Taylor 1981). All he need deny is that we ever learn about the world by learning what we've imagined.

One might worry that refining the claim about imagining in this way ruins the contrast with perception. If imagining can teach us about the world, but not about the world as imagined, shouldn't the contrast turn on the idea that perception teaches us about the world *as perceived* (its teaching us about the world being neither here nor there)? But, while it's clear that perception is the paradigm source of knowledge of the world, it's less than clear that it teaches us about the world as we perceive it. Indeed, we might wonder quite what to make of this last idea. This is a sensible worry to have, but I think it can be met (see Hopkins 2006: §1).

At this point the theme of imagining's relation to feeling enters. In perception, there are two ways in which we learn about the world. We often do so simply by using our perceptual powers, by observing. However, we can also learn by responding affectively to what we perceive. I might discover that someone is attractive by finding myself aroused in that person's presence. I might discover that some creature or substance is disgusting by responding to it with disgust. Or I might discover the aesthetic properties of a thing by taking pleasure in it. I realize, say, that the tie goes with the shirt by trying the pair on, and finding myself pleased at the result. Thus I discover through feeling that someone is sexy, a creature disgusting, or that a tie and shirt look right together. Perhaps in these cases it is not always clear that what I discover has a bearing beyond my own case. Perhaps it would be safer to say that I learn that I *find* the person sexy, or that the animal is disgusting *to me*. But even if some such reference to the feeling subject is unavoidable, there seems no reason to deny that in such cases I learn how things are. A property, or at least an aspect, of what I perceive becomes apparent through my responding to it in a certain way.

In discussing imagining, Sartre concentrates on the idea that we learn from it by observation, by adopting to it an attitude analogous to that we adopt in observing the world perceived. His central claim is that this is not possible (IPPI: Pt 1, ch. 1, §3). But what of learning from affective response? Does this have its equivalent in imagination? To suppose it does is to accept that the following is possible. I might imagine someone I know presented in a certain way, find the result erotically appealing, and thereby learn that as imagined that person holds a certain attraction for me. I might imagine some substance or creature, find myself revolted at the idea, and thereby learn that the thing (as imagined) would be disgusting. Or I might imagine that tie with that shirt, or that painting with the colours altered somehow and, on the basis of the responses thus elicited, learn about the aesthetic properties of those imagined combinations.

There are at least some grounds for thinking that things do happen this way. We do imagine in ways that are somehow bound up with these affects, and we do seem to use such imaginings to help us anticipate the erotic, repulsive, or aesthetic properties of things. Indeed, it is tempting to think that imagining is our only way to anticipate such matters. For the properties in question – beauty, disgustingness, erotic appeal – are not obviously governed by general conditions. What features are sufficient for some sartorial combination to be beautiful, or sufficient to render a creature disgusting? (See Sibley 1959.) But if these properties are not governed by general conditions, we can hardly anticipate which things will have them by knowing whether those conditions will be met. And, if not, how do we come by this knowledge? The idea that we use our imaginations, and then respond as we would before the correlative perceptions, at least provides a clear answer.

Prima facie then, in these cases we learn in the following way that an object or scene that combines a particular set of complex features, F, will also be G (where G is a property such as *disgusting*, *erotically appealing* or *aesthetically pleasing*, a property usually identified in perception via an affective response):

(i) We imagine something F and respond affectively to that imagined object.

(ii) We thereby discover that *the world as imagined* is also G.

(iii) On that basis we draw conclusions about the world: anything F is (or would be) G.

Such cases thus pose a double challenge to Sartre. The specific challenge they offer is as counter-examples to his claim about imagining and learning. We refined that claim as the idea that it is not possible to learn about the world as we have imagined it. (ii), however, suggests that is false. Even if that threat can somehow be deflected, a more general challenge remains. The broad thrust of Sartre's thinking is that imagining and perceiving are very different states, playing radically different roles in our mental economy. The current cases seem counter-examples to that too. For in them imagination stands in relation to feeling very much as perception often does. Feeling can be provoked by presenting a suitable object either in imagining or in perceiving, and in either case the result is that some feature of the presented object is revealed.

Two views of affective imagining

Both the general and the specific challenge turn on a certain conception of imagining's relation to feeling. Let's call the imaginings that interest us, that is imaginings that somehow involve affect, *affective imaginings*. Both challenges to Sartre turn on the idea that what is really going on in affective imagining is this:

> *Response to Imagining account*: We imagine a certain object or scene and are thereby caused to respond affectively to that object or scene.

Claim (i) above clearly invokes this view. Since the specific challenge to Sartre relies on (ii), and since (ii) in turn relies on (i) to explain how learning about the world as imagined occurs, the specific challenge stands or falls with the Response to Imagining view. But so, of course, does the general challenge. Unless imaginings can cause affective responses, as perceptions do, we lose a major point of similarity between the roles imagining and perceiving play in our psychological economy.

Sartre could thus block both challenges were he able to persuade us that the Response to Imagining view is false. What are the alternatives? Although various options will emerge, the main rival has already been sketched:

> *Imagined Response account*: We imagine a certain object or scene and also imagine responding affectively to that object or scene.

Some of what Sartre says in discussing affective imaginings (IPPI: Pt 4, §2) suggests sympathy for this view. He certainly seems committed to rejecting its rival. Considering the view that 'images ... can have the same effect as does a direct stimulation', he says

> [I]ike it or not, this view implies that the image is a detached bit, a piece of the real world. Only a reborn sensation – undoubtedly more feeble than a perception, but of the same nature, could pro-voke the real and perceptible movement that is pupillary dilation. For us, who have distinguished from the outset between the real imagining consciousness and the irreal object, it is impossible to admit a causal relation that would go from object to consciousness.
>
> (IPPI: 136)

Sartre here concentrates on the image's putative *bodily* effects, in particular dilation of the pupils. This is a partially distinct theme, to which we will return in a moment. Nonetheless, it seems clear that his objections to the thing imagined (the 'irreal object') having effects on the body ought to count equally against its having affective consequences. What does Sartre propose to put in their place? At least some of his discussion suggests the Imagined Response view. He claims, for instance, that in affective imagining '[m]y feeling ... is wholly activity ... it is played [*joué*] rather than felt'; and com-pares the situation to that of the psychasthenic suffering from algia, or imagined pain: 'The distress is indeed there, no doubt, but *before* him, in an image, inactive, passive, irreal ... ' (IPPI: 143, translation altered).

Thus, although the exegetical situation will turn out to be complex, there are some grounds for treating Sartre as adopting the Imagined Response account. But how plausible is that account? It faces at least three serious objections.

First, as Sartre has just implicitly conceded, imagining can involve genuine *bodily* changes. Imagining the erotic can lead to erection, imagining the dis-gusting to retching, imagining the fearful to sickness in the pit of the stomach, and so forth. These physiological changes are certainly not imaginary. Moreover, they are precisely the changes that generally accompany the affect appropriate to the imagined object or scene – arousal, disgust, fear, and so on. The Response to Imagining view can easily accommodate these observations: since the affect is really brought about, so are its typical physiological elements or accompaniments. The Imagined Response view, in contrast, seems embarrassed by them. Why do the appropriate bodily changes really occur, if the relevant affect is merely imagined?

Second, what is it to imagine a feeling? Some deny that there is any such state of mind. Imagining affects simply *is* imagining objects or scenes and then really responding to them with some feeling. If this is right, the Imagined Response view is either false or a mere gloss on its rival.

Third, as we've been reading Sartre, he is motivated to adopt the Imagined Response view as a way to defend the refined claim about imagining and learning. The view is supposed to help him maintain that we never learn about the world as imagined, while conceding that imagining can teach us about the world. But can he really walk this tightrope? How can imagining teach us about the world without teaching us about the world as we've imagined it? The Response to Imagining view is part of a story about how it is possible to use imagination to learn about the world, the story told in (i) to (iii). What can the Imagined Response view put in its place?

In much of the remainder (the next three sections), I discuss each of these objections in turn. I attempt to find the resources to deal with them. Often those resources come from Sartre's own discussion of affective imagining, but I do not limit myself to those materials. Nor, indeed, do I restrict myself to the Imagined Response account – other alternatives to Response to Imagining will emerge. The sixth section, 'Matters Exegetical', discusses how far all these materials can be found in Sartre, and thus how far he had available to him the resources for resisting the Response to Imagining view. Of course, it is one thing to make space for alternatives to a view, quite another to show that they are to be preferred to it. In the final section, I briefly review those of Sartre's claims that might be used to argue against the Response to Imagining account, and sketch how they might be developed.

The role of the body in affective imagining

Let's begin with the issue of bodily changes. Sartre notes a range of such changes that imagining has been thought to provoke: dilation of the pupils when imagining darkness; eyes watering when visualizing the sun; discomfort and even retching brought about by picturing something disgusting; and erection in reaction to erotic imaginings (IPPI: 137). Like Sartre, while we might doubt some of these cases, we can hardly dispute them all. At least sometimes, imagining certain things involves a genuine bodily event. Naturally, this is not enough to prove the Response to Imagining view. Such physiological changes are elements in, or accompaniments of, affects such as disgust or arousal, not guarantees of their presence. Vomiting may occur without disgust, as in illness; and erection may occur without arousal. These phenomena do, however, pose a question for the view's rivals, and for the Imagined Response account in particular. Why do these real physiological changes occur if the corresponding affects are merely imagined?

One reply to this challenge draws on materials central to Sartre's account of imagining in general. Sartre holds that imagining involves an 'analogon'. This is a real physiological or psychological element that is a constituent of the imaginative state. The imagining subject is in some sense aware of this element, though not in such a way that its true nature is revealed to him. The subject uses the analogon to make present to himself that which is absent, the imagined object or scene. The case is similar to that of looking at a picture of something. Just as we are aware of the painted canvas or drawn lines, and use them to bring before us the depicted object, we use the analogon in a parallel way in visualizing or imagining sounds. In fact, Sartre thinks these two sorts of case not merely similar, but fundamentally the same: they are both instances of imagining. They differ in two ways. First, whereas we are sometimes aware of the nature of the marks composing the picture, we can never be introspectively aware of the real nature of the physiological or psychological elements that provide the analogon for pure imagining. And second, while the picture is able to act as analogon only because it bears a certain resemblance to the thing depicted, the constraints on the analogon in pure imagining are far looser (IPPI: Pt 1, ch. 2; Pt 2).

What plays the role of analogon in pure imagining? *Inter alia*, Sartre speculates, bodily sensations and movements:

> [T]he image is not a simple content of consciousness among others, but ... a *psychic form*. As a result, the whole body collaborates in the constitution of the image ... It is not because the irreal object appears close to me that my eyes are going to converge; but it is the convergence of my eyes that mimes the proximity of the object.
>
> (IPPI: 137)

This view can be naturally extended to accommodate the physiological phenomena that currently concern us. Those phenomena (retching, sexual excitation, butterflies in the stomach) typically occur as elements in, or accompaniments to, certain affective states (disgust, arousal, fear). As noted, however, they can occur independently. The proposal is that one occasion on which we have one without the other is when these physiological changes serve as analogons for certain affective imaginings. The butterflies in my stomach are not part of a fear really felt in response to imagining some frightening situation. Rather, they are the means by which I imagine fear in response to it. Real bodily change is thus accommodated as a constituent of the imaginative state (IPPI: 137), and affect's role is limited to that which is imagined.

Appeal to the analogon offers the Imagined Response view an interesting and potentially powerful reply to the challenge posed by bodily changes. However, that response is only as plausible as the doctrine of the analogon itself. Like many others, I consider that doctrine to be in some respects highly problematic (Hopkins 1998: Ch. 7, §2). This is not the place to review those difficulties. Suffice to say that they make it worthwhile considering whether there are alternative ways in which actual bodily changes might be accommodated. Not all of the moves we are about to consider will serve the needs of the Imagined Response account. All, however, offer a way to avoid the Response to Imagining view.

Sartre himself offers a quite different way to explain the presence of bodily changes in affective imagining. One repeated theme in his discussion is the idea that often the relevant affect *precedes* our imagining a suitable object for it:

> Desire and disgust exist at first in a diffuse state, without precise intentionality. In being organized with a piece of knowledge into an imaging form, the desire is made precise and is concentrated. Enlightened by the knowledge, it projects its object outside itself. But it must be understood by this that it becomes conscious of itself.
>
> (IPPI: 139)

We are in the grip of some affect, though not really aware of it. The feeling expresses itself in our imagining something appropriate to it. We thereby become aware of what it is we are feeling. And, in consequence, the affect only then comes to find its natural physical expression – say, in vomiting (IPPI: 140).

Here Sartre effectively introduces a third account of imagining's relation to feeling:

> *Imagining as effect*: We are in the grip of an affect, which causes us to imagine an appropriate object or scene (and thereby learn what we feel).

Unlike the Imagined Response view, this position concedes that we really do undergo certain feelings in affective imaginings. It can thus explain the bodily phenomena in the most straightforward way, as constituents or accompaniments of those feelings. Unlike the Response to Imagining view, however, it denies that these feelings are effects of our imagining. Rather, the causal relations go the other way round. There is thus no danger that imagining and perception stand in similar relations to feeling – feelings may colour our perceptions, but they hardly bring them into being. And there is no danger that we learn about the world as we've imagined it by feeling something in response. (Sartre accepts that imagining here leads to learning, but what I learn is *what I feel*, not how I have imagined things to be.)

This Crocean line has its attractions. Certainly we do often imagine in ways that reflect how we already feel (think of the imaginings that are naturally prompted by a heightened state of arousal, or those prompted by anger at some slight one has suffered). And these imaginings can educate us about our own feelings. However, plausible as it is for some cases, the

Imagining as Effect view is not plausible for all. For why think that every case of affective imagining is one in which we already feel the affect, before imagining anything at all? Consider, for instance, the case of imagining the shirt with the tie. There seems no reason to suppose that if I do this and conclude that the two go well together, I must *already* have been experiencing aesthetic pleasure. At least some cases will, it seems, require other treatment.

I close this section by noting one more way in which bodily changes might be accommodated. In one of his discussions of affective imagining, Wollheim suggests that it often exhibits the following structure:

Wollheim's View: We imagine a certain object or scene, imagine responding affectively to that object or scene in some way, and as a result are caused really to feel that way.

(1984: 79–83)

Thus feeling a certain way is a response to imagining some appropriate object or scene. (Wollheim's example (1984: 82) involves an erotic encounter as the situation and arousal as the affect.) It is not, however that the imagined scene brings about the feeling. Rather, the feeling is provoked by one's imagining feeling it. Wollheim thus construes these affective imaginings much as the Imagined Response account does. He adds the idea that nonetheless real affects might result from such activities. He is thus able to explain why real bodily responses are involved: they arrive with the feelings they usually accompany.

Wollheim was not sympathetic to Sartre's claims about imagining and learning (1984: 83–4). Some of his examples of imaginative projects might be taken to put pressure on those claims even in their refined form (1984: 87–8). Nonetheless, adopting Wollheim's View would allow Sartre to avoid the double challenge above. If imagining operates as Wollheim suggests, it differs from perception, since in the latter case the feeling is provoked directly by the presentation of the object or scene. So the general challenge is met. And, since imagining objects and scenes doesn't directly evoke feeling, stage (i) in the story above (p. 103) also goes missing. So the specific challenge also falls away. Thus, at least for those affective imaginings for which Wollheim's View is plausible, Sartre's claims about learning can be preserved.

What is imagining an affect?

The last section explored various ways of accommodating real bodily changes without conceding that we actually respond affectively to what we have imagined. Not all of those suggestions are compatible with the Imagined Response view, but some are – in particular, appeal to the analogon and Wollheim's View. Thus at least something can be said to defend the Imagined Response account from the first objection. I now turn to the second objection: that there is, really, no such thing as imagining a feeling.

This can strike one as bizarre: why would feelings not be the sorts of thing that can be imagined, given all the other things that can be? Nonetheless, I have met folk who expressed puzzlement at the idea of imagining a feeling. Moreover, there has been at least one attempt to articulate that perplexity and to defend it – Currie and Ravenscroft's *Recreative Minds* (2002: Ch. 9, §2).

Currie and Ravenscroft claim that some mental states are 'their own counterparts' in imagining. By this they mean that the only sense in which one can imagine being in such a state is to imagine some suitable object for it and for that state really to occur in response. Amusement plays this role, they say. To imagine finding some situation amusing is to imagine the situation and really to feel amusement in response. And the same, they speculate, is true of affective states more generally. (They mention disgust, anger and 'other paradigmatically emotional states' (2002: 190).) In this respect, affective states contrast with other states we can imagine, such as perceptions and pains. In imagining seeing something or feeling toothache, I do not do so by really seeing anything or by really feeling some pain. Perceptual and pain states are thus imagined by means of genuine counterparts: states of imagining that are distinct from the states thereby imagined.

Are Currie and Ravenscroft right that affective states are their own counterparts in imagining, or do they too have genuine counterparts, as pains and perceptual states do? If the Own Counterpart view is to be plausible, we need to get clear about exactly what it claims. Of course there is some sense in which I can imagine feelings without really feeling anything. I can imagine *that* that I'm angry, without having to engage any real desire or anger on my part. Currie and Ravenscroft don't deny that. Their point is restricted to experiential imagining, i.e. imagining that has a rich phenomenology and that takes something other than mere propositions as its contents – visualizing is the prime example. Nor is it an objection to point out that I can (say) visualize myself being angry, without having really to feel any emotion or desire. The claim intended is restricted to experiential imagining of a given state *from the inside*: imagining that captures the perspective of someone in that state, and captures some of its phenomenology. (On imagining from the inside, see Peacocke 1985 and Wollheim 1984: 72–4.) It is when we restrict ourselves to this understanding of the task, proponents of the Own Counterpart view will say, that we realize that there is nothing more to imagining a given affective state than really feeling it in response to imagining some suitable object.

However, once the position has been clarified, the question remains why we should believe it. As Currie and Ravenscroft concede, many other kinds of mental state do have genuine counterparts in imagining. Why think that perceptual states and bodily sensations are imagined via putting oneself in other states, and yet insist that affective imagining can only operate by really bringing oneself to feel the relevant affect?

Currie and Ravenscroft might first seek an answer in the claim that the phenomenology of affective states can only be fully captured by really putting ourselves in them. However, even if true, how is that relevant? In general it is not required of an activity, for it to count as imagining some mental state from the inside, that it capture its phenomenology *perfectly*. Consider imagining bodily sensations. For some of them, imagining often merely approximates their phenomenology. My imagining seasickness, for instance, captures some of what it's like, but no doubt not all. Yet I have imagined it, from the inside, for all that.

A second unsuccessful answer claims that the Own Counterpart view explains something important about affective imaginings, that they necessarily involve imagining objects for the relevant affects. This last is true, at least for a fair range of affective states. It is also something the Own Counterpart view can explain. In general, these affective states can't really occur without an object – I can't, for instance feel fear or aesthetic pleasure without being afraid of, or taking pleasure in, *something*. According to the Own Counterpart view, imagining these affects involves their occurrence. Hence there has to be an object for them – an object imagining provides. The problem, however, is that we don't need the Own Counterpart view to explain this. Compare perceptual states. These too cannot be imagined (experientially and from the inside) without imagining objects for them. I cannot (in this way) imagine seeing, without imagining seeing something or other. What explains this? Not that the states imagined are their own counterparts in imagining, since that's not true. Rather, the whole explanation lies in the fact that perceptual states necessarily take (intentional) objects. But if that is the whole explanation here, it can be the whole explanation in the case of affective imaginings. We can explain why they necessarily involve objects without supposing that they act as their own counterparts.

A third and final response merits taking more seriously. In affective imagining, not only must there be some object for the affect to be directed at – that object must also be *suitable to* the affect. I cannot imagine from the inside fear, or disgust, or pleasure directed at just *anything*. What I imagine must, it seems, be suitably fearsome, disgusting, or pleasing. If affects are their own counterparts in imagining, this is readily comprehensible. To imagine a given affective state we must induce it in ourselves by imagining something else. Clearly, unless what we imagine is of a nature to induce that state, we won't succeed. If, in contrast, imagining affective states involves other, purely imaginative states as their counterparts, we might expect to be able to imagine any affective state directed at any object or scene. Why shouldn't a given genuine counterpart (imagined fear, say) go with just any imagined object? Here, then, there is something for those who reject the Own Counterpart view to explain. Now, this objection to the idea of affective imagining as a distinct state is very close to the third objection to the Imagined Response view. *En route* to addressing both, let's start with the latter.

Constraints on affective imagining

We turned to the Imagined Response view as a way to allow Sartre to concede that affective imagining can teach us about the world without abandoning his claim that it cannot teach us about the world as imagined. The last of the three objections to Imagined Response above (p. 105) was that it is unclear how it allows us to meet the first of these ambitions. How exactly can imagining an affective response to some imagined object or scene teach me anything about the world? Can't I imagine whatever response I like to the situation I've imagined? Imagination in general is, after all, free to roam wherever I desire. I can imagine pretty much any object or scene I choose. And I can imagine being in pretty much any mental state with which I'm familiar. Why, then, can't I combine pretty much any imagined situation with pretty much any imagined affective state? But if I have that much freedom over the combinations I can imagine, how can imagining any one of them tell me anything about how things really are? I imagine the shirt and tie, and imagine taking pleasure in the result. But, given that I might, it seems, just as easily have imagined hating the combination, how does the fact that I happened to imagine finding it pleasurable show anything about whether the two really go together?

The underlying demand here is for affective imagining to be constrained in some way. Only activities and processes that are subject to constraint can be possible sources of knowledge. More particularly, their outcomes need to be constrained by the nature of whatever one hopes to use them to investigate. The problem for the Imagined Response view is that, on its construal, affective imagining seems to operate free of almost any constraints at all.

Contrast in this respect the Response to Imagining account. It takes affective imagining to involve the real occurrence of some affective state, brought about as a response to what is imagined. Not just any imagined object or scene will elicit that particular response. Affective imagining is thus constrained by whatever mechanism generates our feelings of disgust, anger, pleasure and so on in response to imaginings. But very likely that mechanism is the same as that governing the formation of affective states in response to perception. What shocks when seen, shocks when imagined; what pleases in the one case, pleases in the other, and so on. So affective imagining is not merely *somehow* constrained, but constrained by the very facts we use it hoping to discover: facts about what really (i.e. when seen) disgusts, frightens, pleases, and arouses us. Hence there is no mystery, on this view, how affective imaginings can indeed inform us about these aspects of the world. The Response to Imagining view prospers precisely where its rival struggles.

To tackle this objection, we need to find some constraints on affective imagining, as the Imagined Response view conceives it. To uncover them, let's begin with some thoughts about the nature of affective states.

As noted above (p. 110), the affective states that are our concern (disgust, fear, pleasure, arousal, and so forth) all take an object, some item at which they are directed. But more than this, they all involve that object being *presented in a certain way*. To feel erotic attraction for someone is for them to be presented to me in a certain light, i.e. as desirable. To feel disgust at some creature is for it to be presented under a certain aspect, as disgusting. To take aesthetic pleasure in something is for it to be presented as pleasurable. To fear it is for it to be presented as fearsome. Of course, these descriptions of how the objects are presented are not always very informative. The thought, however, is that, whether or not it is easy to say anything interesting about the way things are presented, there is such a way. Contrast bodily sensations, such as pain. These are experienced as mere accompaniments of the events and things that cause them. The nettle causes the stinging pain, but looks and feels no different in virtue of doing so. Affective states aren't like this. As well as having causes, they are directed at objects, objects they present to us in ways reflecting the feelings thus caused. More, the way the object appears and the feeling it provokes are inseparable.

Now let's return to affective imagining. Above (p. 109) we also saw that our interest is in *experiential* imagining (as opposed to merely imagining that something is the case), *from the inside* (as opposed, say, to visualizing oneself in the grip of some feeling). Now, if imagining a response were a matter of imagining that something is the case, or of experiential imagining from the outside, the inseparability of feeling from the way its object is presented would not matter. I can imagine that I am disgusted whatever I have imagined in other ways; and can visualize myself wrinkling my nose, etc., whatever else I have visualized. But if the relevant imagining is experiential, and from the inside, inseparability places a significant constraint on what response I can imagine having to what imagined object. The object must be imagined appropriately for the response to be imaginable. Not only can I not imagine disgust without imagining something to find disgusting; I cannot imagine finding just anything disgusting. The thing must be imagined as having an appropriate nature – or at least be presented in the right light.

Here, then, is the constraint on affective imagining the Imagined Response view needs. Note that it not only promises to solve the third objection to that view. It also allows us to tackle the only serious argument in favour of the Own Counterpart account. That argument also turned on the claim that, if imagining an affect were different from really feeling it in response to imagining some object or scene, any affect could be imagined with any object or scene. The considerations just given show that conditional to be false. Even though we merely imagine affects as directed at imagined objects, the nature of the objects we imagine constrains the range of affects we can imagine directed at them.

Matters exegetical

What of Sartre? How many of the ideas developed in the preceding as ways of defending him from the double challenge of the first section does he accept?

Sartre certainly recognized the challenge. When articulating his key claim that there is nothing more to the object as we imagine it than we ourselves are aware of (IPPI: 10) he closes the paragraph with a footnote acknowledging that one sort of apparent counter-example is provided by cases in which 'the image comprises a kind of emotional teaching [*enseignement affectif*]'. He promises that such cases will be considered later, and in the passages that do most to fulfil that promise (132–48) he does make some of the moves we have considered. It seems clear that he rejects the idea that affective states are always their own counterparts in imagining, when discussing the psychasthenic and the idea that more generally affects might be merely 'played' (143). (Interestingly, in a nearby footnote (142 n10) he perhaps indicates that he himself had previously doubted whether imagining a feeling really differs from feeling it while imagining something else.) And in discussing the case of apparent aesthetic learning in imagining, he makes quite clear that he rejects at least some of the claims proponents of the Response to Imagining view are likely to make: 'what one can never see as imaged is *the effect* of a top hat *on* Pierre's face' (134). (The same presumably would apply to the tie and the shirt.)

However, there are also grounds for doubting whether Sartre would accept the thoughts we've offered him. Most significantly, at one point he is at pains to point out that he is not denying (at least for the cases then under discussion) that the feelings involved in imagining are themselves real:

> Thus, from the very fact of the extraordinary difference that separates the object as imaged from the real, two irreducible classes of feeling can be distinguished: genuine feelings and *imaginary* feelings. By this last adjective we do not mean that they are themselves irreal, but that they never appear except in the face of irreal objects, and that the appearance of the real is enough to make them flee at once.
>
> (145)

In these cases, then, the feelings we have when imagining are genuine. They are not 'irreal', that is, not merely imagined. They do differ from the feelings we have before real things, in perception. The fact that a feeling is directed towards a person imagined, rather than perceived, affects its development, the demands it makes and its role in our wider mental economy. The passage continues:

> These feelings whose essence is to be *degraded*, poor, jerky, spasmodic, schematic, need non-being in order to exist. Someone will hound his enemy in thought, make him suffer morally and physically; but will be defenceless when really in his presence. What has happened? Nothing, except that the enemy now really exists. Until now the feeling alone gave the meaning of the image. The irreal was only there to allow the hatred to objectify itself. Now what is present overflows the feeling completely and hatred is in suspense, derailed. ... If I strike my enemy in image, blood will not flow, or will flow only as much as I would want it to. But before the real enemy, before this real flesh I anticipate that real blood will flow and that alone suffices to stop me.
>
> (145–6, translation altered)

Thus the development of my feeling when directed at my enemy as I imagine him takes a quite different course from that when he is really before me. But the feeling itself is just as real in either case.

Of course, if Sartre is right about the different economies of feeling operating in the face of the imagined and the real, learning about the world from affective imagining will be less common than we have so far assumed. However, this hardly banishes the challenges to his position. Remember the three-stage account of how, according to those who hold the Response to Imagining view, such learning is possible:

(i) We imagine something F and respond affectively to that imagined object.

(ii) We thereby discover that *the world as imagined* is also G.

(iii) On that basis we draw conclusions about the world: anything F is (or would be) G.

The point about different economies merely suggests that the conclusions drawn in (iii) will be false. That does nothing to dispense with the specific challenge, which turned on stage (ii). And nor does it help very much with the general challenge. Even if imagined scenes provoke different emotions from perceived ones, imagining and perception remain alike in one substantial respect: both provoke affective responses.

Thus Sartre concedes that sometimes we feel real affects when imagining, and any differences he describes between those cases and affective perceptions are insufficient to block the challenges with which we began. What, then, can Sartre do to meet those challenges? There are options open to him. He can concede real affects in imagining, but deny that that the imagining causes the affect (Imagining as Effect). He can allow that affects are caused by imagining, but insist that what does the causal work is not imagining the object, but imagining the affect itself (Wollheim's View). And, of course, in other cases he can deny that the affects are real: he may not adopt the Imagined Response view for all cases, but he certainly seems open to it for some. Anyone attempting to defend Sartre's account of imagining from the threat posed by its affective forms must hope that these three strategies together mop up all the cases.

Why resist responses to imagining?

One attractive feature of the Sartrean approach to affective imagining, as we have now reconstructed it, is that it treats the phenomenon as heterogeneous: different cases require different treatment. But why on earth, one might wonder, wouldn't at least some cases require treating as the Response to Imagining view proposes? Why would one deny that sometimes we imagine something and (without the mediation of imagined feeling) feel some or other affect in response? We've been working to make space for other positions, with a fair degree of success. But why, other than a desire to defend Sartre's claims about learning in imagination, reject completely the Response to Imagining view?

Sartre's own antipathy to the view seems driven by the thought that imagined objects are incapable of standing in causal relations. Remember his refusal (p. 104) to accept 'a causal relation going from the object to the consciousness'. We, however, are unlikely to find this consideration persuasive. Of course, what doesn't exist can't bring about anything. But distinguishing, as Sartre does, the state of imagining from the object imagined reveals the limited force of that objection. The imagined object may not be able to act as cause, but the imagining can. Now, any causal relation here needs to reflect the nature of the imagined object: the idea is that we are (e.g.) disgusted *because we imagine something disgusting*. But we can accommodate that without attributing a causal role to what does not exist. For what effects the imagining has is shaped by its properties, and in particular by its content – by its presenting us with some specific object or scene (in this case, a disgusting one). (At least, this is no more problematic than the idea that quite generally the content of mental states can be causally efficacious.) The possibility that imaginings, in virtue of their content, cause us to feel certain things is surely quite enough for the Response to Imagining view. Sartre's strictures on a causal role for the 'irreal object', however reasonable, thus seem irrelevant.

(Perhaps Sartre here anticipates, at least in part, the more sweeping views of *Being and Nothingness* about consciousness and causation. There he sees consciousness as lying completely outside the causal order that governs the inanimate world of being-in-itself. Perhaps appeal to that broader position might do something to support his antipathy to the causal role of imaginings. Even if so, it would be helpful to be able to counter the Response to Imagining view without appeal to such heavyweight, and controversial, theoretical machinery.)

The sceptic about imagining's ability directly to cause affect would do better, I think, to concentrate on the unavailability, not of suitable causes for those states, but of suitable contents or intentional objects for them. As I've stressed, the affects we are supposedly brought to feel must be directed at something: disgust at some repellent object, pleasure in some pleasing configuration, and so forth. Can imagined objects really play this role? The worry that they can't might take two forms.

First, perhaps affective states require us to take the world to be a certain way. One feels fear, for instance, only if one believes oneself in danger; anger only if one believes oneself wronged; pity only if one believes that someone suffers, and so forth. Perceptual states can induce affects precisely because they claim to show us how things are, and thereby exert control over our beliefs. Seeing that I'm on the icy precipice, I believe that I'm in danger, and thus can feel fear. Imaginative states are fundamentally different in this respect. Picturing myself on the edge of a precipice precisely does not claim to tell me how things are. As Sartre puts it, while perception 'posits as existing', imagining 'posits as nothingness' – it presents me with objects and scenes while clearly not claiming that this is how the world really is (IPPI: Pt 1, ch. 1, §4). Visualizing that scene does nothing, therefore, to persuade me that I am in danger, and so cannot induce fear. (Some (e.g. Walton 1978) use similar considerations to argue against our responding to fiction with genuine emotions. Their debate with their opponents bears close parallels to that opening up here.)

There is much that is attractive in this line of thought. Nonetheless, I doubt that it moves the debate forward. One difficulty is that for at least some affective states, it is unclear what the content of the requisite belief might be. Fear arguably requires taking oneself to be threatened, but what of aesthetic pleasure? What belief does it presuppose? A more serious problem is that, even in cases where there is little dispute about what the relevant belief would be, it is controversial whether having that belief really is necessary for having the feeling. Indeed, those who doubt this will precisely take cases such as imagining myself on the precipice as proof that it is not. Thus anyone who holds the Response to Imagining view is likely already to reject the idea that affect involves taking the world to be a certain way. Appeal to that idea might help sceptics about such responses to flesh out their position, but it is unlikely to do anything to persuade their opponents.

The other form of the worry that imagining cannot provide suitable objects for our affective states is perhaps more promising. It turns on the various undeniable differences between the objects with which perception presents us and those objects as presented in imagination, differences that form a central theme of *The Imaginary*. Perception presents us with objects that have stable natures independent of our access to them and that outstrip that access at every point. Imagining, in contrast, presents us with objects the natures of which shift as our imaginings do, and to which there is nothing more than we have at any given moment conjured into being. (Of course, the letter of that last claim is part of what we've been debating here. But no one would doubt that it is *broadly* true: if there is ever more to what I've imagined than I currently grasp, the extra is limited and marginal, as the unperceived features of perceived objects generally are not.) As Sartre notes, the stability and independence of perceived objects is essential to the development of our affective responses, and determines the nature of those states (IPPI: 139). The very different structural features of objects as presented in imagining dictate a very different life story, and nature, for our responses to them (IPPI: 140). On that basis we might draw the interesting but relatively modest conclusion above (pp. 113–14), that feelings before the imaginary, while just as real as those before the perceived, nonetheless exhibit a quite different economy. But might we not also use these contrasts to infer something stronger: that feelings before the imaginary don't count as instances of those affective states at all? The idea would be that all these states – disgust, aesthetic pleasure, arousal, fear and the other emotions – can only form in response to a world given as independent of them, as stable in the face of their development, and as at every point bearing determinate features that those affective responses have not shaped and have yet to reckon with. If so, then, affective imaginings cannot involve forming genuine affective states in response to imagined objects and scenes. The latter lack the sort of presence that the former require of the world at which they are directed.

This is only the sketch of a line of thought. I offer it tentatively, as the most promising way to try to argue that no cases of affective imagining are correctly described by the Response to Imagining view. I have, of course, offered various alternative accounts of what affective imagining might involve. I hope to have done something to argue that they correctly describe some instances of affective imagining. I do not pretend to have argued that those alternatives cover all the cases. To that extent, my defence of Sartre against the challenge with which we began remains incomplete.

8

THE SIGNIFICANCE OF CONTEXT
IN ILLUSTRATIVE EXAMPLES

Andrew Leak

In a well-known 1965 interview with Pierre Verstraeten, Sartre opines that his *Critique of Dialectical Reason* was a superior philosophical text to *Being and Nothingness* because it remained throughout in a resolutely 'philosophical', that is 'denotative', discursive mode, unlike *Being and Nothingness* which, said Sartre, too often gave in to the temptation of the literary (E&L: 56). Surprisingly, it is the phrase 'Man is a useless passion' (B&N: 636) that Sartre regrets in retrospect (he finds the phrase excessively 'poetic', and thus opaque), but he makes no comment on the 'novelistic' interludes that are such a memorable feature of that work. Whether the sixty-year-old Sartre liked it or not, it was the readiness of *Being and Nothingness* to depart from the aridity of philosophical dialectic in order to illustrate its theses with banal but striking examples that earned it a readership beyond the academy. How many named 'characters' are there in *Being and Nothingness*? Many readers might struggle to name more than the omnipresent Pierre – omnipresent in his omni-absence as it were: Sartre seems to have spent his life waiting vainly in cafés for Pierre to arrive! – but the cast of characters is actually far more extensive: Paul, Simon, Claude, Jeanne, Thérèse, René, Lucien and, of course, Anny (with a 'y', as in *Nausea*); is this the same Annie as the one with an 'ie' at the end of her name? For she, too, appears in *Being and Nothingness*. And does it matter? In *Nausea* it does: the connotation of Englishness imparted by the spelling with a 'y', along with references to the time Roquentin and Anny had spent in London, adds to the unresolved mystery surrounding the character and her origins. But in *Being and Nothingness*, connotation is regarded by the philosopher as an undesirable distraction. Who can forget the café waiter, or the woman on her first date? Who has not continued in their imagination the story of the resistance fighters preparing to storm a white farmhouse set atop a hill? And why is the farmhouse white? – a detail that adds nothing to the philosophical point of the example. Time and again, Sartre conjures up scenes that could be episodes in a story or maybe even starting points for a whole novel. Indeed, some even were. When, towards the start of *Being and Nothingness*, Sartre writes: 'The alarm which rings in the morning refers to the possibility of my going to work, which is my possibility. But to apprehend the summons of the alarm as a summons is to get up. Therefore the very act of getting up is reassuring, for it elides the question, "Is work my possibility?" Consequently it does not put me in a position to apprehend the possibility of quietism, of refusing to work, and finally the possibility of refusing the world and the possibility of death' (B&N: 61), he could hardly have known that he had just summarized a novel that would be written twenty-five years later by a young man who also happened to be the cousin of his erstwhile lover, Bianca Bienenfeld![1]

In fact, *Being and Nothingness* is littered with dozens of literary vignettes, like so many stillborn stories that doubtless served to delude some readers that they actually understood, at least occasionally, what they were reading!

One matter for reflexion when reading *Being and Nothingness* in a time and place removed from those in which it first saw the light of day, turns on what we could call the 'timeliness' of its arguments. Sartre is attempting a description of 'human reality' – full stop – not of 'human reality as it can be observed in mid-twentieth-century France'. At the same time, *Being and Nothingness* partakes necessarily of a certain historical and cultural context. I am not suggesting that readings which bracket off that context in order to attend to the purity of the arguments in themselves are in some way deficient, but I am suggesting that an attention to context enables us to see it as a different kind of textual object than might otherwise have been the case.

The famous café waiter is a case in point: are we expected to *recognize* this figure or *imagine* him? What does a reader of *Being and Nothingness* living in twenty-first-century London, who has never visited Paris, make of this example? Well, in the actual experience of such a reader, the waiter will most likely be a waitress, quite likely a foreign national – as like as not originating in one of the recent EU accession states. Terrorized by the health and safety culture, she is most unlikely to carry her tray 'with the recklessness of a tight-rope walker by putting it in a perpetually unstable, perpetually broken equilibrium which [she] perpetually reestablishes by a light movement of the arm or the hand' (B&N: 82). Once at the table (having not received any training, as waiting table has never been considered a 'profession' in British culture) she will probably struggle to remember who ordered the cappuccino and who the skinny latte ...

A frivolous example, perhaps, but one which can serve a limited purpose: I may personally have visited establishments in Paris where waiters still play at being *the* waiter, but the important point is that this example requires that I use my imagination not my memory. This, I think, was the source of Sartre's own anxiety about the probity of his technique in *Being and Nothingness*: it is one thing to demonstrate a truth by reasoned argument, but quite another to convince by 'participation': that is, simply by producing the required image, the reader is already carried halfway along the path towards consenting to the argument supposedly illustrated by that example. If I were a philosopher, I might be worried by the way *Being and Nothingness* attempts to manipulate my critical faculties. But I am not a philosopher, I am a reader of literature, and this idea that attention to the literariness of *Being and Nothingness* might produce a different text is what I want to explore in this article.

Just after the famous description of the café waiter, Sartre makes what may well be the only joke in *Being and Nothingness*. Having suggested that grocers, like waiters, have their characteristic 'dance', he remarks: 'A grocer who dreams is offensive to the buyer because such a grocer is not wholly a grocer' (B&N: 82). If that statement is amusing it is because it makes concrete an oxymoron: 'the artistic grocer'. To understand the oxymoron, you have first to know that the 'épicier' was the object of contempt for writers and artists throughout nineteenth-century France, from the Romantics to Flaubert and beyond, shorthand for the petty-bourgeois philistine who refused to accept the existence of anything that could not be weighed in his scales – in short, the 'anti-artist'. As late as the 1950s Roland Barthes is still using that stereotype in *Mythologies*. As a starting point, one could take Sartre's phrase and make a couple of minor substitutions: 'A philosophical text that dreams is offensive to the (philosopher-) reader because it is no longer wholly a philosophical text'.

It must be said that, most of the time, *Being and Nothingness* remains in the realm of what Freud called 'waking logic', accomplishing the requisite rhetorical gestures with, as it were, the 'inflexible stiffness of some kind of automaton' (B&N: 82). It is sometimes said – perhaps unkindly – that academics produced by the French 'Grandes Ecoles' system often have little original to say but they say it with absolute formal rigour and with a systematicity of argumentation that affords precious little purchase to would-be critics. If this is true today, it was true *a fortiori* of the generation of Sartre, produced by an École Normale Supérieure under the stern direction of Lanson and at the apogee of its power and influence. The structure of the argument of *Being and Nothingness*, the exposition, the development, the end-of-section recapitulations before passing on to the next logical step – all of this is redolent of classical French academic composition. So, too, is the manner in which Sartre engages with previous work in his field. This engagement provides us with a first 'circle' of examples. Given the philosophical space that Sartre is attempting to occupy, it is not surprising that this space is defined with reference to thinkers such as Descartes, Kant, Hegel, Husserl, Heidegger. These are by far the most frequently referenced thinkers in *Being and Nothingness*. Also to be found in this first circle of reference are 'examples' that would, or should, be instantly recognized by any philosophy undergraduate. Locke and his billiard balls, for example, or various of Zeno's paradoxes, such as Achilles and the Tortoise. These are 'commonplaces' in the proper sense of the term: the reader is not being asked to *imagine* the ball being stopped or diverted from its course by a crease in the baize: he is being asked to access, instantly, an argument that he has encountered in Hume or Locke and to bring forward in his mind what he knows about atomistic theories of causation. No-one would think of asking whether Zeno's arrow is fledged with goose feathers or duck feathers, or what colour the billiard ball is: the examples have an abstract purity that excludes or renders redundant any attempt at visualization.

As I said, there is nothing unusual about this first circle of obligatory references and examples, but, as we know, Sartre did not limit himself to this sphere of dutiful reference to the recognized 'authorities'. Readers formed in a culture where interdisciplinarity has long been considered an enrichment, rather than a 'watering-down', may not grasp just how novel *Being and Nothingness* must have appeared to its first French readers: the French system enforces, even today, tight disciplinary boundaries, such that an academic philosopher would likely declare himself incompetent to venture an opinion on a subject that appears to belong to an adjacent discipline, such as psychology. But, in what we could call the second circle of reference, Sartre freely refers to a long list of psychologists drawn from a range of different traditions: Abraham, Freud, Jung, Stekel, Adler, Janet, Piaget, James, Lewin ... Physicists and other natural scientists: Einstein, Heisenberg ... linguists and philologists ... historians. In so doing, he was demonstrating the extent of his intellectual curiosity and, on occasion, ignorance: despite engaging in a lengthy critique of Freud, for example, we know from Beauvoir's memoirs that at the time he had read only *The Interpretation of Dreams* and *The Psychopathology of Everyday Life*! But most of all, Sartre draws on examples from the literary imagination. The index to *Being and Nothingness* lists as many novelists, playwrights and poets as it does philosophers. Here again, the referenced sources are a good reflection of Sartre's bulimic, if somewhat post-Enlightenment reading habits: Diderot, Rousseau, and Laclos from the eighteenth century; the great nineteenth-century novelists are there in force: Balzac, Stendhal, Flaubert, Dostoyevsky; the big names of the early twentieth century: Proust, Gide, Romains, Malraux. The German Romantics are well-represented: Goethe, Lessing, Schiller, as are the writers Sartre regarded as being in the vanguard of contemporary formal experimentation: Faulkner, Fitzgerald, Kafka, and Joyce. In short, it is worth remembering that this is a philosophical treatise containing more references to Malraux than to Kierkegaard, more references to Proust than to Plato.

But Sartre does not only find examples in the fictions of other writers: there is an important set of illustrative examples in *Being and Nothingness* that are actually drawn from a fictional universe of his own creation.

Readers of the collection of short stories *The Wall* or the novel *Nausea* may have recognized in *Being and Nothingness* many echoes of those works. In an attempt to dismiss the Freudian unconscious as an explanation for phenomena of bad faith, Sartre invokes a work by the renegade psycho-analyst Wilhelm Stekel, *La femme frigide*. Sartre interprets Stekel as arguing that 'frigidity' is in fact a choice made by the woman not to feel pleasure, rather than a passively determined complex – that is, the result of unre-solved unconscious conflicts. The story 'Intimacy' appears to be a literary transposition of that theory: like the women in Stekel's study, Lulu manifests the outward signs of pleasure when engaged in intercourse with her lover Pierre, but subsequently denies (to herself, in her interior monologue) having felt pleasure, because, she says, she cannot: the doctor had confirmed as much. Paul Hilbert, the first-person narrator of another story in *The Wall* – 'Herostratus' – has also been viewed by some critics as a casebook illustration of the Adlerian inferiority complex (as discussed, and dismissed, at B&N: 495).

Being and Nothingness also draws quite extensively on Sartre's own work in progress which had not, at time of writing, been performed or published. For example, the whole of the dramatic conceit of *Huis Clos* is summarized in a few lines of the subsection on 'The Past' in Part II, Chapter 2: Tem-porality: 'We shall see later that we continually preserve the possibility of changing the *meaning* of the past in so far as this is an ex-present *which has had a future*' (B&N: 139). Elsewhere we find in embryonic form the moment when Orestes, in *The Flies*, realizes that the law of Jupiter is powerless against his own liberty: 'I emerge alone and in anguish confronting the unique and original project which constitutes my being; all the barriers, all the guardrails collapse, nihilated by the consciousness of my freedom. I do not have nor can I have recourse to any value against the fact that it is I who sustain values in being ... I have to realize the meaning of the world and of my essence; I make my decision concerning them – without justification and without excuse' (B&N: 63).

Two further examples have particularly strong resonances in Sartre's fictional universe. The first of these is the example of the woman on her first date who abandons her hand to the man 'without noticing it'. It comes at the start of the section on 'Conducts of Bad Faith', just after Sartre's discussion of Stekel's views on female frigidity. This vignette has been adduced by some critics as proof of Sartre's sexism, or even his misogyny, but it is interesting to note that the closest fictional parallel to this scene is to be found in 'The Childhood of a Leader' in a scene of *homosexual* seduction: I refer to the scene where the self-proclaimed Surrealist Bergère 'seduces', or rather assaults Lucien as the latter 'distracts' himself as if he were somehow absent from the scene. The narrative perspective is that of the ironically detached third-person narrator who nevertheless has access to Lucien's innermost feelings. In *Nausea*, this surreptitious taking of the hand as a gesture of seduction is also linked to homosexual desire when the Autodidact allows his contemplative admiration for young boys to pass onto a more physical plane. Here, the perspective is that of Roquentin who looks on horrified as the scene takes its bloody course. A variant on the scene is also presented in *The Age of Reason*, but this time with a further change of perspective: in *Being and Nothingness* we know nothing of what is going through the mind of the lothario, beyond, presumably, his desire to get his date into bed. In *The Age of Reason*, it is the woman (Ivich) who remains entirely opaque. The scene takes place in a taxi. Mathieu put his arms round Ivich but she remains like a lump of wood, or an automaton. Emboldened, or perhaps outraged by her irresponsiveness – it is not clear which – Mathieu proceeds to brush her lips with his own, but Ivich's lips remain cold and closed. Unlike the seducer in *Being and Nothingness*, Mathieu interprets this passivity on the woman's part as a clear rejection rather than a tacit encouragement.

I should like to make two points about this example and the earlier one concerning Lulu and the 'femme frigide' drawing out the differences in treatment in the philosophical and literary registers. First, both are concerned with bad faith but they could equally well be seen as dealing with the experience of shame. Second, if the social context of the vignettes in *Being and Nothingness* is suppressed, abstracted or taken as self-evident, in the fictional register it is the social context that most powerfully informs our reading of the scenes. The bad faith of Lulu is only fully comprehensible when we situate it within her milieu, which is that of the petty bourgeoisie. Why does Lulu have a lover if she finds sex – at one level at least – so humiliating? Why does she return to her dismal marriage at the end of the story? Essentially, because it is expected of her: as her friend Rirette tells her, it is not just her *right* to pursue 'happiness' through sexual fulfilment, it is – in the world of the women's magazines they devour – her *duty*! One way of reading Lulu's actions is to see them as the attempt to retain control – over her life, over her body – in a society where that control is seen as the prerogative of men. As I said, the example of the first date – illustrating bad faith in *Being and Nothingness* – turns into a vignette of *shame* in its fictional avatars. In each case, the Other, in form of the social collective, supervenes to break the spell of seduction. Lucien seems less worried about *being* a homosexual than being *seen* as one:

> Lucien smiled bitterly – you could wonder for days on end: am I intelligent?, am I smug? You can never quite decide. But then, on the other hand, there are labels that stick to you one day and you have to wear them for the rest of your life: for example, Lucien was tall and blond, he looked like his father, he was an only child and, since yesterday, he was a homosexual. People would say about him: 'Fleurier, you know, the tall blond chap who likes men?' And other people would reply 'Yes, of course! The big pansy? Sure I know who you're talking about'.
>
> (TW: 167)[2]

The collective judgement of the Other is later given a distinctly social determination when Lucien imagines how difficult it will be to take over his father's business if his workers – knowing that he *is* a homosexual – snigger behind his back when he tries to give them orders.

A similar collapse into shame occurs in the example from *Nausea*. In the public library in Bouville, the boy appears mesmerized like a rabbit in car headlights; he has abandoned his hand to the Autodidact when, abruptly, the gaze of the Other – in the person of the atrabilious Corsican librarian – breaks the spell:

> 'I saw you', cried the Corsican, drunk with rage, I saw you this time, don't try and tell me it isn't true. You're going to tell me it isn't true, are you? You think I didn't see your little game, do you? … I know your name, I know your address, I've checked up on you, you see. I know your boss, too, M.Chuiller. And won't he be surprised tomorrow morning, when he gets a letter from the librarian, eh?
>
> (N: 235)

A little later, Roquentin imagines the Autodidact wandering the town pursued by the vindictive gaze of the good burghers of Bouville, dying of shame.

> Finally, the attempted seduction of Ivich by Mathieu also ends in shame. Mathieu reads the silent reproach in Ivich's eyes: He thought: 'a married man who touches up girls in taxis' and his arm fell from her shoulders, dead and limp; Ivich's body righted itself like a pendulum returning to its point of balance. 'That's it,' thought Mathieu, 'it's done, I can't take it back.'
>
> (AR: 65)

In light of this, we could revisit the example of the first date in *Being and Nothingness*. The only context provided by Sartre is that this is a first date. We are told nothing of the age of the protagonists, their relative social standing, their physical appearance, etc. But the 'first date' information is clearly important and it becomes more so if we imagine turning the example into an illustration of shame. All that is required to do this is to introduce the gaze of a third person and analyse the awareness of that gaze on the part of the protagonists. This is enough to transform the woman's consciousness of her own position: from being a woman sitting talking to a man in a bar she becomes a Woman on her First Date: should a 'respectable' woman sleep with a man on her first date? Is allowing him to take her hand a tacit acceptance that they will sleep together? On the other hand, if she were to withdraw her hand, would she then not appear, to the observer, to be a frightened virgin or a prude? How would she less rather appear: as a prude or an easy woman? Finally, do we accept that the lack of explicit context in this vignette makes it timeless and universally valid as an illustration of bad faith? I think not: the example would be incomprehensible in Saudi Arabia – except perhaps as proof of the moral decadence of the West. But if we accept the notion of implicit context – the context, say, provided by what we know of Paris in the 1940s – how far are we to go in invoking that context when interpreting the example? For instance, if the eventuality of sexual intercourse is implied by the man's manoeuvring and the woman's reaction, is it relevant that contraception at that period was still predominantly the prerogative of the male and that abortion was illegal? The most problematic moment of this example, for me, is when Sartre writes, 'To leave the hand there is to consent in herself to flirt, to engage herself. To withdraw it is to break the troubled and unstable harmony which gives the hour its charm ... We know what happens next'. Well, do we? When I first read *Being and Nothingness*, I certainly didn't. I envisioned three possibilities: (i) the woman gazes meaningfully into the man's eyes and suggests they go somewhere more private; (ii) she slaps him round the face; (iii) she gently but firmly disengages her hand and suggests that they take things a little more slowly. No doubt, my expectations were conditioned by, amongst other things, my own experiences of women living in a post-1968 age of increased sexual liberation and self-assertiveness. But those expectations were sufficient to prevent me from identifying with the 'we' in Sartre's 'we know what happens next', simply because that 'we' is of a different time and place. The crux of the question here is this: is it possible to form philosophical examples regarding human behaviour (as opposed to 'human reality') that have the timeless purity of the billiard ball or Achilles and the Tortoise? Or will such examples always, necessarily, be reliant on context and, therefore, vulnerable to changing contexts?

The question of context and its relevance to interpretation is also raised by the final example I would like to examine. This example is to be found in the chapter on bad faith in *Being and Nothingness* (Pt 1, ch. 2, §2). It begins – in the English translation, at least – with the words 'Let us take an example: A homosexual frequently has an intolerable feeling of guilt and his whole existence is determined in relation to this feeling' (B&N: 86). The focus of this example is not so much on the bad faith of the homosexual's conduct as on the bad faith inherent, according to Sartre, in the notion of sincerity. It is perhaps the fact that Sartre was trying in this example to kill two birds with one stone that creates the ambiguities that have occasioned so much debate amongst Sartre scholars. Sartre presents his homosexual as a 'serial offender' who is unwilling to draw the inescapable consequences, with regard to his own sexuality, of his multiple transgressions. Sartre imagines a further character whom he calls the 'champion of sincerity'. This man, the homosexual's friend, is also his severest critic and he criticizes, specifically, the homosexual's duplicity: why does the guilty one ('le coup-able' in the original) not simply admit his guilt and speak the words 'I am a homosexual'? But this is where the champion of sincerity reveals his own bad faith: in the name of an ideal of sincerity (being what one *is*), he is for-cing the homosexual into an impossible choice where he is damned if he does and damned if he does not: if he pronounces that admission of 'guilt' he lays himself open to the 'terrible judgement of collectivity' [sic], a price for which the 'indulgence' of his friend may prove to be scant com-pensation. If, on the other hand, he says 'I am not a homosexual' he is appearing to deny both the *fact* of his numerous well-documented trans-gressions and the 'penchant' or 'deeply rooted tendency' of which they are, supposedly, a manifestation. Only if he understands that denial ('I am not a homosexual') in the sense that 'to the extent that human reality can not be finally defined by patterns of conduct, I am not one' (B&N: 87), only then does he escape bad faith. But, of course, in order to do this, he would need to accompany his denial with a lengthy Sartrean gloss – of the kind just quoted – that would doubtless be greeted with thigh-slapping incredulity by the champion of sincerity!

I do not intend to rehearse the scholarly debates around this example. Rather, I would like to decontextualize it. For the encounter between the homosexual and the champion of sincerity has a close counterpart in Sartre's fictional work. A discussion of the latter and, more widely, the 'case' of Daniel in *The Roads to Freedom* will, hopefully, throw a slightly different light on the example in *Being and Nothingness*.

This fictional encounter takes place near to the end of *The Age of Reason*. The first thing to note is that the situation is reversed: rather than being cornered by the 'champion of sincerity' and forced into making a confes-sion, Daniel actually seeks out Mathieu in order to 'confess' to him. Why does Daniel come to confess to Mathieu? It is not, as in the *Being and Nothingness* example, to earn his friend's indulgence or some kind of abso-lution from his 'sins'. Quite the contrary, he seeks Mathieu's outrage or, failing that, his overt contempt. Unfortunately for Daniel, Mathieu is not cut out for the role of 'moral censor'. The best response he can muster is a distracted 'What?' Attempting to provoke the reaction he desires, Daniel continues: 'It disgusts you, doesn't it?', but Mathieu is not playing the game: 'No, it doesn't disgust me, why would it disgust me?' And then, unwittingly, he turns the knife in the wound: 'You can be what you want, it's nothing to do with me' (AR: 294–5). This is precisely Daniel's problem: he cannot *be* what he wants without enlisting the help of the Other to tell him what he is.

This already puts the example in *Being and Nothingness* in a slightly dif-ferent light. The first problem with this example is contained in the asser-tion that introduces it: 'A homosexual frequently has an intolerable feeling of guilt and his whole existence is determined in relation to this feeling'.

Does he? Why? The language of the example with its repeated use of quasi-theological terms (guilt, fault, sin, confession, indulgence) implies clearly that the origin of this 'feeling of guilt' is the moral disapprobation of Judaeo-Christian society: the 'terrible judgement of collectivity' that has been internalized or assimilated by the homosexual and that he now attempts to turn against himself. If so, then perhaps 'shame' would be a better term than 'guilt', for we are dealing with an individual who recognizes, in shame, that he *is* as the Other sees him. Indeed, Daniel tells Mathieu 'All inverts are shameful, it's in their nature' (AR: 297). This, of course, is a caricatural statement of bad faith, but even here Daniel still tries to put himself out of reach: 'it is in *their* nature', not 'it is in *our* nature'. This play on attribution is clearly readable in the French original. Daniel says 'Je suis pédéraste' (where 'pédéraste' is, grammatically, an adjectival attribute) in the way that someone might say 'je suis séropositif' ('I am HIV-positive') – that is, as if his sexual proclivities were an affliction that he has 'caught' from somewhere. This contrasts with the extract from *Being and Nothingness* which establishes an equivalence between two substances: 'I' and ' pederast'.

Sartre's choice of a homosexual tormented by guilt for this example clearly makes it dependent on certain contingent factors. The guilt, and therefore the example itself, would be meaningless in a society where the collectivity, far from condemning homosexual liaisons, tolerated or even promoted them – such as ancient Greece. While France in 1938 (the year in which *The Age of Reason* is set) may not exactly have promoted homosexuality – and it probably would not have been a good 'lifestyle choice' for a stockbroker like Daniel – it was, since the rewriting of the criminal code in 1791, one of the few countries in Europe where homosexuals were not treated as criminals on account of their sexual inclinations. But not for long: on 6 August 1942, the Vichy regime made homosexual relations with anyone *under the age of 21* illegal. In light of this, a certain terminological drift observable in *Being and Nothingness*, as elsewhere in Sartre, is worth mentioning. *Being and Nothingness* uses the terms 'homosexual' and 'pederast' interchangeably, as does *The Age of Reason*, but in the latter work it is clear that Daniel – like the Autodidact in *Nausea*, like Bergère in 'The Childhood of a Leader' – is a pederast, in the sense that he is attracted only to adolescents and very young men. I think this also points to Sartre's own 'deeply-rooted tendency' to view male homosexuality nearly always in this 'Socratic' manner, that is, as an uneven relationship between a young boy and an older male.

In the example from *Being and Nothingness*, it is not, however, the specificity of the homosexual's desire that should retain our attention, but rather a feature of his conduct that normally passes entirely without comment: namely, its iterativeness. As I have said, the text presents the homosexual as a serial recidivist. To understand why this should be, we need to return to an earlier chapter in which Sartre discusses the origins of negation. There he gives the example of the gambler (most likely based on Dostoevsky) who has resolved to give up gambling. But every time he finds himself in the vicinity of a gaming house, he realizes the vanity of that resolution: 'I must remake it *ex nihilo* and freely. The not-gambling is only one of my possibilities, as the fact of gambling is another of these, neither more nor less' (B&N: 59) And this is because of the discontinuity of human reality, the fact that, in the psychic duration, any given instant is *not* determined by the one that precedes it: the resolution has not disappeared – we remember it – but it can only be effective if it is re-affirmed in the here-and-now by a fresh choice. This, says Sartre, explains the anguish of the gambler when faced with the temptation of the gaming table: that anguish is the realization that, literally, nothing stops him from gambling again. Anguish, then, is consciousness of freedom. Daniel is tormented by the iterative nature of his choices, despite his resolutions. There is a clear textual link between the gambler of *Being and Nothingness* and Daniel the pederast. That link consists in the single word 'jeu' (rendered by two words, 'gambling' and 'game' in English). As he wanders through Paris, he *knows* that his feet will lead him to the *kermesse* – the seedy games arcade where he goes to pick up his juvenile conquests. As he watches the boys pump money into the slot machines, he understands the nature of this compulsive activity: 'Daniel understood only too well how one could get caught up by one of those machines, and, little by little, lose all of one's money, and start over again and again, one's throat dried out by this fever, this obsession: Daniel understood a thing or two about obsessions' (AR: 129). Daniel actually earns his living from gambling – he plays the stock market – but the reason he understands the nature of addiction is that this is how he experiences his own desire: constantly denied, constantly reborn, repetitive and tedious. In *Iron in the Soul*, Daniel's judges, the bourgeois, the 'gens de bien', have fled Paris leaving the sky above his head empty, but his anguish persists. Having picked up Philippe, he is now sure of his conquest but he is abruptly overcome by the hideous predictability of it all: '"Not this again!" It was all starting over, he already knew everything, he could foresee everything, he could recount minute by minute the tedious years of unhappiness that would follow' (IS: 167).

What the homosexual in *Being and Nothingness* refuses to recognize is not that his repeated misdeeds are the manifestation of a very un-Sartrean 'deeply rooted tendency' but that they are nothing other than the repeated re-affirmation, *ex nihilo*, of his desire. It is not surprising that he does not recognize this. For it is not only resolutions *not* to act in a certain way that need to be constantly reaffirmed (e.g. the resolution not to gamble): if Sartre's theory of the radical discontinuity of 'psychic duration' is rigorously applied, then every choice we make – including our choice of objects of desire – has constantly to be made afresh, *ex nihilo*. This is where Sartre's phenomenology of consciousness seems, to me at least, to fall short of the mark: Sartre did not *discover* freedom as constitutive of human reality in *Being and Nothingness*: it was his oldest and most enduring intuition, a continually renewed oath, and *Being and Nothingness* was written in order to reaffirm that oath. To that end, the radical discontinuity he establishes at the heart of the process of temporalization is crucial, but it runs counter to another, more banal intuition: namely that existence is mostly repetition.

Notes

1 The young man in question was Georges Perec; the book was *Un homme qui dort*, published in 1967. That novel contains allusions to many writers, including several to Sartre. It is perhaps of interest to Sartreans that the book the anonymous protagonist is reading when he first falls asleep is by Raymond Aron (see Perec 1990).

2 Translations of passages from the short story collection *The Wall* (TW) and two of the novels of the *Roads to Freedom* tetralogy (AR and IS) are my own, though the page references given are to the English translations listed in this volume's Bibliography of Sartre's Works Cited. The individual stories from *The Wall* referred to here are: 'Intimacy', 'Herostratus', and 'The Childhood of a Leader'.

9

THE GRACEFUL,
THE UNGRACEFUL AND
THE DISGRACEFUL

Katherine J. Morris

Sartre's intertwined concepts of shame, being-for-others, and the Look have of course been much discussed in the Sartre literature. The majority of such discussions focus on his most thoroughly developed example, that of the voyeur (B&N: 282ff.). Sartre's initial examples – the 'awkward' or 'vulgar' gesture and 'ugliness' (B&N: 225–6) – receive rather less direct attention.[1] My aim here is to rectify that omission, and to explore the consequences for our understanding of shame, being-for-others and the Look.

I begin by showing how Sartre's description of awkwardness or ungracefulness provides phenomenological depth to the observations of those whose job it is to work with very clumsy individuals and how his account can be extended, with the help of some tantalizing hints from both himself and Bergson, to provide a parallel phenomenological description of ugliness. In the second section, I argue that shame is indeed a central feature of the experience of clumsy and ugly people, thus to an extent upholding Sartre's conception of shame not as an awareness of wrongdoing but simply 'the original feeling of having my being outside'. In the third, I argue that such aesthetic qualities as clumsiness and ugliness allow us to make good sense of Sartre's claim that 'the Other is the indispensable mediator between myself and me' while also indicating a way – one that has some considerable support in Sartre's writings – of understanding qualities that are not in any obvious sense aesthetic as likewise indispensably ontologically mediated by the Other. Finally, in the fourth section, I return to Sartre's description of grace and explore its relationship to shame and the Look via a group of notions of 'visibility' and 'invisibility', tentatively drawing some conclusions about the Look that may be surprising.

The ungraceful and the ugly

This section examines clumsiness and ugliness phenomenologically as genera of being-for-others.

The body of a clumsy person in motion often has certain characteristic perceptible qualities. We talk of someone as simply *looking* 'gawky' or 'uncoordinated' when they walk or run; they lack 'rhythm'. Most of us have not paused to analyse what gives rise to this impression; among those who have are those educational psychologists and occupational therapists whose concern is with the diagnosis and treatment of developmental dyspraxia – what used to be called 'clumsy child syndrome' or 'congenital maladroitness'.[2] They note that clumsy people perform actions inefficiently, expending unnecessary effort and engaging in extraneous, non-functional 'accessory' movements: for example, when running, their hands may flap about uselessly above waist level (Portwood 1996: 105). If asked to 'sequence each finger against the thumb of the same hand', the child will 'mirror' this movement in the opposite hand (Portwood 1996: 50; see also 25). And, quite simply, they seem to move in 'unnatural' ways: when they walk on their toes their 'arms [often] move outwards and hands bend at the wrist away from the body' (Portwood 1996: 48), when they jump they often hold the elbows 'tightly into [the] waist, arms upwards and fists clenched' (Portwood 1996: 52). Again, whereas non-clumsy people 'naturally' move their arms and legs in opposition (that is, when they stride forward with one leg, the opposite arm tends to go back), clumsy people's arms tend to go forward *together* (Portwood 1996: 25).

Sartre's description of the ungraceful (*disgracieux*) or the awkward (*maladroit*) considered as a genus of being-for-others (B&N: 421) enables us to find a phenomenological depth in these analyses. He begins with a characterization of grace, nodding en route to Bergson:

> In *grace* the body appears as a psychic being in situation ... Each movement ... is apprehended in a perceptive process which in the present is based on the future. For this reason the graceful act has on the one hand the precision of a finely perfected machine and on the other hand the perfect unpredictability of the psychic ... [T]hat part of the act which has elapsed is implied by a sort of aesthetic necessity which stems from its perfect adaptation. At the same time the goal to come illuminates the act in its totality ... In grace the body is the instrument which manifests freedom. The graceful act in so far as it reveals the body as a precision instrument, furnishes it at each instant with its justification for existing.
>
> (B&N: 422)

Concomitantly, the ungraceful 'appears when one of the elements of grace is thwarted in its realization' (B&N: 422). On the one hand, the body may become purely mechanical without the unpredictability; think of Bergson's man who stumbles and falls while running along the street, thereby displaying 'a certain *mechanical inelasticity*, just where one would expect to find the wide-awake adaptability and the living pliableness of a human being' (Bergson 1911: 10). Although the fall is not what we expect of a wideawake, adaptable human being, there is a mechanical predictability in the whole scene, often exploited in certain genres of comedy. On the other hand, the body can become purely unpredictable without the machine-like element, if for example the actions are 'abrupt and violent': 'If jerky movements are wanting in grace, the reason is that each of them is self-sufficient and does not announce those which are to follow' (Bergson 1910: 13). Here we can see in general what the Other is trying to do – 'it is always in terms of the future that we perceive the Other's gesture' – but still have little idea what will actually play itself out before us, so 'the justification of the gesture and the being of the Other is imperfectly realized'. Thus in witnessing an awkward movement, 'we suddenly encounter the unjustifiable contingency of an unadapted presence' (B&N: 423).[3] This captures rather precisely our earlier observations of dyspraxic movement.

What then of ugliness? Charmé (1991: 27) reminds us that ugliness had a personal significance for Sartre: after his first haircut did away with his long golden locks, transforming him from 'a wonder child' into a 'toad', his mother was no longer 'able to deny the existence of my ugliness' (W: 66). Sartre unfortunately does not provide us with a phenomenology of ugliness parallel to his description of the ungraceful. There are some provocative remarks on ugliness in *The Family Idiot* which we pick up later; they do not, as Sartre admits, amount to 'a true phenomenology of ugliness' (FI: Vol. 1, 299). Nonetheless there are some tantalizing hints in *Being and Nothingness* and, once again, in Bergson.

Bergson begins by admitting that 'ugliness is not much easier to analyse than is beauty' (1911: 22). However, certain *types* of ugliness suggest a mechanical rigidity somewhat similar to that of the ungraceful. (Bergson's focus is on *comic* ugliness which, as I suggest here, is not unconnected to shame.) The back of the hunchback, for instance, 'seems to have contracted an ugly stoop' in which it persists '[b]y a kind of physical obstinacy' (1911: 23); likewise, some ugly expressions 'make us think of something rigid and, so to speak, coagulated, in the wonted mobility of a face … Some faces seem to be always engaged in weeping, others in laughing or whistling, others, again, in eternally blowing an imaginary trumpet' (1911: 24–5). If we can accept as a very crude index of ugliness the reasons why people seek cosmetic surgery, it is noteworthy that some cosmetic surgery narratives somewhat confirm Bergson's point here, e.g. the woman who wanted eyelid surgery 'because her five-year-old son was always asking her "why she had been crying"' (Davis 1995: 70), or the man who sought a facelift because 'the lines around his mouth made him look "hard" – "like one of those criminal types"' (Davis 1995: 71).

Sartre juxtaposes *obesity* with ugliness in his casual reference to the 'gross and ugly passerby shuffling [*en sautillant*] along toward me' (B&N: 300; see Gilman 2004 for historical examples of coupling obesity both with ugliness and with clumsiness). Again it is noteworthy that liposuction (the removal of fat from the body through a tube and vacuum device) is one of the most sought-after cosmetic surgery procedures.[4] Sartre also explicitly connects obesity with *obscenity*, which he takes to be a species of the ungraceful (B&N: 421–2): 'a deformity in [the body's] structure (for example the proliferation of the fat cells) which exhibits a super-abundant facticity in relation to the effective presence which the situation demands' (B&N: 423) is a case where the whole body is made flesh, meaning unjustifiable facticity, a concept at the heart of his analysis of the obscene. Sartre's initial example of the obscene is this: 'certain involuntary waddlings of the rump are obscene ... because then it is only the legs which are acting for the walker, and the rump is like an isolated cushion which is carried by the legs and ... can not be justified by the situation' (B&N: 423). (It is striking too that something like 'unjustifiable contingency' is also at the heart of the way in which many individuals who are considered or consider themselves ugly view their *own* bodies. 'Prior to surgery, she [Sandra] saw her breasts as "this piece of your life that you just really hate", a "pair of sagging knockers" that just "hang there", an alien piece of flesh which "sticks to your body"' (Davis 1995: 74).) Roquentin, a past master at spotting unjustifiable contingency, finds it while regarding his own face in the mirror: 'Admittedly there is a nose there, two eyes and a mouth, but none of that has any significance ... The eyes in particular, seen at such close quarters, are horrible. They are glassy, soft, blind, red-rimmed; anyone would think they were fish-scales' (N: 31).[5]

These comments hardly amount to a full-fledged phenomenological description of ugliness as a mode of being-for-others, but they do suggest that a Sartrean–Bergsonian analysis might see ugliness, rather like ungracefulness, as gravitating between the two poles of 'mechanical rigidity' and 'unjustifiable contingency'.

The ungraceful, the ugly, the shameful and the disgraceful

Sartre introduces his notion of shame with this scenario: 'I have just made an awkward [*maladroit*] or vulgar gesture. This gesture clings to me; I neither judge it nor blame it. I simply live it ... But now suddenly I raise my head. Somebody was there and has seen me. Suddenly I realize the vulgarity of my gesture and am ashamed' (B&N: 245). (One would have liked to have had more specific examples.) The subsequent paragraph introduces the term 'ugly' alongside 'vulgar' and 'awkward' as a shame-inducing quality.[6]

For those of us used to taking the man caught peering through the keyhole as Sartre's central paradigm of a shame-inducing situation, and especially for those of us inclined to understand shame in *this* case as closely akin to guilt, it may be awkward to be reminded of Sartre's opening scenario. We might even be inclined to resist the idea that ugliness and clumsiness are really shame-inducing. (What has a clumsy or ugly person got to be ashamed *of*?)

And yet shame is a fundamental aspect of the experience of clumsy and ugly people. The term 'shame' (also 'fear', another basic aspect of Sartrean being-for-others) is a leitmotif in narratives of developmental dyspraxia.[7] It is equally so in narratives of many individuals seeking cosmetic surgery (cf., up to a point, Martin 1999), many of whom would be considered, or consider themselves, 'ugly'.[8] The sociologist Kathy Davis interviewed a number of women in the Netherlands who wanted to have such surgery and noted that '[m]any women were ashamed of how they looked, experiencing their bodies as inherently deficient or faulty. The women I talked with often described their problems as a kind of disgraceful secret' (Davis 1995: 83); one cosmetic surgery seeker explained: 'I always had this deep-rooted feeling of dissatisfaction, of *shame* … you look in the mirror and you feel so totally humiliated. And you start thinking, God, if only it could be a little less – just a little less – *shaming*' (quoted in Davis 1995: 85). Of a woman seeking liposuction: 'Pamela … referred to her thighs as "these mountains of fat". As she put it, "Your ass shakes all over the place when you walk and you look totally unappetising. It's all so *unaesthetic*, so completely unacceptable, *dirty*"' (Davis 1995: 74; think here of those 'involuntary waddlings of the rump' which Sartre deemed 'obscene'). Some of these women might well have been called 'ugly' by other people; others of them might be diagnosable with 'body dysmorphic disorder' (BDD), whose sufferers, perfectly 'normal' or even distinctly attractive in appearance, feel themselves or some part of their body to be monstrously ugly.[9] (Sartre apparently shows an appreciation of BDD when he says that 'pure nausea can be surpassed toward a dimension of alienation; it will then present to me my body-for-others in its "shape", its "bearing", its "physiognomy"; it will be given then as disgust with my face, disgust with my too-white flesh, with my too-grim expression, etc.' (B&N: 380–1).[10]) Shame characterizes the experience of BDD as well: 'shame is so common in BDD, it may even be intrinsic to the disorder' (Phillips 1986: 82). 'Whenever I see myself, I see something very inadequate. The one word I associate with my body is shame' (a BDD sufferer, quoted in Phillips 1986: 82–3).

One might add here that although Bergson's descriptions of the ungraceful and the ugly were explicitly in the context of his theory of the *risible*, there is a clear relationship between shame and laughter, at least what might be called 'laughter-*at*'.[11] And clumsy schoolchildren, as well as ugly ones, are frequently the targets of 'laughter-at', teasing, taunting and outright bullying. Many of those seeking cosmetic surgery as adults 'remembered being teased mercilessly as children. ("Rabbit face", "Dumbo".)' (Davis 1995: 83); and this from a young woman diagnosed with dyspraxia: 'As the door swung shut behind me they burst into loud laughter ... Some of the milder nouns that were substituted for "Vicky" were "reject", "spaz", and "retard"' (Biggs 2005: 109). Fat children are likewise seen as fair game for laughter-at: think of Piggy in William Golding's *The Lord of the Flies*. Bergson (1911: 23) at one point suggests imitability as a criterion of (comic) ugliness; such imitation is itself used as a form of mockery, to induce others to laugh at the one so imitated: a schoolteacher seeking dental cosmetic surgery said, 'Kids tell it like it is ... that you have a rabbit face, that you're Bugs Bunny. And they start imitating you all the time' (quoted in Davis 1995: 83). The clumsy too are the target of such mocking imitation: a dyspraxic teenager in a karate class noted that the teachers 'began to make fun of me in front of the class, mimicking my moves and saying thing like, "Look, the new downward block!"' (quoted in Biggs 2005: 160). For Bergson, laughter-at is a 'sort of *social gesture*. By the fear which it inspires, it ... softens down whatever the surface of the social body may retain of mechanical elasticity' (1911: 20). 'Fear' is a wonderfully perceptive term in this context; 'shame' fits equally.

Thus Sartre is clearly on firm ground when he identifies shame in the experience of awkward and ugly people. In addition, however, many sufferers from BDD experience what Phillips calls a 'double whammy' of shame: 'some people with BDD feel it's wrong – even immoral – to be so focused on how they look ... Many ... consider themselves morally weak and defective because they're so preoccupied with something they feel is so trivial. They feel ashamed of being ashamed' (Phillips 1986: 83). There is a striking concordance here with the experience of the cosmetic surgery seekers interviewed by Davis: 'Some women I talked with were not only ashamed of the way they looked ... They were also ashamed for feeling ashamed in the first place' (Davis 1995: 85). This point might resurrect the earlier concern about whether the ugly and the clumsy really do feel ashamed of their ugliness and clumsiness. Surely, we might urge, shame is a *moral* emotion, closely linked to (though often, variously, distinguished from) guilt,[12] and only makes sense when one has or takes oneself to have done something *wrong* or to possess a vicious character trait. Those who describe themselves as 'feeling shame on account of their shame' are using the word correctly in the first instance – they take themselves to be vain or petty – but incorrectly in the second. There is nothing disgraceful about being ungraceful and nothing sinful about being 'ugly as sin'.

There is much that could be said; here I will make just three points.

First, even if we accept that shame is a 'moral emotion', it does not follow that it is confined to cases in which one has or takes oneself to have done something *wrong* or to possess a vicious character trait. Phil Hutchinson (2008: 56) quotes Primo Levi who refers to 'the shame the [Nazi] Germans did not know, that the just man experiences at another man's crime' and discusses at length what is called 'survivor shame': e.g. the shame felt by Levi and other survivors of the Holocaust.[13]

Secondly, as Sartre points out in *The Family Idiot*, there is a kind of 'folk wisdom' which sees a *kinship* between aesthetic and moral qualities, according to which an ugly woman is 'responsible for her ugliness' (FI: Vol. 1, 297). Gilman calls attention to a related bit of 'folk wisdom' which connects particular character traits with specific facial features: 'the shape of the nose is generally regarded not alone from an aesthetic point of view … to many minds it conveys an idea of weakness or strength of character' (quoted in Gilman 1999: xviii).[14] (This expression comes from the late nineteenth century, but lest we imagine it to have disappeared, consider this, from a recent study of Asian American women seeking cosmetic surgery: 'They all stated that an eyelid without a crease and a nose that does not project indicate a certain "sleepiness", "dullness", and "passivity" in a person's character' (Kaw 2003: 189).) Gilman also reminds us of the 'ugly laws': 'the infamous Chicago municipal code 36–34 … imposed fines on persons who appeared in public who were "diseased, maimed, mutilated, or in any way deformed so as to be an unsightly or disgusting object"' (Gilman 1999: 24); this law came into force as recently as 1966 (although it was repealed in 1974). However much we may feel we have progressed beyond such 'ugly laws', those who are or feel themselves to be ugly continue to (be made to) feel 'responsible for their ugliness'; *a fortiori*, those who are fat. Let us recall too Bergson's striking expression 'physical sympathy' to characterize 'the feeling of grace', the feeling which grace gives to observers: in dance, 'when the graceful movements submit to a rhythm and are accompanied by music … the regularity of the rhythm establishes a kind of communication between him [the dancer] and us [the viewers]' (1910: 12); he suggests that there is an 'affinity' between physical sympathy and *moral* sympathy (1910: 13). The ungraceful and the ugly live an awareness of others' lack of 'moral sympathy'.

Finally, let us remember what Sartre himself says about shame: 'shame is only the original feeling of having my being outside' (B&N: 312). It is by no means confined to the awareness of sin or vice. We may say, and many commentators have said, that Sartre is here *extending* the ordinary use of the word 'shame': but this is the spirit in which we are also going to say that the notion of 'survivor shame' is a misnomer and in which we will quarrel with the use of the word 'shame' by the clumsy and the ugly to describe their everyday experience. We could look at this in a quite different spirit, and urge that Sartre has actually captured something deeply important about the experience of shame.

Being-for-others and aesthetic qualities

Certain of Sartre's examples of shame-inducing ways of being – ungracefulness, ugliness and even vulgarity – are straightforwardly 'aesthetic', in the sense that they are qualities that apply to artworks as well as to human beings. I argued in the previous section that Sartre is right to see these qualities as shame-inducing. In this section I want to argue that there are distinct exegetical advantages of taking these qualities, as opposed to (say) virtues and vices, as *paradigmatic* being-for-others qualities: doing so allows us to make better sense of a number of claims which Sartre makes about being-for-others. Here I develop just one, albeit a central one, although I think that the argument carries over to other such claims.

The claim I will consider is this: 'The Other is the indispensable mediator between myself and me' (B&N: 246). This is clearly central to Sartre's explication of being-for-others. Two prior clarifications:

First, 'mediation' can be understood as *epistemological*, or as *ontological*; the first emphasizes the idea that 'the Other teaches me who I am' (B&N: 298); the second suggests that the Other is partially *constitutive* of 'who I am'. I take it that Sartre intends both – 'the Other has not only revealed to me what I was; he has established in me a new type of being which can support new qualifications' (B&N: 246) – but also that it is the latter which is more fundamental (assuming that 'what I am' is prior to 'knowledge of what I am'). Ontological mediation implies that I and the Other are internally related, connected by a bond of *being*: there is an aspect of my being, namely, my being-for-others, that I would not possess at all if it were not for the Other.

Secondly, 'the Other' is ambiguous between the Other-as-object and the Other-as-subject, but I take it that it is primarily the latter which is intended here, as it is the Other-as-subject who *looks* and whose Look brings about shame.[15] There are qualities such as kindness and cruelty which are easily seen to be ontologically mediated by the Other, but not *obviously* by the Other-as-*subject*: roughly speaking, one can only be kind or cruel *to* another person, but it is the Other-as-*object to whom* one is cruel or kind. (Other qualities, for instance vanity, seem not to be mediated in this way: one is not 'vain to others' in the sense that one might be kind or cruel to others.) It seems that in order for a quality to be ontologically mediated by the Other-as-*subject*, it must be such that a necessary condition for possessing it is that others respond to one in characteristic ways; and it is far from clear that any of these – vanity, cruelty or kindness – meets this condition. Indeed the obvious paradigms for explicating ontological mediation by the Other-as-subject are, precisely, aesthetic qualities.

Sartre is said to have observed 'that for a man, to be ugly is to have been rejected by many women' (P. S. Morris 1976: 141; compare, up to a point, Roquentin's statement 'I think it [my face] is ugly, because I have been told so' (N: 30).). This is too crude for at least three reasons: it applies at best to heterosexual men; it ignores other reasons for 'rejection by many women', such as being a nerd, or ungenerous, or failing to wash properly; and it ignores reasons why women might not reject him despite his ugliness (e.g. his charm, his sparkling intellect, or his money). Nonetheless it serves to make the point: that part of what it is to *be* ugly is for others (and this clearly means: Others-as-*subjects*) to find one's appearance repellent or risible. (Part of what makes BDD a *disorder* is precisely that others do *not* find the individual's appearance distasteful.) Arguably *all* aesthetic qualities (whether applied to artworks or to human beings) depend simultaneously on non-aesthetic properties (say, marked asymmetry or disproportion in the features) and viewers' responses. Thus when it comes to the aesthetic qualities of human beings, the Other-as-subject really is an *indispensable* mediator.

Isn't there a problem, however? If being-for-others qualities were confined to aesthetic qualities, we would have achieved an interpretation of Sartre's claim that carries real conviction. But they are not: apart from kindness, cruelty and vanity which I have already said are *not* obviously ontologically mediated by the Other-as-subject, Sartre himself instances, alongside being ugly or handsome, clumsy, vulgar, and having 'insignificant features' (B&N: 548), being 'evil', 'jealous', 'sympathetic', 'antipathetic' (B&N: 298), 'Jew, or Aryan, ... one-armed, etc.' (B&N: 544), 'a civil servant, untouchable', a professor or a waiter in a café, 'spiritual, ... distinguished' (B&N: 548), and such properties as 'infirmity' and one's 'race' (B&N: 549).

This objection, however, misses the point. I want to argue that if we *begin* with qualities like those just canvassed, we are unlikely to see how to make full sense of Sartre's claim; whereas it is straightforward (and plausibly true) if we *begin* with aesthetic qualities. Once we see what the claim involves, we can return to these other qualities and show that each of them can be understood in a way that makes the Other-as-subject an indispensable ontological mediator. This would involve showing, for example, that being vain *in the relevant sense* (that is, *as* a being-for-others quality) is not simply spending a great deal of time in front of the mirror or thinking a great deal about how one looks, but for others to find these characteristics off-putting. Again, 'being kind' as a being-for-others quality is more than treating others (as-objects) in a helpful or understanding way, but involves others (as-subjects) finding one's helpfulness or understandingness *sympathique.*

Parallel moves can be made in respect of the more obviously socially and politically resonant being-for-others qualities: e.g. 'being a Jew' in the relevant sense is not simply being an adherent of a particular set of practices or possessing a certain family background, but being responded to by others in certain characteristic ways: in an anti-Semitic society, perhaps with disgust (cf. A&J: 10–11), 'justified' by the bad-faith reasoning which Sartre dissects so brilliantly that Jews are dishonest (A&J: 11–12), or dirty ('the Jew contaminates all that he touches with an I-know-not-what execrable quality', A&J: 34), or evil (A&J: 39ff.). Likewise, 'being black' as a being-for-others quality is not simply possessing a particular skin colour (see Gordon 1995 for a classic treatment of what it is to 'be black' in an antiblack society). From this perspective, we may be struck forcibly by Bergson's unselfconscious 'What is there comic about a rubicund nose? And why does one laugh at a negro?' (1911: 40).

I have made this argument only with respect to one particular, albeit an important and central, claim that Sartre makes about being-for-others. The case for saying that it can be made with respect to his other claims about being-for-others must await another occasion.

Grace, invisibility and the Look

I want, finally, to return to Sartre's description of grace, and to make some speculative suggestions about its relation to shame and to the Look. Grace

> forms an objective image of a being which would be the *foundation of itself in order to –*. Facticity then is clothed and disguised [*masquée*] by grace; the nudity of the flesh is wholly present, but it cannot be seen ... The most graceful body is the naked body whose acts inclose it with an invisible garment while entirely disrobing its flesh.
>
> (B&N: 422)

Thus grace involves a paradoxical interplay between 'visibility' and 'invisibility' which I will label 'grace-visibility'. Remarkably, however, one could make exactly the same claim about ungracefulness and ugliness: to be ugly or clumsy is to be visible in the sense of being stared at; it is also to be invisible in the sense of being bypassed, ignored, 'looked right through'; this combination I will label 'ungracefulness-visibility'.[16] Thus a dyspraxic child may complain that the others 'ignored me or teased me' (quoted in Biggs 2005: 47, cf. 107), which covers both invisibility and visibility; they are frequently the target for bullies (Biggs 2005: Ch. 7), which might feel like excessive visibility, but treated as invisible when it comes to choosing sports teams (Biggs 2005: 52f., 107). The same interplay is found in those who consider themselves ugly: prior to cosmetic surgery, '[m]any women described the agony of feeling that everyone's eyes were glued to that one body part ... Even when they were alone, many women could not shake the feeling that they were being observed ... [They felt] permanently on display' (Davis 1995: 82). But others, for example, women with 'flat' chests, may feel invisible: 'I always saw other girls walking down the beach, and saw a man looking at her, and thought, "Well, no one's going to look at me because I'm flat as a board"' (quoted in Gagné and McGaughey 2002: 823). Again, those who were attractive to men when younger but have now aged may complain of being 'invisible' to members of the opposite sex: a 52-year-old woman said 'I've felt for the last 10 years that I'm completely invisible to men ... Nobody even sees me. ... I get introduced to somebody but they're looking at somebody across the room. It's as though you're invisible' (quoted in Clarke and Griffin 2008: 661). And this same interplay of visibility and invisibility is perceptible elsewhere, for example, 'being black' in an antiblack society: Lewis Gordon highlights, on the one hand, Fanon's 'Look, a Negro!' ('Fanon's problem seems to be a problem of his presence. He is *seen*. Wherever he goes, he is seen by everyone, including himself, when he catches himself, as a black' (Gordon 1995: 99)), and on the other, Ralph Ellison's 'I am an invisible man ... because people refuse to see me' (quoted in Gordon 1995: 98).

The cultural historian Sander Gilman has coined the term '(in)visibility' – yet another way of intertwining visibility and invisibility – to characterize what is sought by those who undertake cosmetic surgery. It is linked to a notion of 'passing': '*Passing* was the nineteenth century's pejorative term for the act of disguising one's "real" (racial) self' (Gilman 1999: 20), as in a light-skinned 'black' individual 'passing himself off as white' or (more neutrally) 'being able to "pass as white"'. 'Such a notion of "passing" is not becoming "invisible" but becoming differently visible – being seen as a member of a group with which one wants or needs to identify' (Gilman 1999: xxi), or 'moving into and thus becoming invisible within a desired "natural" group' (Gilman 1999: 22). We need not think only of Michael Jackson to spot the connection between 'passing' and cosmetic surgery: Gilman (1999: esp. Ch. 3) records a whole history of surgery which was sought to make noses look 'less Jewish' or 'less Irish'. If one looks at recent cosmetic surgery statistics, similar interesting patterns emerge: breast augmentation is among the top three procedures sought by Caucasians and Asian Americans, but breast *reduction* one of the most popular for African Americans; rhinoplasties are among the most popular procedures for both African Americans and Asian Americans, but the former group tend to have surgery to make their noses smaller, the latter have surgery to build up the bridge and refine the tip; blepharoplasty (eyelid surgery) is widely sought both by Caucasians and by Asian Americans, but in the former the aim is apt to be to counter the appearance of ageing, whereas eyelid surgery on Asian Americans is usually so-called 'double-eyelid surgery' which produces a crease, making their eyelids look 'more Caucasian' (see Kaw 2003).[17]

Those who seek cosmetic surgery confirm that '(in)visibility' is their goal: after surgery, some comment: 'It was such freedom. I could finally just move around in my body. I felt so *free*. No one was looking at me' (quoted in Davis 1995: 82). 'What I noticed right away was that no one noticed me. Now *that* was a great feeling ... Finally, nobody is there looking at me' (quoted in Davis 1995: 102). Davis reports that '[t]he women I spoke with invariably told stories of terrible suffering which came about because they experienced their bodies as different or abnormal' (Davis 1995: 91); she notes that '[o]ne of the surprising features of women's explanations for their suffering was their unanimous reluctance to connect it with beauty' (Davis 1995: 88). After cosmetic surgery, they hope to have 'reentered the field of the ordinary looking' (1995: 112). It really is (in)visibility, not the special visibility of beauty, that they are after.

Another telling Sartrean example comes in his discussion of what he calls the third dimension of the body, the body as it is lived in awareness of being looked at by the Other. Sartre's principal example in that section is shyness (*timidité*).

> To 'feel oneself blushing', to 'feel oneself sweating', etc., are inaccurate descriptions which the shy person uses to describe his state; what he really means is that he is vividly and constantly conscious of his body not as it is for him but as it is *for the Other* ... I seek to reach it [my body-for-the-Other], to master it ... in order to give it the form and the attitude which are appropriate. But it is on principle out of reach ... Thus I forever act 'blindly', shoot at a venture without ever knowing the results of my shooting. This is why the effort of the shy man after he has recognized the uselessness of these attempts will be to suppress his body-for-the-Other ... he longs 'not to have a body anymore', to be 'invisible'.
>
> (B&N: 376–7)

This man's effort to 'give his body-for-the-other the form and the attitude which are appropriate' is an effort to achieve through (in)visibility what the 'socially graceful' possess 'naturally' (and its failure may lead him to wish for literal 'invisibility').

We seem to have *three* visibility/invisibility 'packages', but they are themselves interrelated. What I have called 'grace-visibility' (possessed as well by the ordinary-looking, the white in an antiblack society, the socially graceful, etc.) is the opposite of what I have called 'ungracefulness-visibility' (possessed equally by the ugly, the black in an antiblack society, the shy, etc.). Gilman's '(in)visibility', it seems to me, as the goal of those who aim to 'pass' (*as* graceful, ordinary-looking, white, socially graceful, etc.), is the grace-visibility possessed 'naturally' by the graceful, the ordinary-looking, the white, the socially graceful, etc.[18]

I want finally to sketch very briefly four linked tentative conclusions.

First, given that visibility and invisibility surely have much to do with the Look, the existence of different modes of visibility and invisibility appears to imply different types of Look. There is not just the hostile or ridiculing stare, but the Look which recognizes a fellow human being. (Some might prefer to say that not every look is a *Look*.)

Secondly, 'not-Looking' is often as significant as Looking: there are profoundly different ways of *not-being-Looked at*. To be ignored ('Did something squeak?') is importantly different from simply being nodded through.

Thirdly, if to be Looked at is, by definition, to be 'made into an object', then it also follows that there are different ways of being an object. Women in patriarchal societies, as feminists have insisted, are 'made into objects' or 'objectified'; that is, they are 'ungracefulness-visible'. But as Phyllis Morris points out, given that many girls and women 'say, for instance, that they are ignored by male teachers in the classroom or by colleagues or supervisors who do not hear what they have to say … part of what feminists might be considered to hope for is *more*, not less, objectification' (1999: 80). In the terms I have been developing, what they seek is (in)visibility. From this perspective, consider this: one woman who had had a breast reduction 'explained that before her surgery, people would stare at or "talk to" her breasts. She said that since her surgery, "People are paying attention to [me] and not a part of [my] body"' (Gagné and McGaughey 2002: 822).

Finally, not all types of Look are shame-inducing. The Look directed upon one who is 'naturally' (in)visible is not shame-inducing; the graceful dancer whose facticity 'is clothed and disguised by grace' is immune to shame, at least as long as the dance lasts. Likewise (with similar qualifications about context) for others who possess grace-visibility.[19]

These conclusions, in and of themselves, are hardly surprising. They may however be surprising as implications drawn from *Sartre*.

Notes

1 A notable exception is Stuart Charmé (1991); he takes *vulgarity* as central – vulgarity understood not aesthetically, as I take it for present purposes, but as opposed to 'civility'. His analysis contains much to admire, but I cannot engage with it in detail here. The context of the reference to ugliness that I have cited leaves it unclear as to whether it is seen as shame-inducing (Sartre is here *contrasting* my being-for-others with 'a bad portrait of myself which gives to my expression an ugliness or baseness which I do not have' and which might simply irritate me or make me angry), but other references, especially those in the subsection entitled 'My Neighbour', clearly support this idea.

2 'Dyspraxia' refers to an (alleged) clinical entity (or set of entities). Under the name 'developmental coordination disorder' or DCD, it appears in the fourth edition of the *Diagnostic and Statistical Manual of Mental Disorders* (or DSM-IV), the standard psychiatric manual, although dyspraxia and DCD are sometimes distinguished, with dyspraxia indicating a specific difficulty with motor planning

(see Drew 2005: 2). It appears in the tenth revision of the International Classification of Diseases (or ICD-10), used by the World Health Organisation, as 'specific developmental disorder of motor function', where it is classified as a 'disorder of psychological development' under the larger category 'mental and behavioural disorders'. Other authoritative textbooks classify it as neurological. An older term for 'developmental dyspraxia' (by contrast with adult-onset dyspraxia which may be diagnosed, for instance, after a stroke) is 'clumsy child syndrome' (see ICD-10); another is 'congenital maladroitness' (Drew 2005: 2). I will consistently use 'dyspraxia' in the text to avoid confusion. See Drew 2005: ch. 1 for the complex history of its nomenclature, diagnostic criteria and classification.

3 The facticity of the awkward person 'is not yet flesh' – not yet wholly an 'unjustifiable facticity'. The obscene body is *wholly* flesh: 'The obscene appears when the body adopts postures which entirely strip it of its acts and which reveal the inertia of its flesh' (B&N: 423). Thus, arguably, the obscene is not so much a *species* of the ungraceful as its upper limit.

4 The other most popular types of cosmetic surgery are rhinoplasty (nose-reshaping), breast augmentation, blepharoplasty (eyelid surgery) to remove sagging skin from above the eyes or fat from bags below the eyes or to alter the shape of the eyelid, and rhytidectomy ('facelifts') which remove 'excess' fat, tighten muscles and redrape the skin on the face – although with the development of non-surgical procedures such as Botox®, microdermabrasion, and soft tissue fillers, facelifts have become rather less frequently sought. This information comes from the American Society of Plastic Surgeons (ASPS) website (www.plasticsurgery.org); statistics from professional bodies in many other regions, including the UK, are not publicly available on the Internet.

5 This passage is altogether remarkable; Roquentin might well have been diagnosed with body dysmorphic disorder (see pp. 134–5).

6 He also introduces the term 'base', which I ignore for present purposes; it could be understood as equivalent to 'vulgar'.

7 Drew 2005: 82–4. The fear experienced by clumsy people includes not simply fear of failure (which may be 'paralysing'), ridicule (all too often justified), and rejection (likewise), but 'fear of being found out' (Drew 2005: 83). 'Many will have known all their life that something was "different about them"' (Drew 2005: 26). See K. J. Morris 2010 for a fuller phenomenology of clumsiness.

8 There are multiple motivations for cosmetic surgery; some simply see it as increasing their opportunities for a decent job or mate. For present purposes I will focus on those whose primary motive is felt unattractiveness.

9 See e.g. Phillips 1986. DSM-IV gives these diagnostic criteria for BDD: '1. Preoccupation with some imagined defect in appearance. If a slight physical anomaly is present, the person's concern is markedly excessive. 2. The preoccupation causes clinically significant distress or impairment in social, occupational, or other important areas of functioning. 3. The preoccupation is not better accounted for by another mental disorder (e.g. dissatisfaction with body shape and size in anorexia nervosa).' For a full discussion of BDD from a Sartrean perspective, see K. J. Morris 2003; see also Fuchs 2003.

10 This needs qualification as it seems likely from the context that Sartre is here referring specifically to one's awareness of one's own body-for-others in *illness*.

11 A recent study by the psychologist M. D. Ross, described in the *Daily Telegraph* of 12 January 2010 under the headline 'Only Humans "Use Laughter to Mock or Insult Others"', suggests that what I have called 'laughter-at' is both distinct from laughter which expresses enjoyment and is uniquely human.

12 Others suggest that the term 'shame' forms part of a family that includes both guilt and embarrassment. Embarrassment is a concept badly in need of a phenomenological analysis.

13 Hutchinson himself suggests that we can begin to understand this in terms of the Nazis' systematic undoing of a life at whose core was an internal relation between 'human' and 'humanity', to be replaced by a life centred on an internal relation between 'human' and '(the possibility of) inhumanity' (2008: 116–17). It would be worth considering whether the shame of the clumsy and the ugly can be understood in a parallel way.

14 The quotation continues by noting that the shape of the nose also conveys social status: 'Certain types of nose are "better bred" than others … a man with a "good nose" is more likely to gain immediate respect than one with a "vulgar" nose'.

15 Phyllis Morris notes correctly that being-for-others qualities – what are indicated by what she terms 'outside-view predicates' – are 'relational properties, applicable in a social context but not otherwise' (1976: 141), but she forgets the Other-as-object/Other-as-subject distinction at this crucial juncture.

16 I could perhaps have used labels that referred to *stigma*; the labels I have chosen are less weighted down with a history and literature.

17 See the ASPS website mentioned in note 4.

18 Needless to say, this notion of 'naturalness' is heavily loaded; and perhaps also needless to say, any (in)visibility achieved by those who do not possess it 'naturally' is forever vulnerable (see Gilman 1999: esp. ch. 1); to pursue these points here would take me too far afield.

19 It goes without saying that no individual is immune to shame in all contexts: the most graceful of individuals stumbles on occasion, even the ordinary-looking person has 'bad hair days', and all human beings belch, get ill, and grow old. Moreover, the 'grace-visible' and the 'ungracefulness-visible' groups intersect as well as (in a certain sense) interact. Additionally, the possession or non-possession of a being-for-others quality, as well as its status as grace-visible or not, is hugely society-dependent and variable over time. All of these qualifications are vital, but I cannot develop them here.

10

MAGIC IN SARTRE'S EARLY PHILOSOPHY

Sarah Richmond

Although Sartre does not present magic as a major theme in his early philosophy, it is striking how frequently he refers to it. The best-known and most sustained example is in *Sketch for a Theory of the Emotions*, first published in 1939, where Sartre characterizes emotional experience as the manifestation of a magical strategy, whose aim is to transform some difficult situation in which the person finds him or herself. Towards the end of that work Sartre further amplifies the role of magic, in the following remark:

> It must not, indeed, be supposed that magic is an ephemeral quality that we impose upon the world according to our humour. There is an existential structure of the world which is magical. We will not now enlarge upon this subject, which we are reserving for treatment elsewhere. However, we are able here and now to point out that the category of 'magic' governs the interpsychic relations between men in society and, more precisely, our perception of others.
>
> (STE: 56)

I will return to this later, but first I would like to point out some other, less familiar references to magic in Sartre's early work.

In *The Transcendence of the Ego*, published in 1936, and usually regarded as Sartre's first philosophical publication, he describes the structure of the ego as magical:

> We readily acknowledge that the relation of hatred to the particular *Erlebnis* of repulsion is *not logical. It is, to be sure, a magical link.* But our aim has been simply to describe and nothing more, and, in addition, we shall soon see that *it is in exclusively magical*

terms that we have to describe the relations between the me and consciousness.

(TE: 26, my emphasis)

In the same paper, Sartre also states that '*man is always a sorcerer for man ...* That is also why we are sorcerers for ourselves, each time that we take our *me* into consideration' (TE: 35, my emphasis). The phrase I have empha‑sized – 'man is always a sorcerer for man' – appears verbatim in the *Sketch*, which shows that Sartre's commitment to the idea that magic inheres in interpersonal relations was not fleeting. (Indeed, although magic is not mentioned in Sartre's celebrated account of the Look in *Being and Noth‑ingness*, it is clear from his description there that the Look is an extremely strange, non‑natural phenomenon, something capable of establishing me in 'a new type of being' (B&N: 246).)

In *The Imaginary*, published in 1940, Sartre suggests in the following pas‑sage that the subject depicted in a portrait is experienced by the viewer as magically incarnated in it:

> The first bond posited between image and model is a bond of emanation. The subject has ontological primacy. But he incarnates himself, he descends into the image. This explains the attitudes of primitive people towards their portraits and certain practices of black magic (the effigy of wax pierced with a pin, the wounded bison painted on the walls to make the hunt more fruitful). *It is not a question, moreover, of a way of thinking that has disappeared today. The structure of the image remained, with us, irrational and, here as almost everywhere, we are restricted to making rational constructions on pre‑logical bases.*

(IPPI: 24, my emphasis)

These examples – which do not exhaust Sartre's references to magic in his philosophical writings prior to *Being and Nothingness* – suffice to show that the concept of magic plays a significant role in his thinking during the 1930s. My aim in this paper is, first, to examine and elucidate the surpris‑ingly central role accorded to magic in Sartre's philosophical writings prior to *Being and Nothingness*. I will go on to discuss the fate of magic in *Being and Nothingness* where, although some references remain, its role appears to be reduced. However, there is a noteworthy change in the emphasis and implications of the references to magic in *Being and Nothingness*, and I offer a possible explanation for this change.[1]

Sartre's familiarity with the concept of magic in the 1930s is easily explained; many leading thinkers, whose work Sartre knew, discussed it in the early decades of the twentieth century. Here, as always in his career, Sartre's thinking was heavily influenced by his intellectual habitat. To understand what Sartre does with the concept of magic, it is helpful to look at what he found in the writings of others.

The concept of magic: Sartre's sources

Lucien Lévy-Bruhl

Lucien Lévy-Bruhl (1857–1939) was trained in philosophy, and taught the history of philosophy for a while, before his interests turned to anthropology. He became a much-read 'armchair' anthropologist, associated with the 'French school' that also included Durkheim and Mauss. Lévy-Bruhl hypothesized that the inhabitants of primitive societies had a radically different way of thinking to ours: theirs was a 'pre-logical mentality'. By this, Lévy-Bruhl meant a style of thinking that would be rejected by civilized Westerners as 'irrational': contradictions, for example, could be tolerated within it, and inferences that we would regard as logically mandatory could be rejected. This idea of a 'pre-logical mentality' imputed to primitive peoples was well known to Sartre. (Lévy-Bruhl advances it throughout his career, and it is reflected in the titles of some of his books, such as *Mental Functions in Primitive Societies* (published in France in 1910) and *Primitive Mentality* (1922).)

Simone de Beauvoir recalls in her memoirs Sartre's interest in this idea. In Sartre's view, 'pre-logical mentality' was not a feature of 'primitive' societies that human beings had now outgrown, but something that remained widespread and apparent in contemporary society. Beauvoir mentions a murder trial in France that she and Sartre were following in the press, and their disgust at the irrationality of the judicial process:

> The murderer was not so much tried as made a scapegoat. Sartre used to collect, diligently, all the examples of prerational mentality that abound in this civilised world of ours. If he repudiated the kind of rationalism practised by engineers, this was in the name of a more justly conceived intelligibility. But by superimposing upon logic and mathematics the surviving features of a frankly magic-aligned mentality, our civilisation was doing nothing but show its contempt for truth.
>
> (Beauvoir 1962: 131)

Sartre's account of emotion, which interprets this fundamental human experience as the manifestation of a magical strategy, instantiates his generalization of Lévy-Bruhl's 'pre-logical mentality'. If, as Sartre claims, every emotional episode involves an unreflective use of magic, human beings in civilized societies exhibit a 'pre-logical' mentality throughout large tracts of their lives.

Henri Bergson

Henri Bergson (1859–1941) was one of the most prominent French philosophers in Sartre's formative years, and Sartre studied many of his works in great depth. The extent of his influence on Sartre's early philosophy has not yet, I think, been sufficiently documented.[2]

Bergson knew Lévy-Bruhl himself, as well as his ideas, and his response to the theory of 'pre-logical mentality' anticipates Sartre's. In his *The Two Sources of Morality and Religion* (which was only published in 1932, just seven years before Sartre's *Sketch*), Bergson formulates exactly Sartre's objection: he insists, against Lévy-Bruhl, that 'primitive' mentality has not been superseded, but remains in force in contemporary society.

Bergson's ideas are extremely close to those that Sartre presents in the *Sketch*: he maintains, as Sartre will just a few years later, that throughout history people have turned to magic when they encounter a difficulty that seems insuperable by other means. As an example of a difficulty (that often confronted people in traditional society), Bergson cites the problem of *distance*. Suppose A desires to kill his enemy, B, but realizes that B is currently too far away for him to reach. In this situation, A's magical solution will be to use an effigy of B as a proxy, and to harm the effigy in the belief that this action will achieve the goal of harming B himself. A modern example that shows, Bergson says, that we have not entirely abandoned magical thinking, is that of the gambler who attributes his success or failure to good or bad *luck* – which he understands, Bergson says, as 'a favourable or unfavourable intention' (Bergson 1977: 145). For Bergson, magic is 'innate in man, being but the outward projection of a desire which fills the heart' (1977: 168). Sartre's *Sketch* differs from Bergson's focus insofar as it associates the phenomenon of magic particularly with our capacity for emotion.

Alain (Emile-Auguste Chartier)

Sartre was familiar with the work of Chartier (who published under the name Alain). Alain (1868–1951) was trained as a philosopher, and through his work as a lycée teacher, in addition to his journalism, he influenced a great many students and readers. Sartre mentions Alain approvingly several times in *Being and Nothingness*. And in the *Sketch*, Sartre quotes a sentence from Alain to characterize magic: 'The magical, as Alain says, is "the mind crawling among things"; that is an irrational synthesis of spontaneity and passivity' (STE: 56).

Throughout his writings, Alain's descriptions of human experience are attentive to the colossal part played by the imagination. In *The Gods*, published in France in 1934, he explores the childhood origins of beliefs in magical forces and divinities. It is because the child, in his powerlessness to affect the world, experiences the godlike interventions, requiring no effort on his part, of the adults who surround him, that he forms a belief in magic that never wholly leaves him. According to Alain, the child learns that *incantation* – in the form of a shout or a cry – is an effective means of translating his will into action, by the intermediary of the adults charged with his care: in other words, he learns how to achieve his wishes 'magically'. The sentence quoted earlier – 'Man is always a sorcerer for man' – that Sartre uses in two different essays, has been thought to be a quotation from Alain, although I have not been able to verify this.[3]

Sigmund Freud

Freud (1856–1939) had read many anthropological accounts of primitive thinking and, in his *Totem and Taboo* (1913), he set out to show how 'the point of view and the findings of psycho-analysis' might further illuminate it. (Although Freud was most familiar with the 'British' school of anthropology, represented by Tyler and Frazer (both of whom he mentions) his ideas are equally applicable to the characterization of magic developed by the French school.) The third chapter of *Totem and Taboo*, entitled 'Animism, Magic and the Omnipotence of Thoughts', is of most relevance here.

Although I have not been able to establish whether Sartre read this particular Freudian text, we know of course that he was familiar with psychoanalytical theory more generally, and deeply engaged with it: he voices his disagreement with it several times in his early philosophy. It seems likely that Sartre had come across Freud's explanation of the belief in magic. But whether or not he had, it is important to note Freud's view, especially in light of Sartre's official repudiation of psychoanalysis, because it is so remarkably similar to Sartre's own.

Freud follows anthropological convention in holding that the three successive views of the universe to have been espoused by men are: first, animism, then religion, and then science. Magic belongs especially to the animistic world view, in which things behave as spirits. Freud agrees too with the anthropologists that the starting point for this system of thought was probably an attempt to understand death, an event that naturally gives rise to the belief in the separability of spirit from body. (Faced with a lifeless corpse, the belief that something – their *spirit* – must have left the person, so that nothing but their body remains, arises naturally.)

Freud canvasses the 'special procedures' instantiated in magic. One example is the well-known use of an effigy to represent an enemy: whatever is done to the effigy is then thought to occur to the corresponding part of the enemy's body. In this instance, Freud says that the principle at work here is 'imitative'; elsewhere, for example in the practice of injuring an enemy by damaging one of his belongings – a piece of his clothing for example – the type of link is 'contagious'. Both sorts of case exhibit a single mistake, which Freud describes, following Frazer, as the substitution of an *ideal* connection for a *real* one. Men 'mistook the order of their ideas for the order of nature, and ... imagined that the control which they have ... over their thoughts, permitted them to exercise a corresponding control over things' (Frazer, quoted by Freud (1913: 83)).

Freud's distinctively psychoanalytical contribution to the understanding of magic is to point out that magical thinking resembles the wish-fulfilling thinking that psychoanalysis attributes to infants and children, for whom it is a normal developmental stage. According to psychoanalytical theory, children, who are limited by their undeveloped motor and intellectual capacities from fulfilling their desires in reality, often engage in hallucinatory satisfaction of their wishes. Not yet having fully adapted to reality, they misrepresent the power of their wishes, and by means of this 'centrifugal excitation of their sense organs' they are able to summon up the experiences they desire, and thereby avoid unwelcome experiences of need and deprivation. For Freud, the primitive man who engages in magic, uses just this method although in his case, as an adult, he has greater opportunity to use *actions* as well as sensations to represent the desired result.

Children of course are not yet aware of their 'mistake' – and neither, Freud says, are primitive men, because animistic thinking belongs to a stage at which science has not yet developed – but from our modern point of view, their common error is the 'overvaluation of mental processes', otherwise known as 'omnipotent thinking'. Freud notes that the disregard in magical practices for the challenge presented by spatial distance is an indication of the overvaluation of thinking; he points out that 'distance is of no importance in thinking – since what lies furthest apart both in time and space can without difficulty be comprehended in a single act of consciousness' (Freud 1913: 85). (As we will see, this idea of 'action at a distance' is prominent in Sartre's account of magic.) Freud also makes a suggestion to which he is very attached – also advanced in his other writings – that is, that ontogenesis, the development of the individual, recapitulates phylogenesis, the history of the species. Animism then represents the 'childish' stage of human cultural development.

While the overvaluation of thinking represents a normal development stage in children, and was a 'normal' feature of adult thinking in primitive cultures that had not yet developed scientifically, in *modern* adults it is a symptom of neurosis. Freud describes the peculiar beliefs of neurotic patients who fear that real harm will occur to people merely as a result of their having had hostile thoughts towards them. The excessive sense of guilt frequently found in neurotics is derived from the same source; not from any actual misdeeds, but from unconscious death-wishes that are 'overvalued'. 'The primary obsessive acts of these neurotics are of an entirely magical character' (Freud 1913: 87).

Sartre's magic: two lines of thought

The amount of anthropological interest in primitive magical practices during the period in which Sartre grew up makes it unsurprising that, along with Bergson, Alain, and Freud, he made a place for magic in his own work. As we have seen, the concept of magic appears throughout Sartre's philosophical writings of the 1930s, and plays its most central role in the *Sketch*. It is here that Sartre boldly asserts that magic comprises an 'existential structure' of the world, and that it 'governs the interpsychic relations between men' (STE: 56).

This claim, however, occurs towards the end of the text and it is easy, if one takes it out of context, to be misled by it. In fact, it represents a departure from the dominant line of thought in Sartre's account of the emotions. The existence of these two lines of thought about magic in the *Sketch*, and the conflict between them, has not often been noted or discussed.[4]

The dominant line of thought

According to the 'phenomenological' theory of emotion that Sartre proposes in the *Sketch* to replace the existing psychological theories that he regards as defective, emotion is a way of responding to an experience of difficulty. It is an 'escapist' solution that presents itself, albeit unreflectively, when the obstacles to achieving one's ends by normal, practical means appear insurmountable. The alternative course of action that emotion offers the subject is the magical *transformation* of his or her situation. Instead of changing the situation directly – by acting upon it – the subject changes her *consciousness* of it, and through this means its *meaning or appearance*. With the transition to an emotional consciousness, the difficulty magically vanishes.

To illustrate this, Sartre retells the fable of the fox and the grapes: some tempting grapes hang before my eyes, generating a desire to eat them. It turns out, however, that they are out of my reach and, there being no ladders to hand, this problem seems insuperable. Yet, by changing my perception of the grapes, the problem can be made to disappear: all that is required is that I adopt an attitude of disgust, in which the grapes are represented as unripe, sour, 'too green' – and therefore no longer desirable. The difficulty vanishes and the experience of frustration has been sidestepped.

Emotion's magic replaces our normal mode of relating to the world – in which, Sartre says, we have a 'pragmatic intuition of [its] determinism' (STE: 39) with an attempt to live 'as though the relations between things and their potentialities were not governed by deterministic processes but by magic' (STE: 40). In this respect, the non-scientific world view instantiated by emotion, with its misapprehension of causal efficacy, resembles that of the primitive societies studied by Lévy-Bruhl, and Sartre's use of the word 'magic' invites this association. However, while the belief in magic, in primitive society, was an element within a *shared* understanding of the world, in the context of the modern world Sartre presents it – as Freud does – as an evasive strategy on the part of an *individual.* Indeed, in spite of his explicit rejection, in the same text, of 'psychoanalytical theory', Sartre encourages the reader at several points to note his proximity to it; for example, when he remarks that in emotional states – *just as in dreams and in hysteria* – consciousness 'is captured by its own belief' (STE: 52).[5] The allusion to dreams and hysteria, states of consciousness to which Freud pays so much attention, highlights the interest that Sartre shares with Freud in the latent meaning of these states. With Freud, Sartre holds that the meaning of many conscious episodes is not apparent to the subject; there is a 'discrepancy between … signification and … consciousness' (STE: 33) that psychoanalytical theory is right to elicit. The disagreement between Sartre's theory of emotion and Freud's view of wish-fulfilling behaviour is not about the (purposive) *function* of the behaviours in question but rather about whether their meaning is unconscious (as Freud maintains, and Sartre denies).[6]

It is often remarked (correctly in my view) that Sartre's theory of emotion is an earlier version of the account of bad faith developed four years later in *Being and Nothingness.*[7] There are many parallels: emotion, like bad faith, is a strategy of motivated misrepresentation, and as such, Sartre cannot allow it to be fully lucid, even while he insists that it cannot be unconscious. Also, both in emotion and in bad faith, consciousness *denies its own freedom*, not at a cognitive level but *practically,* by *making itself* less free. Although this idea is not as prominent in the *Sketch* as it is in *Being and Nothingness* (where the denial of freedom is bad faith's single goal), it is nonetheless present. It can clearly be seen in Sartre's discussion of Janet's 'psychasthenic' patient, who bursts into tears in order not to confess to the doctor. In doing this, Sartre, says, she avoids the need to acknowledge that the act of confessing is in fact in her power. Sartre compares her behaviour to that of 'one of those domestic servants who, having admitted burglars to their master's house, get them to bind them hand and foot, as a clear demonstration that they could not have prevented the theft' (STE: 45). The patient *makes use of her body to* transform her options, just as the woman on the date in *Being and Nothingness* abandons her hand lifelessly in the hand of her male companion so that, having become an entirely bodily object, she will not have to decide how to respond to the man's sexual advances. According to Sartre, the purposive use of one's body in emotional episodes *debases* and *obscures* consciousness (STE: 51). Although Sartre accommodates the bodily aspect of emotion in his account, he follows the western philosophical tradition in regarding it as an inferior mental capacity, a 'clouding' of consciousness, and a diminishing of awareness: 'a consciousness becoming emotional is rather like a consciousness dropping asleep' (STE: 51).

These ideas comprise the well-known content of Sartre's account of emotion. It follows both the anthropologists and Freud in regarding 'magical thinking' as inferior to a rational engagement with reality. While Sartre disagrees with Lévy-Bruhl that this kind of irrationality is confined to primitive peoples, his account retains the traditional western philosophical view of emotion as an unreliable attitude to the world, a bodily 'degradation' of consciousness. Despite his rejection of Freud, Sartre's account of magic resembles Freud's wish-fulfilment, insofar as its misrepresentation of reality serves a defensive psychic role.

The innovative line of thought

It is only in its last five pages of the *Sketch* that Sartre casually introduces a new dimension to the account. Given their lack of prominence, it is not surprising that these few pages have attracted little attention, especially as Sartre presents them as merely an addition to a unified account, 'compatible', as he puts it, 'with the ideas we have been discussing' (STE: 56). In my view this appended section is *not* compatible with the first line of thought, but rather shows an indecisiveness in Sartre about whether to stick to the classical anthropological account of magic (in which it is repeatedly contrasted with scientific understanding, as the most effective instrument for engaging with the world) or whether to reject that account in favour of a more positive and innovative view, that magic genuinely belongs to the 'fabric of the world' and requires recognition within our ontology.

The motivation for this final section seems to have been Sartre's thought that, without it, his theory would be obviously incomplete. For Sartre's account makes it clear that in all cases of emotion, it is *both* terms of the relationship between consciousness and world that are transformed: a conscious state that is experienced as *sad* for example, has as its counterpart a world that is defined by '*Bleakness*' (STE: 44). (Borrowing Husserl's terminology, Sartre calls this the 'noematic correlative' of the conscious state (STE: 44).) In Sartre's example, consciousness makes itself 'sad', in order to render the world 'bleak': finding myself in an intolerable situation of loss, and 'lacking both the ability and the will to carry out the projects I formerly entertained', I may resort to sadness in order to apprehend a bleak universe that 'requires nothing more from me' (STE: 44).

It is natural to wonder whether there are situations in which the order of dependence described in this example is reversed; that is, where a quality perceived in the world is the cause, rather than the effect, of the counterpart emotion in the subject. Might the bleakness of the world cause me to feel sad? (In fact this pattern fits our everyday understanding of emotion better: we more readily think of emotion as a response to the world than as an attempt to transform it.)

Sartre's view is that emotion can indeed work this way round, and to illustrate this he introduces a strange example: a person catches sight of a grimacing human face behind a window pane, experiences it as *horrible*, and is overcome with terror. Magic, Sartre claims, is present in this case too: in fact, as we have seen, he believes that our perception of an Other *always* involves magic. (So it turns out that Sartre's choice of a *face* as an example of an object in the world that presents *itself* to us as magical is not accidental.) In perceiving an Other, Sartre says, we confront an 'altered, degraded' consciousness that belongs to the medium of emotional 'magic': although we know ourselves to be dealing with another *consciousness*, it is, in the embodied aspect in which it appears to us, 'rendered passive' (STE: 56). It is at this point that Sartre repeats the phrase that he used three years earlier in *The Transcendence of the Ego* – 'man is always a sorcerer to man' – adding that 'the social world is primarily magical' (STE: 56).

Sartre invokes Alain's definition of magic as 'the mind crawling among things' to argue that this is what perception of the Other reveals: a mind, reified in an expressive face, manifests 'an irrational synthesis of spontaneity and passivity' (STE: 56). But this is not the only magical characteristic of the experience: in seeing an Other, I also experience the 'magical' phenomenon of *action across a distance*. This magical property which, we saw, figures in the anthropological accounts as well as in Freud and Bergson, is one of Sartre's favourite descriptive resources. He uses it repeatedly, across many texts, to characterize the transformation of the world brought about by the encounter with the Other. Here, in a passage that prefigures the well-known description of the Look in *Being and Nothingness*, Sartre describes how, in seeing the face at the window,

> we do not at first take it as that of a man, who might push the door open and take thirty paces to where we are standing. On the contrary, it is presented … *as acting at a distance*. The face … is in *immediate relationship* with our body … [its signification] *annihilates the distance* and enters into us.
>
> (STE: 57, my emphasis)

Sartre, following Husserl and Heidegger, believes that it is not only when we are directly confronted with other people that we 'experience' their presence. By virtue of this extended signification, one can come up against a world that is 'magical' when no Other is physically present: for example, Sartre says, in a room 'which retains the traces of some mysterious visitor' (STE: 58). (This observation recalls the depiction of Pierre's 'haunting' of the café in *Being and Nothingness*, and suggests that ghosts, for Sartre, are also a supernatural feature of the real.) Nonetheless, in an entirely inhuman world there would be no magic.

Although it is presented almost as an afterthought in the *Sketch*, this part of Sartre's theory of emotion is in many ways the most satisfactory. It portrays a type of emotional experience that, unlike Sartre's best-known examples from the earlier part of the text, does not distort or misrepresent the world.[8] The emotion elicited by the grimacing face at the window is an appropriate response to it; the element of magic is not conjured up to serve a wishful alteration of the subject's perception of reality but is found there, in the extraordinary experience of the Other. Sartre's account of emotion at this point of the text has some of the features of Heidegger's *Befindlichkeit* in *Being and Time*: affective experience is credited with a cognitive role in 'disclosing' the world. (Sartre appears to have noticed this parallel, as he remarks himself in this section that 'Emotion is ... one of the ways in which consciousness understands (in Heidegger's sense of *Verstehen*) its Being-in-the-World' (STE: 61).)

The magic that 'governs the interpsychic relations between men in society' is for Sartre an existential structure of reality. His account of our perception of the Other does not suggest that we have *any choice* but to experience him or her 'magically' – and emotionally. Unlike the regressive emotional episodes described earlier in the text, Sartre does not disparage this experience of the Other, or describe it in terms associated with bad faith.[9]

And this is the source of the conflict between the two lines of thought in the text, for Sartre cannot maintain both that emotion is to be accounted for in terms of an escapist magical strategy on the part of the subject who experiences it, and that it is a justifiable response in any of us to the encounter with the Other, a legitimate way of disclosing the world. The account that starts from the 'noetic' side of consciousness is not symmetrical after all with the one that goes in the other direction.

Sartre's second line of thought is, in relation to traditional thinking about magic, original and audacious. Although he presents the *Sketch* as an exercise in phenomenological psychology, and invokes Husserl and Heidegger as pioneers in this approach, his phenomenology of the Other is distinctively his own, and quite unlike Husserl's or Heidegger's accounts of interpersonal experience.

Magic in 'faces'

Although this account of the magic at work in interpersonal contexts plays a minor role within the *Sketch*, other writings from the same period show that Sartre took the idea seriously. Even within the *Sketch* Sartre promises – in the passage quoted at the outset – that he is reserving this topic 'for treatment elsewhere'. Beauvoir remarks in her memoirs that the *Sketch* represents the only published part of a huge manuscript entitled 'The Psyche' on which Sartre was working at the time (Beauvoir 1962: 253). The rest of the work did not survive. Although we may never know – and although Sartre is notorious for his unfulfilled promises to develop a subject 'elsewhere' – I think it likely that 'The Psyche' contained further discussion of the theme of interpersonal magic.

I have already mentioned that Sartre's claim in the *Sketch* that 'man is always a sorcerer for man' appears three years earlier in *The Transcendence of the Ego*; disappointingly, he also leaves the idea largely undeveloped there. But in 'Faces', a less well-known, and beautifully written short text published in 1939 in a magazine called *Verve*, Sartre provides a detailed description of the experience of the human face that confirms his view that magic is an essential part of the experience. 'A society of faces, a society of sorcerers' (F: 67) he writes, stating a few lines later that faces are like other 'magical objects', 'deep in the rut of their dumb ordinariness and yet [possessing] spiritual properties' (F: 68). (This phrase evokes, again, Alain's idea of the 'synthesis of spontaneity and passivity'.) For Sartre, faces are 'natural fetishes' (F: 68). And Sartre insists that these claims are to be taken *literally*: 'I beg you not to take the following considerations for metaphors. I am simply saying what I see' (F: 68). He insists, that is, that an unprejudiced description of the perception of a human face must include its magical elements.

'Faces' also emphasizes the special role, among all the features of the human face, of the *eyes*; once again, the magical power of the Look – its capacity to act across a distance – is invoked: 'But now the eyes are opening and the gaze appears. Things leap backward … The gaze is the nobility of faces because it holds the world *at a distance* and perceives things *where they are*' (F: 70, my emphasis). Sartre contrasts his phenomenology of the face with the derisory investigations of psychologists who 'are only at ease among inert things, and … have made a mechanism of man and an articulate nutcracker of the human face' (F: 67). Sartre's dismissal of the methodology of psychologists is the germ of a critique of the scientific perspective that is fully developed in *Being and Nothingness*.

Magic in *Being and Nothingness*

Magic is still mentioned in *Being and Nothingness*, but it has less prominence and a less important role than in the *Sketch* and other early writings. It could be that there is no interesting explanation for this: perhaps, by the time Sartre was writing *Being and Nothingness*, the idea of magic had simply ceased to have the same grip on his imagination, and had been displaced by other concerns. In my view, this dismissal is inadequate, and there is more to be said about the shift in Sartre's use of the concept of magic between the earlier writings and *Being and Nothingness*. (Moreover, the fact

that references to magic continue to appear in texts published subsequently to *Being and Nothingness* shows that the idea had not left Sartre's mind.)

One notable aspect of the development of the theme of magic in *Being and Nothingness*, which only shows up when it is compared with the earlier writings, is that in many of the contexts where Sartre had previously invoked it, he no longer does – even though the 'magical' elements of the descriptions he provides are still present. In other words, there are passages in the text where the *content* of the idea of 'magic' remains, but Sartre does not use the *word*.

If one looks at the account of 'The Look', for example, which is a lengthy section in *Being and Nothingness* and which, as we saw, the passage about the face at the window in the *Sketch* and the description in 'Faces' prefigure, we see that Sartre continues to present the experience of the Look as something deeply extraordinary. The Other's Look has the capacity to affect me in my being, as 'essential modifications appear in my structure' (B&N: 284). It brings about a radical disturbance in my world, such that '*I am no longer master of the situation*' (B&N: 289). The spatiality of my world is reorganized (B&N: 290), I am enslaved (B&N: 291), I experience myself as '*in danger*' (B&N: 291), and so on. Sartre compares the transformation of my world brought about by the appearance of the Other to a *haemorrhage* of the meanings I have established – my world 'bleeds' into the hole brought into it – yet despite all these features, Sartre *doesn't* describe the experience as magical.[10] It seems that he no longer wishes to insist on the twice-repeated claim that 'Man is always a sorcerer for man'.[11]

Sartre's characterization of bad faith is, seen in the light of his earlier works, even more interesting. As we saw, the idea of bad faith is rehearsed in the *Sketch*, and inherits many of the features Sartre had attributed to emotional experience in 1939: in both cases reality is purposively misrepresented, to escape an unpleasant reality, by a consciousness that affects itself. Some details in the two texts are identical: Sartre applies to bad faith, for example, the comparison with falling asleep that he had used in relation to emotion in the *Sketch*: 'One puts oneself in bad faith as one goes to sleep' (B&N: 91). One might expect, then, that Sartre would also extend the idea of magic that he had found so useful in the *Sketch* to describe the irrationality of this type of evasion. But while he maintains that bad faith is 'a certain art of forming contradictory concepts' (B&N: 79), the accusation of magical thinking is withheld. The contradictions entertained by the person in bad faith seem not to invite comparison with the contradictions of primitive beliefs in magic.

If the ordinary person in bad faith is not accused of magical thinking, however, Freud does not escape the charge. He is the one character in Sartre's discussion of bad faith whose views *are* explicitly criticized for their explanatorily 'inferior' reliance on magic. As Sartre puts it, in his dismissal of psychoanalytical theory: 'By rejecting the conscious unity of the psyche,

Freud is obliged to imply everywhere a magic unity linking distant phenomena across obstacles, just as sympathetic magic unites the spellbound person and the wax image fashioned in his likeness' (B&N: 77).

In *Being and Nothingness* Sartre retains 'magical' as a pejorative term that describes an irrational mentality but while his earlier writings drew attention to its role in the everyday conduct of ordinary human beings, *Being and Nothingness* highlights its presence in certain *theoretical* constructions that Sartre wants his readers to reject. The complex ontological theory that Sartre develops in *Being and Nothingness* is shown to be vulnerable not only to the purposive distortions of ordinary human beings, for many of whom, Sartre says, bad faith is 'the normal aspect of life' (B&N: 73), but also to the methodologically generated distortions of scientists.

Freud, we have seen, is a case in point. According to Sartre, his 'materialist mythology' does not fit the characteristics of consciousness. A fundamental methodological flaw in psychoanalytical theory is its application of an *external* point of view to the explanation of 'my' subjectivity. In Sartre's view this inadmissibly combines two distinct perspectives, thereby manifesting the irrationality characteristic of magical thinking.

This accusation recurs later in *Being and Nothingness*, in the chapter on 'The Body', where experimental psychologists are ridiculed for committing the same error. Sartre offers a highly comical account of the type of experiment scientists conduct in their research on human subjects; in this case, the scientists are seeking to confirm a theory of sensation. But the concept of 'sensation', Sartre argues, is an incoherent construct that arises, like Freud's interpretations, from a flawed theoretical model that once again seeks to account for 'my' experience from an external perspective. The conflation of the two perspectives produces the incoherence in the concept of 'sensation' which, Sartre says, is a 'hybrid' notion that tries to combine subjective and objective elements. In order to explain how consciousness is implicated in the 'inert' series of sensations that they hypothesize, these psychologists resort to the concept of 'life' but, Sartre points out, in resorting to this 'biological vision' they are postulating mechanisms that are magical. 'Thus *life* is a magical connection [established] between a passive environment and a passive mode of this environment' (B&N: 337), Sartre writes, and reinforces the accusation a few lines later: 'The unity of the "lived" and the "living" … is a magical inherence' (B&N: 337–8).

These uses of the concept of magic to discredit the theories of Sartre's opponents in *Being and Nothingness* exhibit an interesting reversal of the rhetoric used four years earlier in 'Faces': Sartre's contempt for the scientists remains constant but while the earlier text criticized them for their failure to respect the *genuinely* magical phenomena they deal with – conscious beings – the complaint in *Being and Nothingness* is that these scientists' concepts are as incoherent as the concepts used in magic and on that account to be rejected.

In *Being and Nothingness* Sartre develops an ontology that is self-consciously opposed to naturalism and, we have seen, beyond the reach of scientific method (at least as it is applied to human beings). In *Being and Nothingness* Sartre holds that the correct description of our being requires the use of contradiction: in the Introduction he claims that the 'principle of identity' applies only to *one region* of being, being in-itself (B&N: 21). As being *for-itself*, on the other hand, is 'defined as being what it is not and not being what it is' (B&N: 21), the principle of identity does not apply to it. This is what makes Sartre's account of the error involved in bad faith so complicated: the 'contradictory concepts' it trades in are not inadmissible because they are contradictory, but because of the way in which they combine the elements of 'human reality'. As Sartre puts it: 'These two aspects of human reality are and ought to be capable of a valid coordination. But bad faith does not wish either to coordinate them nor to surmount them in a synthesis' (B&N: 79).

Sartre's apparent retreat in *Being and Nothingness* from the bold claim, advanced towards the end of the *Sketch*, that magic is an existential structure of reality is, I think, connected with the fuller elaboration of his ontology. In *Being and Nothingness* Sartre has not abandoned his conviction that consciousness must be understood in non-natural terms, and that interpersonal encounters reveal a kind of magic: on the contrary, he presents a fuller and more detailed defence of that view. What Sartre has come to realize, however, is the inappropriateness, given his philosophical purposes, of affirming a concept of magic that traditionally implies the superiority of science. But if the affirmative use of the word 'magic' is, for the most part, absent from *Being and Nothingness*, its pejorative use is retained to criticize the very people – the scientists – whose thinking is widely supposed to have left magic behind. Using a strategy that anticipates the deconstructive movement that had not yet begun in France, Sartre challenges the opposition between magic and science by claiming that civilized scientific theory itself is, despite its pretensions, an example of primitive magical thinking.[12]

Notes

1 This paper deals only with Sartre's philosophical texts up to and including *Being and Nothingness*, but it should be noted that magic also crops up elsewhere in his work, such as in his 1944 play *The Flies* (TF: *Passim*), and his 1961 Preface to Frantz Fanon's *The Wretched of the Earth* (WE: *Passim*).

2 For discussion of Bergson's influence on Sartre's conception of nothingness in *Being and Nothingness*, see Richmond 2007.

3 Vincent de Coorebyter (2003: 192n75) says the phrase is a quotation from Alain, but no reference is provided.

4 Coorebyter (2000: 485–90) provides a short discussion of Sartre's general 'ambivalence' towards magic in his early philosophy. To my knowledge, the only discussion of these two lines of thought in the *Sketch* is Mazis 1983.

5 Sartre's supposition of the 'unbearable tension' of the situation, that emotion works to release, is a further element that his theory has in common with Freud's (STE: 40).

6 Against psychoanalytic theory, Sartre argues in the *Sketch*, exactly as in *Being and Nothingness*, that one cannot maintain at the same time that consciousness has any *comprehension* of its meaning and account for that meaning in terms of *causal* processes, such as mechanisms of association. While Sartre insists that consciousness cannot but comprehend its own symbolization – so an account in causal terms is out of the question – he claims that the psychoanalysts incoherently include both types of process within their account.

7 This continuity of theme, in combination with the greater accessibility of the *Sketch*, has led critics to suggest this latter as a helpful introduction to *Being and Nothingness* (see Contat and Rybalka 1974: Vol. 1, 65).

8 It is this aspect of the main part of Sartre's account that leads Wollheim to describe it as being in fact applicable – although Sartre does not see this – only to deviant, 'malformed' emotions (Wollheim 1999: 83).

9 At least, in Sartre's description of the experience of seeing the face at the window there is no mention of distortion or bad faith. The connection is however clumsily reintroduced just before the 'Conclusion', where Sartre says – in keeping with the main line of thought in the text – that 'the reflection that we direct towards the emotive consciousness is accessory after the fact', and contrasts this with the 'purifying reflection of phenomenological reduction' (which is said to be 'rare'). I think Sartre must have become aware at this point of the conflict between the two parts of his theory, and made an attempt to resolve it.

10 Much later in the text, however, Sartre alludes in passing to a magical (or at least divine) aspect of the Look when he states that the 'petrifaction' that it causes is the 'profound meaning' of the myth of Medusa (B&N: 451).

11 In other words, the 'innovative' use of magic present in the *Sketch* virtually disappears from *Being and Nothingness*. But not entirely: Sartre describes language (part of the 'First Attitude toward Others' explored in Part III, Chapter 2, of *Being and Nothingness*) as an aspect of the interpersonal relationship that involves magic, and action at a distance.

12 I would like to thank Jonathan Webber for inviting me to contribute this paper and for his friendly and efficient organizational and editing assistance. I am also most grateful to Sebastian Gardner and Neil Vickers for helpful discussion of the paper.

11

ALIENATION, OBJECTIFICATION, AND THE PRIMACY OF VIRTUE

Alan Thomas

This paper examines the ways in which Sartre's philosophy of mind supports some of the foundational claims of virtue ethics. Virtue ethics understands the idea of character as being explanatorily and normatively prior to the concepts of rightness and of value. This sharply distinguishes it from other approaches to normative ethics such as deontology and consequentialism. My aim is to show how Sartre's philosophy of mind is structured around a basic asymmetry between first and third personal ascriptions of mental predicates in a way that is very important to the phenomenological plausibility of virtue ethics. I will further argue that Sartre's claim that there is a sense in which one cannot think of one's own character as an 'object' is important to establishing the priority of virtue ethics over other normative theories.[1]

The tragedy of consciousness

There is a clear sense in which Sartre's philosophy as a whole has an ethical basis: he places a tragic diremption at the very basis of consciousness. Conscious experience, structured as it is by our capacity intentionally to represent, is divided from itself in a way that it seeks to overcome but cannot. This tragic failure of the 'for-itself' (conscious experience) to achieve the self-identity characteristic of the 'in-itself' (the world of non-mental objects) is grounded in Sartre's account of negation.[2] Negation introduces the freedom to think other than in the way one thinks when the object of thought is manifestly present to mind. However, the cost of this achievement is that negation also introduces division into consciousness. It is the internal structure of consciousness, explained in terms of negation, which explains why it self-defeatingly aspires to the condition of the non-conscious, non-mental world. That world is comprised of what simply *is*: the non-conscious world is made up of objects that are necessarily self-identical because they simply are.[3] This tragic failure to

161

achieve self-identity lies at the very basis of intentional representation and conscious thought.[4]

Sartre's treatment of the connection between intentionality and consciousness is highly distinctive. Consciousness is properly to be identified as the *act* of positing an external object that extinguishes itself in that object. This account of intentional consciousness explains why, when we attempt reflectively to focus on consciousness, it is systematically elusive. First, there is the problem posed to our reflection on consciousness by the passage of time. When we attempt reflectively to grasp our consciousness we are always too late; we always find a 'consciousness reflected on', not consciousness itself. All we can find at the time of reflection is a trace of consciousness in short-term memory. Secondly, we fail to grasp our intended object: we sought consciousness, but instead we find the external object in which consciousness has been extinguished. For these two reasons we never seem to grasp consciousness itself in reflective thought. Consciousness has an elusive, evanescent quality: Sartre calls it a 'nihil', or nothing.[5]

Sartre treats consciousness as both analogous to an activity and as functioning as a transcendental condition for the representation of objects. His analogy for consciousness is light:

> I am as inseparable from the world as light, and yet exiled as light is, gliding over the surface of stones and water, never gripped and never held.
>
> (TR: 308)

Consciousness is translucent, a nothing, but a something without which we cannot 'see' the objects of consciousness.[6] It enables awareness of objects, but plays that role transcendentally (J. Rosenberg 1981; Longuenesse 2008). Using the somewhat unhappy English translations of Sartre's central terms, all 'positional' consciousness directed towards an object is 'non-positionally' self-aware. However, the latter is an insight into an activity, not properly a matter of knowledge (J. Rosenberg 1981; Thomas 2006a).

From consciousness to self-knowledge

Sartre's general account of mentality can be interpreted as a reaction against Cartesianism. Common sense would seem to support Sartre's view that the asymmetry between my knowledge of my own mind and other people's knowledge of my mind has to be reconcilable with a low-key 'realism' that mandates that these are two ways of knowing specific instances of a more general thing – a token instance of minds in general. However, a long tradition of philosophical reflection seeks to replace these truisms with a contested, philosophical re-description of the subject matter.

This view abandons the common sense truism that access to my own mind is knowledge of an instance of a more general type. It has bequeathed to us two contested issues. First, how can there be cognitively substantial *knowledge of self* with the characteristic features of such knowledge? Second, how can there be knowledge of *other minds* given the presumed inaccessibility of one's own mind that seems implied in any convincing answer to the first question? Sartre thinks that a description of our ordinary practices suffices to dissolve these problems. The way forward is to treat the asymmetry of first and third personal *access* to the mind as basic and to work with that idea while dispensing with the metaphors of 'inner' and 'outer' (Moran 2001: xxxiv–xxxv; Sacks 2005a).

The constraint of objectivity in this context is that any philosophical account has to preserve the datum that first and third personal ascriptions of one and the same mental state answer to the same objective and cognitively substantial facts that makes each true. My talk of my headache and your talk of my headache are both about the same thing – a token headache that simply happens to be mine. First personal and third personal ascriptions of mental predicates are answerable to the same fact.

It is true that Sartre has a distinctive ontological gloss on this claim, but it respects the minimal form of objectivity internal to the way we think and speak about minds. This minimal objectivity blocks the proposal that mental facts are perspectival through and through; that would be a mistaken interpretation of the metaphor of consciousness as a 'for-itself'.[7] The 'for-itself' and the 'in-itself' are essentially complementary, just as the metaphor of perspective has to be complemented by that upon which it is a perspective, namely, something non-perspectival (in this case the world of objects). Sartre's insight is that if we are going to be drawn into using metaphors like 'perspective' or 'point of view' when we think about the mind, then we must, essentially, see such metaphors for the 'for-itself' as being contrastive with, and complementary to, the 'in-itself'.

The real work done by the distinction between the 'for itself' of conscious experience and the 'in-itself' is to hold apart consciousness and the world in a way that respects the basic asymmetry between first personal and third personal perspectives as two distinct perspectives on one and the same mental reality. But that reality, too, is elusive. Sartre's account of the intentional objects of thought is shaped by his radical externalism. Sartre's externalism is expressed by his explanation of consciousness as an intentional positing that both culminates in, and is extinguished by, its objects. This emphasis on activity is distinctive of Sartre's view and opens up some of the most interesting of his claims, notably that there can be no 'inertia' in consciousness. For any of your mental states, the question arises as to whether you affirm it: the norm governing the rational standing of each of your mental states holds you responsible for the states in which you acquiesce as well as those that you actively endorse. This norm reflects the

fact that your mind is yours to make up: mental action and inaction (acquiescence) are on a par (Moran 2001: 59, 63, 75–6, *passim*).

This is a crucial aspect of Sartre's view for what follows. Sartre seems prepared to advance the radical claim that all of your mental states are reason-sensitive, including emotions and moods, arguing that these are structured responses to situations that also invoke this norm of responsibility (see Webber 2009: 38–41). The idea of responsibility that Sartre appeals to here works at a deeper level than a superficial voluntarism that claims (falsely) that you can change your emotional responses or moods at will. The basis of Sartre's claim is that in so far as we can speak of consciousness as having a nature, then its nature is to be thoroughly active. Therefore, for any mental commitment of yours we can ask whether it can be connected to your rational endorsement of that commitment via Sartre's notion of a project. Projects are structured hierarchies of normative commitments (Webber 2009: 51–3).

This claim about the mind directly connects to the most well-known element of Sartre's philosophy as a whole, namely the centrality to his work of the idea of freedom. From an interpretative point of view, Sartre's talk of 'freedom' can be interpreted in this context as referring to the idea of reason-sensitivity and its connection with projects. (This may, indeed, help to make Sartre's extended uses of terms such as 'freedom' and 'choice' seem more plausible.) A mental state can be sensitive to reason without being acquired by reason or passing through some filter of rational endorsement. For example, the perceiving subject is usually simply assailed by beliefs from her environment without an ongoing process of rational endorsement. The key issue is that such beliefs are sensitive to further rational assessment (Thomas 2005: 38–40). In particular, choosing to acquiesce in those beliefs once you have become aware of them can be interpreted as a rational commitment on the thinker's part. As Jonathan Webber has pointed out, Sartre's idea of a rationally assessable project to which one can take an agent to be committed extends to such 'projects' as staying alive (2009: 49). That is not a purposive, goal directed activity, but a commitment rationally to underwrite acquiescing in a given state of affairs. It is, in that sense, a helpful example of the reason-sensitive nature of a mental commitment even in a case where it seems 'passive'.

Building on these points, it can be seen why, for Sartre, we have to take the asymmetry between first personal and third personal perspectives on mentality as basic. That is because you have a kind of direct rational control over your own mental states that others do not. But this notion of a perspective needs to be handled carefully. It is an inherently realist metaphor: perspectives are perspectives on something non-perspectival. Your first personal perspective on the world is not a perspective *for* you. Nor is it captured by some other metaphor such as a 'point of view' or a 'standpoint'. You do not occupy your mental life or view things *from* it; you *are*

it. Sartre's externalist treatment of consciousness emphasizes this further point: first personally your consciousness is opened out onto its objects in the world.

However, at this point a problem arises for the internal consistency of Sartre's view. When the conscious subject reflectively turns his or her thoughts to consciousness itself, it permanently escapes our grasp. Phenomenologically convincing though this may be, it does seem threatening to Sartre's fundamental commitment to treating the asymmetries of first and third personal knowledge of mind as basic. Our aim was to make sense of two perspectives on a common subject matter. Given the systematic elusiveness of consciousness, the threat is that we cannot locate in the first personal case any distinctive subject matter at all. Sartre has a particularly subtle treatment of this problem that connects his philosophy of mind with the foundations of virtue ethics, namely, his treatment of the connection between self-knowledge and knowledge of the Other. It is to that theme that I now turn.

Sartre on alterity

From a first personal perspective your attention, qua rational agent, is simply opened out on to the world and the objects of your conscious experience. Yet, reflectively, you know that your mind is one instance of mentality in general. However, given that from our first personal perspective we find simply the world, and that whenever we turn our reflective thought onto consciousness it always slips through our fingers, what are the materials for substantiating that thought? I cannot improve upon the succinct summary Mark Sacks gives of Sartre's conception of the problem:

As long as my awareness is rooted solely in first personal thought I cannot, by reflection, dissociate myself from my subjective stance and identify myself as an object. Every object that I come to perceive as an object, is presented as essentially distinct from me, the perceiver; and just insofar as it is presented to me as a distinct object, it is presented as in principle alienable from me. The only item that is not presented as separable from me in that way, the only thing that is given to me with an immediacy that precludes the coherence of my thinking it away, is my own point of view. But that is always given as a point of pure subjectivity: it is behind the lens, so to speak, whereas anything captured as an object is always in front of it.

(Sacks 2005a: 288)[8]

Sartre both appreciates this problem and solves it in a way that respects the objectivity requirement for mental ascriptions. He does so solely for those mental predicates where the idea of a common subject of ascription across the first and third person has an application. Sartre is aware that it does not apply to mental dispositions or mental capacities where the basis of ascription is as third personal for me as it is for you (see Gardiner 1977: 72ff). Setting that class of cases aside, how is self-knowledge to be reconciled with the evanescence of conscious experience as a 'nihil'?

Sartre's solution is to turn to the interdependence of the first and third personal perspectives on mentality to argue that those patterns of your past behaviour that constitute your character are, *for you*, an interpretative artefact of how *others* view you. The only solution to the envisaged problem compatible both with the phenomenology of the first person and with treating the first/third person asymmetry as basic to our idea of mentality is to form a conception of oneself *as one is seen by others*.

The very idea that I can so much as refer to mentality in my own case depends on my being the subject of the interpretative gaze of the Other, dramatized by Sartre's famous account of 'the Look' (Sacks 2005a). The solution to the problem of other minds is to be found in an unlikely place: the moral psychology of shame. It is in the experience of being ashamed that I feel ashamed of myself through and through, as a whole person, in the gaze of another person.

The Other in this example need not actually be present, but can be surmised. Shame can be triggered by the fact that I could be observed. That phenomenological fact, in turn, is part of seeing the world as structured around other centres of consciousness each of which is a 'for-itself' that transcends its own reality just as I transcend mine. Solipsism does not need to be refuted: an account of its presuppositions exposes it as a view that claims to arise from our ordinary conception of mentality and the latter's claim to objectivity while it actually silently repudiates that concept of objectivity in an unacknowledged way. In the only sense in which I am given to myself, I am given to myself 'as for another'.

One aspect of Sartre's claim is that when we reflexively mirror our own character in the guise of how we seem to the Other, we resist such descriptions as falsely objectifying. This is the part of Sartre's treatment of the idea of character that has been picked up on by situationist sceptics, notably Gilbert Harman (2009).[9] Sartre's view of character traits is that they are reason-responsive patterns of action and motivation, comparable to Dennett's 'real patterns' (Dennett 1991). We pick out such patterns from a background of 'noise', irrelevant information that obscures the pattern that we discern. In classifying another person's actions as 'typical' of her, as 'out of character', or as 'throwaway' actions that simply do not bear on the idea of character, we interpret the presence of a pattern in a person's responses that simultaneously involves treating other actions as irrelevant to the patterns that we seek.

Sartre objects to two forms of false objectification of this process: one models patterned rational responses on the idea of a fixed inner causal mechanism grounded in a person's 'nature'. But the other form of false objectification is our justifiable recoil from having this process of interpretation applied to our own case. When we discover that others find us 'cranky' or 'charming' we refuse to identify with such ascriptions simply because we take ourselves to transcend any such pattern.[10] The reason for Sartre's emphasis on this point is his distinction between transcendence and facticity that I will discuss further below.

Given Sartre's unique achievement in describing this area of moral psychology and conceiving of a range of 'pathologies of self-regard' that other moral psychologists had neglected, it is tempting to allow these diagnoses to overshadow the fact that there is a positive sense in which one is presented to the Other as object. However, there is such a positive aspect: one is presented as an irreducibly whole person, a basic subject of reference. It is as oneself that one is presented to the Other (Theunissen 1984: 224–7, 230, 236–7; Sacks 2005a: 285–90). The pathologies of self-regard arise only when one views oneself merely as an object. The key idea for Sartre is that we are never self-identical in this sense: we know ourselves both as transcendence and as facticity. The pathologies of self-regard result from a collapse of one of these aspects of subjectivity into the other.

Given the richness of the territory in moral psychology that Sartre explored in his account of bad faith, it is understandable that a great deal of the literature on his moral philosophy focuses on the nature of these pathologies. However, for my purposes it is the positive sense in which one is presented to another, such that this is how one can conceive of oneself, that is of greater importance than his explanation of bad faith. If Sartre is correct, then there is a plausible basis in the philosophy of mind for two arguments that are helpful for the development of a virtue ethic.

The first is the claim that there is a fundamental asymmetry between the first and third personal use of virtue terms; this would be a corollary of Sartre's more general thesis that this asymmetry holds true for a wide range of mental ascriptions. The second is the claim that there is a sense in which one cannot think of one's own character as merely an object for oneself. But to understand both of those claims we need to understand a more basic Sartrean distinction between the self as transcendence and as facticity.

Transcendence and facticity

If the first personal point of view is a rational openness to the world, then this seems to problematize self-knowledge. Sartre's solution appeals to the Other's conception of oneself. This puts in play the fundamental distinction in Sartre's account of character of knowledge of your own facticity versus insight into your own transcendence. With this distinction substantiated Sartre can go on to generate all of his diagnoses of bad faith as involving the affirmation of 'facticity as being transcendence and transcendence as *being* facticity' (B&N: 79).

I have explained Sartre's emphasis on freedom by invoking the idea of reason-sensitivity. Consciousness is an openness to the world in the sense that one is rationally oriented to that world in a way that imposes the norm for reason-sensitive mental states that the agent cannot acquiesce in any such state. They are all, in principle, connected to reason-sensitivity via the idea of a project. When this thought is combined with the idea that the asymmetry between first and third personal access to the mind is basic, the consequence is that in integrating another person's conception of you as your conception of yourself, the latter must have the capacity to outstrip the former. This is because the pattern in your conduct that the other has discerned in your past actions and reflexively 'returned' to you was, after all, a pattern in your past rational responses to situations. It is only in so far as you are an appropriate subject for such rational interpretation that this conception of yourself for another has any salience for you. But you have not ceased to be such a rational subject and thereby open to the demands, not of your own past character, but of the world. In knowing your own character via the way you are interpreted by the Other, then you must, thereby, transcend that character. That is the basis of Sartre's distinction between facticity and transcendence.[11]

Practical deliberation is, in fact, the most helpful case for making this kind of point even if Sartre's eventual aim is to generalize it for responsibility for all your rational commitments, practical and theoretical. If your virtues are oriented to a situation via sound practical deliberation about what to do, then in any particular instance of practical decision the circumstances call upon one or more of your virtues. Sartre actually thinks that the entire perspective of deliberation will be so structured by the prior commitments expressed by your virtues that there is not much of a task left for the deliberative process itself (B&N: 472–3).

Responsible decision, that which Sartre calls authentic choice, always involves both facticity and transcendence. Your aim, qua deliberator, is to be rationally sensitive to the demands of the situation. This is largely predetermined by the patterns of relevance and salience in the situation to which you are attentive that have been established by your virtues. This represents your facticity, the real pattern within your rational responses to past situations that forms the reality of your character for another. However, from your first personal, engaged, situation your engagement is with *the situation*. In that respect you must transcend your facticity: you must do so because what you are responsible to is a correct response to this situation, regardless of how much your apprehension of this situation has been structured in advance by your prior facticity.

Sartre's insight into transcendence and facticity has been taken up and explored by, amongst others, Stuart Hampshire (1975) and Richard Moran (2001). Both Hampshire and Moran emphasize that one can form a belief or intention from an engaged perspective *from* one's own character. However, this engagement must also be informed by knowledge *of* that character as an 'object' for one. (Where the relevant notion of character encompasses the very normative commitment that one is about to make.) That this practical question is irreducibly first personal is brought out by noting that even in the case of facticity, it is one's perspective on one's own character that is in question, even if it is modelled on other people's knowledge of your character. Your mind is yours to make up the way that the minds of others are not. Only your decisions are expressive of a capacity for direct rational control of your intentions, decisions, and actions.

I have noted that Sartre's view is that responsibility for decision (authenticity) always involves both facticity and transcendence. Richard Moran explains why, using the idea of intention formation as involving 'answerability' to evidence:

> ... When I avow my belief I do not avail myself of psychological evidence of any kind, I nonetheless take what I say in that context to be *answerable* to whatever psychological evidence there may be ... Since an expression of intention is not a prediction, it is not contradicted by a contrary prediction (but by the expression of an opposed intention). To say this is not, however, to deny that in declaring the intention the person is committed *both* to the practical endorsement of the action and to the expectation of a future event.
> (Moran 2001: 87–8)

Denying answerability is precisely to commit oneself to transcendence without facticity or vice versa. These constitute the two general patterns of bad faith as two different forms of ethical evasion.

On the one hand, there is the empty, illusory 'transcendence' of a normative commitment in decision that is simply insensitive to the evidence as to whether one will, in fact, act as one's commitment dictates (Moran 2001: 81–2, 88). This is an ethical error as a first personal avowal of intention creates an expectation as to one's future action. Therefore the agent's responsibility includes sensitivity to the *same* range of facts appealed to in establishing his or her 'facticity'.

On the other hand, there is the pretence of submerging one's transcendence in one's facticity, as if one's active role in sustaining a normative commitment has been submerged in a mechanism beyond one's own control. This second general form of ethical error is, to borrow Moran's helpful phrase, a 'tactical substitution' of one's facticity for one's transcendence. Here one reflects that one simply cannot help being the kind of person that one is. This is a particularly subtle form of bad faith as it can assume the guise of a hard-headed realism about one's own motivations, simultaneously self-aggrandizing and evasive.

In this second kind of bad faith there is an evasion that seeks a guarantee for one's resolve by absorbing it into facticity. It is as though one had put in place of one's ongoing rational commitment a mechanism to whose operation one is now indifferent. This can only lead to the undoing of one's resolution. Attention has been diverted from where it ought to be directed: to your reasons. Those reasons, in turn, direct you outwards to those evaluative features (reasons) to which your rational judgement is a response. Paradoxically, reliance on knowledge of one's character as 'facticity' (as an external mechanism to back up one's reasons analogous to alienated action control) succeeds only in qualifying whether there was a commitment there in the first place. As both Hampshire and Moran note, if a person seeks to strengthen her resolve by the subterfuge of tactically substituting facticity for transcendence then I, your interpreter, ought, rather to conclude that your avowal is insincere or at least significantly hedged (Hampshire 1975: 52; Moran 2001: 81–2). All you achieve with this tactical substitution is to raise doubts in your interpreter's mind as to whether you sincerely undertook a normative commitment at all.

Underpinning these diagnoses of bad faith is a positive ideal of authentic choice that reflects the following principle:

> When I *avow* a belief, I am not treating it as just an empirical psychological fact about me; and to speak of a *transcendental* stance towards it is meant to register the fact that it commits me to the facts beyond my psychological state; and as a commitment it is not something I am assailed by, but rather is mine to maintain or revoke.
>
> (Moran 2001: 89)

The important issue is that one can derive from Sartre's work a positive model for responsible, authentic decision-making that is as interesting as his diagnoses of the pathologies of self-regard. My interest in this ideal is the light it casts on the fundamental rationale for virtue ethics for reasons that I will now explain.

Sartre and virtue ethics

The foregoing account of Sartre's moral psychology offers two powerful arguments in support of virtue ethics. If it can be proved that Sartre believes in the reality of moral character, interpreted not as an inner causal mechanism but as an interpretative pattern in a person's actions that is sensitive to reasons, then he offers two considerations of central importance to an ethics of virtue.[12] The first is the robustness of his claim that there is a deep asymmetry in first and third personal uses of virtue terms. The second is the claim that it is an ethical error always to think of oneself *merely* as an object. I will now set out these claims, describe why they are important to virtue ethics, and how Sartre's views can be put to use in resisting an attempt to undermine the distinctiveness of virtue ethics as a self-sufficient approach to normative ethics.

Given the priority he attaches to freedom, Sartre is consistently hostile to the idea of independently existing values. It would, then, be completely alien to his thought to interpret the kind of openness to the world characteristic of his externalist view of consciousness as capable of being extended to the idea of openness to values.[13] However, given that Sartrean freedom is rational freedom, there is less strain in interpreting a Sartrean account of rational deliberation as openness to those features of a situation that are the basis of her reasons.

Virtue ethicists since Aristotle have noted that it is characteristic of the majority of virtue terms that they do not figure in the first personal rational deliberation of agents. That which figures in such deliberation are those features that ground an agent's reasons: that another person is in distress, is easily helped, and so on. The concept of a particular virtue, whether it be kindness, compassion, helpfulness, is not part of how the agent conceives of the situation calling for action with the exception of some special cases such as justice or righteousness. This phenomenological point is basic to an ethic of virtue that conceives of virtues as a sensitivity to those features that ground an agent's responses of the kind found, for example, in the work of neo-Aristotelians such as John McDowell.

If, as Bernard Williams argued, virtue terms *are* asymmetric across their first and third personal uses, then any use of a virtue term in a person's first personal ethical deliberation is, in his memorable phrase 'a misdirection of the ethical attention' (Williams 1985: 11). Sartre's moral psychology offers a grounding for that claim. Attention to one's character is properly a part of learning to be good.[14] However, it is not a part of a mature ethical understanding when that process is completed. That consists, as John McDowell puts it, in an 'an ability to recognize requirements which situations impose upon behaviour' (McDowell 1979: §2).

This phenomenological argument is important to virtue ethics, as it is the first step one can take as a response to views that seek to deflate the importance of virtue ethics as a self-sufficient ethical view. The claim of first and third person asymmetry in the ascription of virtue terms is not simply true to our ethical experience. It also points to some of the difficulties in store for any view that simply wants to adopt the idea of a virtue and make it a derived concept in a wider framework in which other concepts (such as duty or optimal consequences) are described as being normatively and explanatorily prior to that of a virtue.

Any view of this kind requires your own character to be merely an object for you in a way that Sartre exposes as illusory (whether that object is valued instrumentally or intrinsically). Later in the work in which Williams argues for the first/third personal asymmetry in the use of virtue terms he suggests this more general form of argument. It takes as its target precisely that family of views that seeks *indirectly* to model a virtuous sensitivity to reasons with a theory that attaches derivative importance to virtues:

> Is there anywhere in the mind or in society that a theory of this kind can be coherently or acceptably located? The theory finds a value for these dispositions, but it is still an instrumental value. The dispositions are seen as devices for generating certain actions ... That is what those dispositions seem like when seen from outside ... But it is not what they seem from the inside ... The dispositions help to form the character of an agent who has them, and they will do the job the theory has given them only if the agent does not see his character purely instrumentally, but *sees the world from the point of view of that character*. Moreover, the dispositions require the agent to see other things in a noninstrumental way. They are dispositions not simply of action, but of feeling and judgement, and they are expressed precisely in ascribing intrinsic and not instrumental value to such things as truthtelling, loyalty and so on.
>
> (Williams 1985: 108, emphasis added)

This argument is unsatisfactory as it stands: it is possible for an indirect theory to model virtues as intrinsic goods, as Williams recognized in his later work on the epistemic virtues (Williams 2004; Thomas 2008). However, I think that the phenomenological force of Williams's critique remains powerful, notably in the sentence I have emphasized concerning the necessity of the agent's 'see[ing] the world from the point of view of that character'. That remark suggests a connection with Sartre's conception of the rational agent as open to the world and those considerations that ground her reasons.

This phenomenological point suggests a deeper Sartrean argument against moral theories that seek indirectly to model the value of virtue. They require a standpoint from which your character is *merely* an object for you, qua deliberating agent. That distinctively Sartrean claim would be tantamount to the claim that theories that assign an indirect, derivative role for virtue (even qua forms of intrinsic value) are in bad faith. That would be a powerful argument for the priority of virtue ethics if it could be made good. However, the claim that one's character cannot be an object for one's own reflection seems, on the face of it, very implausible. It is to an assessment of this Sartrean claim that I now turn.

Treating oneself (merely) as an object

Sartre's moral psychology underpins the asymmetry between the first personal and third personal ascription of virtue terms. Furthermore, his account suggests a novel counter-argument against the attempt to model virtue ethics in an impartialist ethical theory, to be developed along the lines that Williams suggested in the passage I have cited. Those sympathetic to the priority of virtue ethics over other normative views need to show that any attempt to model virtue ethics in an impartialist theory is falsely objectifying. Sartre seems to offer a basis for this argument but, unfortunately, it involves interpreting one of his less clear claims, namely, that an ethical agent cannot treat him- or herself as an object.[15]

Critical reaction to this claim is, understandably, that it is a paradigm instance of Sartre exaggerating a claim such that a genuine insight is lost in an empirical falsehood (Gardiner 1977: 77; Moran 2001: 174). Nothing could be more commonplace than the thought that one ought to work on being a better person. However, I have emphasized two points throughout this chapter. First, that in the case of exposure to the Other in the Look, the sense in which one is presented to another can be in a positive and not an objectifying sense. So there is one respect in which Sartre is quite happy to defend the view that one can reasonably be thought of 'as an object'. Secondly, the key formulation is that one ought *not* to regard oneself (to borrow a Kantian formulation) as *merely* an object. There is an acceptable sense in which one thinks of oneself as an object, but not merely as an object, when one thinks of oneself in the light of the two complementary aspects of transcendence and of facticity.

So Sartre can agree with the common sense thought that one can think of one's own character as an object while disambiguating that claim and finding another sense in which it is always an ethical error to think of oneself always as merely such. Patrick Gardiner critically examined Sartre's claim in his 'Sartre on Character and Self-knowledge'. I think that some of the concerns that Gardiner expresses there can helpfully be allayed by some of the considerations that I have canvassed. He describes Sartre's view as follows:

> [Sartre] seems to be saying that there are really only two alternatives here: either the putative self-ascriber is referring to a stretch of his past history or else he is giving expression to what amounts to some kind of resolve or intention concerning his future conduct. The third possibility, that he is treating himself as the subject of certain evidentially based predictions, is considered to be one which is in some sense not open to him.
>
> (Gardiner 1977: 75)

Gardiner gives the putative counter-example of a person with a tendency to irascibility who sometimes tries to control himself and succeeds, or tries and fails, or who simply expresses his character trait:

> In each [case] it would not merely seem natural for the man in question to conclude that he was irascible: it would also seem odd to propose that, if he expressed this opinion, he should *not* be understood to be implying anything with predictive import.
>
> (Gardiner 1977: 71, emphasis added)

If, in these examples, a person concludes that he or she is irascible, why is this not an empirically grounded regularity with 'predictive import' about the future actions of the person involved, who just happens to be me? If Gardiner is right about that, then Sartre's claim that there is some in principle difficulty about knowledge of one's own character that makes it categorically different from knowledge of another person's character seems indefensible. Thus we can think of our own characters as objects, namely, by thinking of them in exactly the same way as we think of other people's characters. Therefore Sartre's claim about the distinctiveness of the first personal case lapses.

However, I have already noted points that address Gardiner's concerns and, indeed, move one towards the more sympathetic reconstruction of Sartre's own views at the conclusion of his paper. First, we need a very weak interpretation of the thesis that the point of our ascribing mental states to others is to predict their behaviour if we are not to run very quickly into the serious difficulties posed by the extreme complexity of such iterated predictions (Morton 1996). Secondly, Sartre does recognize the issue of 'predictive import'. Consider a remark of John McDowell's in the course of his discussion of Wittgenstein's rule following remarks:

> When I claim understanding of someone else, and construe this as knowledge of the patterns to which his present utterance owes allegiance what I claim to know is not that in such and such a circumstance he will do so and so, but rather at most that *that is what he will do if he sticks to his patterns. And that is not a prediction at all.*
>
> (McDowell 1984: 349, emphasis added)

McDowell's concluding moral seems to me wrong: in this case one *does* make a prediction, but only a conditional prediction. However, this point suffices to restore the asymmetry that Sartre emphasizes. In the case of predicting the actions of others, those predictions are conditional on the other person 'sticking to his or her patterns' in his or her own case in a way beyond your direct control. First personally, however, that normative commitment is yours to maintain or revoke. The direct relevance of this observation to Sartre's ideal of authenticity is that the latter views us as always both facticity and transcendence. Therefore, if you are a reason-sensitive agent whose intention formation is appropriately sensitive to reasons then, in the light of your forward looking commitment, I can predict what you are going to do, all other things being equal. However, that prediction cannot simply leave out the normative commitment, your transcendence, from the picture. That would be to leave out precisely that which Moran called 'answerability to evidence'. This is, moreover, disanalogous to one's own case. Gardiner later softens his criticism of Sartre:

> The solution of the problem of what we are going to do or be cannot appropriately appear to us as some-thing which we can merely 'read off' in a theoretical fashion from knowledge of our past history; *for all that, an awareness of how we are prone to behave may play a crucial role in contributing to the decisions we actually take.* ... For to try to treat the question of what one will do as if it were essentially a matter of investigation and discovery, answerable solely on the basis of data provided by one's past behavior, is necessarily to be precluded from treating it at the same time as if it were genuinely a matter for decision which one is called upon to make in the light of reasons.
>
> (Gardiner 1977: 79–80, emphasis added)

This more nuanced assessment seems to be exactly right and to converge with the interpretations of Sartre's view by Hampshire and Moran that I described above. But now there is a clear sense in which Gardiner has vindicated the claim that one's character cannot be *merely* an object for oneself. Therefore, there is a significant asymmetry between your knowledge of your own character and your knowledge of the character of others.

How does this Sartrean argument connect with the attempts to undermine the priority of virtue ethics that I described in the previous section? It does so in this way: the Sartrean counter-argument would be that any such view, even if it values the exercise of virtue as an intrinsic good, is committed to requiring a deliberating agent to treat her character as merely an object for her. The deliberating agent would be required to see her character merely under the guise of facticity.

Suppose, for the sake of argument, that an impartialist ethical theory captures all the evaluatively relevant features of situations in a finite set of finite general principles (Holton 2002). Suppose, further, that the theory is liberal enough to include the fact that these principles are applied via the exercise of virtue as a further intrinsic good, perhaps to be built into the outcomes thus brought about (Hurka 2001). What directives does such a theory issue to the deliberating agent? To try and do the right thing. Now, admittedly, the virtuous agent will not try and do the right thing under that description. For example, he or she will, rather, try and alleviate the suffering of a particular person in a particular context (in a way consistent with the first person and third person asymmetry in the use of virtue concepts). However, if the theory is true, then that does not matter: if all evaluatively relevant features are indeed truly captured by the principles, and if the theory intrinsically values the exercise of virtue, then in doing what is in fact the right thing by her own lights, the agent *will* have done the right thing as the theory conceives of it even if that is not how *the agent* conceives of it. How does this involve, at any point, an agent thinking of herself 'merely as an object'?

In this sense: Sartre's norm of epistemic responsibility for any reason-sensitive state of the agent's requires any conclusion, or verdict, to be underwritten by the agent's first personal executive authority. The role of that authority is ineliminable even where, as in the case described, the verdict determined by the application of theory and the verdict determined by practical judgement coincide. By not requiring the operation of this capacity and the implication that the agent could have judged otherwise, the indirect modelling of a competence requires the agent to view him- or herself as merely an object in the sense that a privilege of the first person standpoint has been suspended. Such a theory thereby violates the agent's integrity even where the verdict derived from the theory and the agent's own judgements are the same.[16] However, Sartre takes the role of the first person in underwriting one's own rational verdicts to be ineliminable.

I conceded the hypothesis that there could be a finite specification of a finite set of general principles for the sake of argument. In doing so, I accepted the kind of epistemological modesty that such views now advertise. We are now told that the aim of the theorist is not to say anything about practical reasoning, or deliberation, but rather to describe what are in fact the right making features of actions (Bales 1971). An account in terms of general principles has nothing to say to the deliberating agent going forward in the process of decision, but is an attempt to show, *ex post facto*, how any true moral verdict can be derived from moral principles and 'the facts' (Holton 2002). A further response to these views would be to challenge this modesty: it is not simply that an indirect impartialist theory does not address these issues, but that it *cannot* do so. It is a very serious cost that a theory of this kind can say nothing about the process of practical deliberation (Thomas forthcoming).

By way of contrast Sartre's focus is primarily on forward-looking deliberation and how it is structured by character. It is true that he does not say very much about practical deliberation, but that is because of the point noted above that he believes that the ensemble of projects that make up one's character have *already* structured one's experience in terms of the patterns of relevance and salience that they dictate so that the task of deliberation is relatively complete. That is one explanation of why the truly interesting cases for Sartre are dilemmatic where the situation places incompatible demands on the way in which your projects have structured the situation.

However, it is this epistemological role of character in forward-looking deliberation that my hypothetical indirect theorist faces particular difficulty in accommodating. In a deliberative context, character works as a filter on practical options, a determinant of relevance and salience. Your character is expressed as much by that which you do not consider in a particular context and by the quality of your deliberation as it is by your actual choices. It can play this role only if it is not an object for you in the sense of an explicitly thematized 'filter' on your options. You do not solve the problem of relevance by suggesting that a deliberating agent inspect every piece of potentially relevant information and classify it as relevant or not: that is evidently a self-defeating strategy. (It is not a solution, but a restatement of the problem.) The same is true of salience: an expert chess player focuses on only one salient situation or pattern in a chess game while a tyro looks all over the board, failing to grasp the key strategic overall pattern in play (Groot 1965). A virtuous person displaying sound practical reason has the same focus on the salient aspects of a situation as the expert chess player has of her strategic position. How are those epistemic roles of character to be captured by theory? These roles are functions that general principles simply *could not* discharge (Thomas forthcoming).

This epistemic role of character does not reduce it simply to a facticity even though relevance and salience are products of past decision. The deliberating agent is focused outwards on those reasons called for by the situation just as his or her sense of relevance and salience are determined by past sensitivity to such reasons. Given that the deliberating agent is always both a facticity and a transcendence, he or she is 'answerable' to the determinations of relevance and salience, but they are not finally determining for him or her. In Sartre's terms, you know yourself in not being merely that facticity, and the final all-things-considered practical verdict of the agent that expresses a capacity for executive decision is never determined in advance. In that sense Sartre's ideal of authenticity respects what I have called his requirement that any reason-sensitive state of yours can be rationally underwritten, reflecting the deeper fact that you have a rational control over your own mind that you do not have over the mind of another.[17]

Notes

1 I will restrict my focus to the account presented in *Being and Nothingness* and will not, here, attempt the very different task of interpreting the change in Sartre's later ethical views consequent upon his adoption of a Marxist conception of politics and hence his very different later conception of the circumstances of ethical choice.

2 For the sense in which the conscious self exists, but is not an object amongst other objects, see Fraassen 2004.

3 This 'fundamental project' for the conscious, rational, subject to achieve the condition of such a being that is internally unified in the way that the 'in itself' is forms part of Sartre's critique of our aspiration to a form of divine nature (B&N: 587). This is our 'futile passion' (B&N: 636; translation amended as per Webber 2009: 107).

4 This pessimistic reading places tragedy at the very basis of our conscious experience. For an alternative interpretation of this aspect of Sartre's view in which this desire for the for-itself to take on a God-like combination of the for-itself (being conscious, rational, and active) and the in-itself (being self-identical), see Webber 2009: 108–10. On this reading this aspiration is only typical of those in bad faith; existential psychoanalysis can reveal to us the self-defeating nature of this aspiration that is contingent and hence avoidable.

5 I discuss the way in which Sartre's account of consciousness reconciles two basic intuitions about consciousness in Thomas 2006a.

6 Fraassen takes this quotation from *The Reprieve* as his epigraph (Fraassen 2004: 453). Bergmann's discussion, that focuses on Sartre's externalism, also develops the same Sartrean metaphor (1982: 156).

7 I take this to be the moral of a series of insightful papers by John Biro (1991, 1993, 2006).

8 'Consciousness does not know its own character – unless in determining itself reflectively from the standpoint of another's point of view. It exists its character in pure indistinction non-thematically and non-thetically in the proof which it effects of its own contingency and in the nihilation by which it recognizes and surpasses its facticity' (B&N: 372).

9 The situationist critique of virtue ethics is not as sensitive as it could be to *which* concept of a virtue is embedded in folk psychology. That is why Sartre is a good example of a theorist who is sensitive to the indeterminacy of character ascriptions and the tendency of folk psychology falsely to objectify their determinacy who, nevertheless, vindicates realism about character. This is, however, a realism about character that embeds it in the wider perspective of a virtuous person as precisely one who intelligently copes with situations in the light of sound practical reason.

10 As Gardiner puts it, 'Thus for another person "I am ill-tempered, hypocritical or frank, cowardly or courageous" … and the shock we are liable to experience when such judgments are made is of immense consequence. For through them we are forced, as if by a mirror, to recognize that others see us as the repository of determinate tendencies and routines which can be expected to govern our actions and responses in the future as surely as they have governed them in the past. But this is a conception of what we are with which we are unable, in the last analysis, to identify ourselves' (Gardiner 1977: 72).

11 It is also the entry point for Sartre's account of embodiment that, for reasons of space, I cannot discuss here. For a general perspective, see Wider 1997. For an analysis with a direct bearing on transcendence and facticity, see Longuenesse 2008: 10–12.

12 For an insightful defence of that interpretation of Sartre's account of character see Webber 2009: Ch. 2.

13 Of the kind defended in Thomas 2006b.

14 In response to the objection that the asymmetry claim is simply false, I have argued elsewhere (Thomas 2009) that when people use virtue terms in their first personal deliberations these are instances of moral perplexity and thus analogous to recapitulating the process of learning to be good.

15 I am indebted to Richard Moran's discussion of Sartre's view that impartialist ethical theories are not demanding enough and represent bad faith (Moran 2001: Ch. 5, esp. 164–74). However, Moran thinks that Sartre's critique fails precisely because he cannot identify precisely what is wrong with thinking of oneself as an object.

16 For further discussion of this claim see Harcourt 1998, Chappell 2007, and Thomas 2009.

17 I have benefited from discussing the issues covered in this paper with Sean Gould. Special thanks are due, as ever, to Kathryn Brown for her critical comments on all versions of the paper.

12

BAD FAITH AND THE OTHER

Jonathan Webber

One of the characteristic features of Sartre's philosophical writing, especially in *Being and Nothingness*, is his use of extended narrative vignettes that immediately resound with the reader's own experience yet are intended to illustrate, perhaps also to support, complex and controversial theoretical claims about the structures of conscious experience and the shape of the human condition. Among the best-known of these are his description of Parisian café waiters, who somehow contrive to caricature themselves, and his analysis of feeling shame upon being caught spying through a keyhole. There is some disagreement among commentators on Sartre's philosophy, however, over precisely what these two examples are intended to convey and over how they relate to one another. The waiter is usually taken to provide an example of bad faith, on grounds that he is taking himself to have a fixed nature that determines his actions, but this reading has recently been challenged. The description of shame is usually understood as an account of the revelation of the existence of another mind and as at the root of the conflictual basis of interpersonal relationships, though commentators are divided over just how this revelation is supposed to work and why it is supposed to lead to conflict.

My aim here is to defend and enrich the interpretation of these vignettes and their associated theories that I offer in my book, *The Existentialism of Jean-Paul Sartre*. On this reading, the waiter should indeed be understood as he usually has been, but the significance of this discussion of bad faith is much greater than has generally been recognized. For we should read the discussion of shame and interpersonal relations within the framework sketched in the discussion of the waiter and other characters in bad faith. Other people are hell, Sartre thinks, unless we abandon the project of bad faith. We should read *Being and Nothingness* not as a series of discussions of discrete issues, but rather as progressively elaborating a single view of the ontology of human existence and the ways in which we think and behave as a result of that ontology. The book is a work not only of phenomenological ontology, but also of existential psychoanalysis. It is intended not only to show what we most fundamentally are, but also to provide a cultural critique aimed at exposing the roots of many personal and social problems. Quite how we should understand this aspect of his work more than half a century later and from within a different linguistic community is a matter for careful consideration, since the question of the acuity of Sartre's cultural critique at the time is matched with the question of the significance of the cultural distance between Sartre and ourselves (see Leak, this volume). Although we will not address this question here, we will see that readers of *Being and Nothingness* are apt to misunderstand the book if they overlook this cultural dimension of it.

Defending this view of the relation between bad faith and interpersonal relations, however, does require us to consider a different methodological concern rooted in the cultural aspect of Sartre's work. Critics have argued that some of the central stories that Sartre presents are distorted by prejudice. Sartre has been accused of being unfair to waiters, for example, and indeed of showing through this vignette a condescending and demeaning attitude towards working people in general (Phillips 1981). Critics have denounced a similar vignette of his, in which a woman on a date wants simultaneously to enjoy her companion's advances while overlooking his intentions, as patriarchal fantasy (Moi 1994: 127–33; Doeuff 1991: 72–3). Reviewing a recent production of Sartre's play *Kean*, an influential theatre critic declared that 'there is nothing remotely original in Sartre's ideas', on grounds that the play merely propounds 'the discredited myth of the actor as an echoingly empty vessel' (Billington 2007).[1] These criticisms are clearly misplaced: Sartre argues that people in general, not just particular groups of them, are guilty of the bad faith that these characters represent in their different ways. But these criticisms do raise a deeper question: just why does Sartre think he can surmise someone's motivations on the basis of brief observations of their behaviour across the café floor? According to his own phenomenology, the world as they experience and respond to it is not immediately accessible to anyone but themselves. According to his own theory of existential psychoanalysis, these motivations are accessible to others only through careful analysis of the whole range of their behaviour.

We will see that Sartre's use of these examples is compatible with his overall philosophical theory after all. He does not consider the overt behaviour of these characters to show that they are in bad faith, but rather considers it to be equally compatible with the recognition and affirmation of our lack of any fixed nature. Appreciating this point will help us to see where recent commentators have gone wrong in denying that the waiter is intended as an illustration of bad faith, but also to see what is right about their reasoning. Moreover, it will help us to see that Sartre's famously gloomy discussion of interpersonal relations cannot be arguing for the pessimistic view that human interaction is necessarily conflictual, but is rather intended to show that such frustrating and alienating relationships are all that is available within the project of bad faith, a theory that Sartre sketches in his account of the waiter and other characters in bad faith but only fully elaborates in the discussion of shame and the subsequent discussion of sexuality much later in the book.

One challenge to this reading of *Being and Nothingness* is presented by Matthew Eshleman's recent claim that the discussion of various characters in bad faith – the most detailed of which is the depiction of the waiter – would be much better placed towards the end of the book. To understand that chapter correctly, he argues, we need to read it in the light of the discussion of shame and interpersonal relations, since the theory of bad faith is dependent upon the outcome of that later discussion. Sartre would therefore have followed his method of progressive exposition more closely, on this reading, if he had established the theory of the look before introducing bad faith and the example of the waiter (see Eshleman 2008a, 2008b). In terms of our two vignettes, Eshleman's claim is that the earlier presupposes the later. This seems to challenge my view that the later should be understood within the framework sketched by the earlier, unless we are to accept both points and reject Sartre's existentialism as fundamentally circular.

Once we clarify the sense in which each vignette is dependent on the other, however, we will see that there is no circularity here at all. For we will see that the aspect of shame that is born of bad faith is distinct from the aspects of shame on which that bad faith relies. Sartre would have made his position clearer, of course, had he discussed the two aspects of shame separately, but his running them together is no mere accident of exposition. It results from the overall structure of *Being and Nothingness*. Eshleman is right to draw attention to the way in which Sartre's phenomenological ontology progresses from the highly abstract to the fully concrete, and to point out that we are apt to misunderstand it unless we allow for the development of the central phenomenological and ontological concepts through this progression (2008a: 18, 2008b: 44–5; see also this volume, p. 43). But we should also be aware of the further complication that this is accompanied throughout by a critical account of the ways in which this ontology is manifested in modern life. Borrowing terminology from Martin Heidegger, we can say that Sartre's discussion weaves a concern with the ontic facts of our current existence into his investigation of the ontological structures of our kind of existence (see Heidegger 1962: §§3–4).

To put it another way, *Being and Nothingness* is as much in dialogue with Sigmund Freud as it is with Edmund Husserl. The discussion of various characters in bad faith provides an excellent illustration of this. Sartre introduces these vignettes by saying that they will help to 'fix more exactly the conditions for the possibility of bad faith' (B&N: 78). This has led some commentators to argue that these vignettes are solely, or at least primarily, aimed at uncovering the ontological structures of the kind of existence we have. Rather than trying to present a complete picture and analysis of a pervasive psychological phenomenon, on this reading, Sartre is pursuing the much more limited aim of showing that certain actual behaviour patterns reveal something peculiar and fundamental about our existence, namely that we are what we are not and are not what we are (e.g. Eshleman 2008a: 16–18). Other commentators, however, point out that Sartre's concern with the detail of bad faith pervades his philosophical and other writings throughout his career, which implies that detailing it is not a secondary or subsidiary issue in these vignettes but is part of a wider concern with bad faith itself (e.g. Santoni 2008: 36). This latter point seems right and should be made more broadly: Sartre's concern with existential psychoanalysis is closely bound up with his phenomenological ontology, but is not merely a means to it; his concern with ontology, after all, seems at least partly aimed at getting psychoanalysis right. It is no accident, therefore, that the two concerns are often woven together in a single discussion.

Bearing this in mind, we will see that Sartre describes two aspects of shame. One is the revelation of the existence of what Sartre calls 'the Other'. This is part of his phenomenological ontology: the claim that the structure of the experience essentially involves the Other is both phenomenological, since it is about the structure of experience, and ontological, since this experience reveals part of the structure of our existence. The second aspect is the ascription to another person of a particular kind of attitude towards me, one of seeing me as having some fixed characteristics that explain my current behaviour, even though I cannot know exactly which characteristics that person sees me as having. This aspect presupposes the first, since without the revelation of the Other there could be no question of ascribing anything to any other person. But this second aspect is neither an essential structure of feeling shame nor constitutive of my existence. It is merely the way in which our experience of the Other is played out within the project of bad faith.

Understanding the behaviour of the waiter in the light of this distinction is rather complicated. The issue is best approached through consideration of the recent claims that the waiter is not intended as an illustration of bad faith at all. For these readings emphasize the role of the waiter's clientele in the story. Customers demand that the waiter behaves in a certain way, writes Sartre, 'as if we lived in perpetual fear that he might escape from it, that he might break away and suddenly elude his condition' (B&N: 83). Two commentators have recently argued that the waiter Sartre describes in the chapter on bad faith does not take himself to have a fixed waiterly nature that determines his actions, but is rather acceding to the demands of the clientele in a superficial and ironic way in order to deny that he has such a nature. 'The waiter succeeds in rejecting the attempt to reduce him to nothing more than being a waiter', according to Robert Bernasconi, 'not by refusing the role, but by highlighting the fact that he is playing it to the point that he escapes it' (2006: 38).

There are two ways in which the waiter could be behaving as Bernasconi describes. He could be rejecting the attempt to identify him with being a waiter because he wants to identify himself with some other fixed nature, such as that of a writer or a musician, and emphasize that he is only work-ing as a waiter to make ends meet. In this case, he would still be an example of bad faith, since he would still be taking himself to have some fixed nature. Alternatively, he could be rejecting the very idea of a fixed nature underlying his actions. Gary Cox interprets the passage in this second way: the waiter is intended to illustrate the correct attitude of authentic recogni-tion and affirmation of one's true condition, he argues, since the exag-gerated display is at once a rejection of the idea that he has a fixed nature and an emphatic identification with the social position that he does in fact occupy (Cox 2006: 101–4, 137).[2]

Bernasconi and Cox are certainly right that Sartre's philosophy does not rule out the possibility of a waiter having precisely the motivations they give for his over-inflated routine. Towards the end of *Being and Nothingness*, Sartre briefly characterizes behaviour in the absence of bad faith as a form of play. 'The point of these remarks', he tells us, is 'to show us that in play … the function of the act is to make manifest and to present to itself the absolute freedom which is the very being which is the person' (B&N: 602). A waiter 'playing at being a waiter' (B&N: 82), therefore, could be playing this role in an attitude of authenticity. Sartre does not claim, how-ever, that this is the *only* way in which one can play (see his brief discussion at B&N: 601–2). So it seems that the very same behaviour could be engaged in with the aim of manifesting and presenting freedom or with the aim of denying that freedom and identifying with the role played; the difference here is not in the act but in the function of the act.

This might seem to leave us at an impasse: we have competing ways of understanding this waiter's behaviour and no way of deciding between them from our external perspective. Perhaps it is for this reason, however, that Sartre abruptly switches from a third-personal description of 'this waiter in the café', in the midst of his initial description of this behaviour, to the first-personal account of 'this person who I have to be (if I am the waiter in question)' (B&N: 83). Shortly after this switch, Sartre refers to the motivations behind the behaviour. 'What I attempt to realize', he writes, 'is a being-in-itself of the café waiter, as if it were not in my power to confer value and urgency upon my duties and the rights of my position, as if it were not my free choice to get up each morning at five o'clock or to remain in bed' (B&N: 83).

We should continue to read this version of the waiter example, there-fore, as presenting a way of denying one's freedom to choose how to see and react to one's situation. The vignette illustrates the strategy of seeing oneself as having a fixed nature that fits and explains one's current condition, as possessing the being-in-itself, in this case, of a waiter. We should see this waiter as being in bad faith. But this is not the claim that one can recognize bad faith in the behaviour of a waiter: that behaviour itself is compatible with any of a number of motivations. It is rather the claim that bad faith is among these motivations and that in this passage bad faith is the motivation Sartre is interested in. By couching this part of the passage in the first person, Sartre signals that external observation of such behaviour alone will not settle the question of motivation. This issue is more acute in the case of the waiter than in the case of Sartre's other examples, since only this one begins as a description of the behaviour of a real person. The other vignettes are more clearly fictional and therefore stipulative, allowing Sartre the novelist's insight into his creations' motivations.

Reading the waiter as wanting to deny his freedom to do otherwise, however, leaves us with a second puzzle: why does Sartre here draw attention to the expectations of the customers if the waiter's motivation is independent of these expectations? In order to answer this question, we need to consider the reasons one might have for denying one's ability to change course in life. By this point in *Being and Nothingness*, Sartre has not explained why we should want to deny our freedom. He has provided vivid examples, of course, in which people find their freedom disconcerting: confronted with the ability to destroy oneself, or with past resolutions that seem to provide no barrier to the actions they proscribe, or with our responsibility for the ways in which we see the world and behave in it, he argues, we become reflectively aware of our own freedom and this awareness is the feeling of anguish (see B&N: 53–69). But why should this be anguish? Why should it be unpleasant at all? Why should we not celebrate our freedom with all the openness, all the possibilities, and all the responsibility that it brings? What is more, there is another option open to the waiter that does not even involve asserting his freedom. Soon after the vignette of the waiter, Sartre provides an example of someone who refuses to accept the social identity that his friends confer on him in the light of his actions, a man who insists that he is not homosexual but merely sexually adventurous and unlucky enough not to have found the right woman (B&N: 86–7). The waiter could likewise insist that he is by nature something else entirely and only working at this job to make ends meet.

To see why Sartre casts the waiter as he does and to see why he mentions the expectations of the customers, we need to take seriously his claim towards the end of *Being and Nothingness* that all positive and negative feelings are manifestations of one's projects. 'Generally speaking there is no irreducible taste or inclination', Sartre tells us. 'They all represent a certain appropriative choice of being' (B&N: 636; see also B&N: 589–90).

Negative feelings are triggered, he argues, by the awareness of anything that itself challenges our deeply held beliefs and values, even when this challenge is wholly symbolic. Sliminess is abhorrent, for example, because it symbolically represents the impossibility of consciousness having the solidity of being-in-itself and therefore challenges our pretence to having fixed natures (B&N: 630–2). Sartre has here generalized to all affective states the theory he initially developed in studying a particular class of them, the emotions (see STE: Pt 3). Whatever we think of his psychoanalysis of aversion, we cannot properly understand the role anguish plays in Sartre's philosophy unless we see it in this context: the reflective apprehension of freedom is anguish only because the object of that experience, the freedom of which one is directly aware in that experience, conflicts with some project one is pursuing. What project could this be? Clearly, a direct awareness of one's freedom would conflict with a project of denying one's freedom. Sartre thinks that such a project is widely pursued: central to his existential psychoanalysis is the idea that the denial of freedom is widespread or even ubiquitous. The aversive tenor of reflective awareness of freedom is explained by the subject of the experience aiming to avoid acknowledging that freedom.[3] Anguish is a product of bad faith.

Part of the way in which bad faith perpetuates itself, therefore, is by making any evidence of freedom unpleasant and so unlikely to be faced. Anguish is thereby a sustaining cause of bad faith, but since it results from bad faith it cannot also be an initiating cause of bad faith. So we are left with the question of where bad faith comes from in the first place. Some commentators argue that Sartre considers bad faith to result from the structures of our ontology. Lacking a fundamental nature, writes Ronald Santoni, 'human reality' as Sartre understands it 'is immediately and perpetually disposed to flee from its nothingness, to fill its emptiness, to become *something*' (2008: 30). An 'original or primitive ontological bad faith', he claims, which is 'congenital' or 'natural', underpins any particular projects of bad faith (2008: 31; see also Thomas, this volume, pp. 161–2). Indeed, towards the beginning of *Being and Nothingness*, Sartre does say that bad faith 'is essential to human reality' (B&N: 71). Nearer the end of the book, he reiterates this when he argues that 'human reality is the desire for being-in-itself' (B&N: 586). He does think that the structure of 'human reality' involves the desire to have a fixed nature, the desire for being-in-itself, the desire that drives the project of bad faith.

We should not conclude from this, however, that Sartre thinks of this as part of the ontology of our existence. For that would contradict his claim that we can 'radically escape bad faith' through the 'self-recovery of a being that was previously corrupted' that he calls 'authenticity' (B&N: 94n9). We should rather bear in mind that Sartre is offering not only a phenomenological ontology of existence but also an existential psychoanalysis of the way in which that ontology is played out in our culture. We should not take his term 'human reality' to denote the deep and necessary structures of our existence, but rather to refer to the whole of our current socially structured existence built upon that ontology; it is an ontic term, not an ontological one.[4] He is claiming in these passages, therefore, that bad faith is endemic in the lives of people in his culture even though it is not necessitated by the basic structures of human existence. Far from being an occasional act of self-deception, it is part of the very fabric of everyday life as he sees it. But this is only contingently the case: bad faith is the corruption from which authenticity is recovery.

If bad faith is not a necessary result of ontology and is not originally a response to anguish, then where does it come from? It would seem plausible to suggest that one initially understands people in terms of their fixed natures as a result of upbringing and social pressure. Having learned to see people in general this way, one sees oneself as having some particular fixed nature or other. One attempts to discover who one truly is, while skewing the evidence to ensure that one does not find anything one does not want to find. Since other people generally see the world this way, moreover, the other people one encounters are likely to see one as having some fixed nature or other. Bernasconi, Cox, and Eshleman are right to emphasize the role of other people's expectations and demands in Sartre's illustrative examples of bad faith. For faced with such a view of oneself, one must either accept the nature they ascribe, reject the nature they ascribe, or reject the very idea of a fixed nature altogether. In his discussion of various characters in bad faith, Sartre presents the waiter as an example of the first response and the unhappy homosexual as an example of the second. The third response, of course, is an authentic affirmation of the true human condition. But this is likely to be unusual – even though Sartre ultimately thinks it best – since it runs against the demands, expectations, and teachings of one's society.

As with everything else that one encounters, Sartre argues, this nature that others ascribe to me cannot simply be something I am aware of as it is in itself. Rather, it is through the lens of my projects that this nature appears to me in this or that way. I may be aware of it 'in fury, hate, pride, shame, disheartened refusal or joyous demand', or indeed in any of 'an infinity of ways', depending on how that nature fits with my conception of myself and with my aims in life (B&N: 550). In becoming aware of this nature that other people confer upon me, therefore, I subsume it within the projects that I pursue. In so doing, I 'assume' that nature even if I aim to deny it. This is what Sartre calls 'interiorization': taking up some aspect of the world as I find it, and as it has been constructed by other people, within the ambit of my projects, which does not require any explicit decision to do so (see B&N: 544, 547–50). Authenticity would involve interiorizing such natures within the project of affirming my genuine condition of lacking any such nature. Bad faith, on the other hand, subsumes the nature others ascribe to one either through affirming it or through denying it in favour of some other nature.

Bad faith, therefore, is a social disease rather than an individual failing, in Sartre's view, and is an ongoing condition rather than a sporadic activity. But this cannot be fully explained or justified until the end of *Being and Nothingness*, by which point Sartre has elaborated enough of his phenomenological ontology to be able to detail his notion of existential psychoanalysis. Since the waiter's project of bad faith is originally motivated, and perhaps also partly sustained, by the expectations other people have of him, it seems that Eshleman is right: explaining the waiter's behaviour requires reference to his understanding that other people see him as having some fixed nature or other. If this is right, then how could it also be the case that the experience of shame that grounds this understanding is itself a manifestation of bad faith?

To answer this question, we need to distinguish two things that Sartre considers to be implied by the experience of shame. One of these is that another person is looking at me and categorizing me as having certain fixed properties, such as being a snoop or a voyeur, on the basis of my behaviour, even though I cannot know exactly what properties they ascribe to me. The feeling of shame implies that this is occurring, but that implication might be false; there may even be nobody there at all (B&N: 300–1). Shame also implies a dimension of my existence that Sartre calls my 'being-for-others'. This implication is infallible; my being-for-others is essential to shame. Shame is therefore a genuine revelation, a discovery of an aspect of my existence that is not manifested in my absorbed engagement in the world. Shame presents me with the very fact that an external perspective can be taken on me, that my existence is not simply my awareness of a world but is also my appearance in the world. In addition to my experience 'on the inside', to put it another way, there is how I look 'from the outside'.

Interpretation of this aspect of Sartre's philosophy is particularly delicate, partly because Sartre uses the term 'being-for-itself' sometimes to mean one's engaged unreflective consciousness of the world and other times to mean the being that is conscious of the world in this way. He has been understood as claiming that conscious experience of the world is ontologically dependent upon being-for-others (e.g. Gardner 2005: esp. §1). On the other hand, he has been claimed to view being-for-others as no part of the ontological structure of the individual at all (e.g. Santoni 2008: 26–7). To render the account coherent, however, we should read such claims as that 'being-for-others is not an ontological structure of the For-itself' (B&N: 306) as asserting the independence of *one's consciousness* from one's being-for-others, while reading such claims as that 'we are talking of objective characteristics which define me in my being-for-others' (B&N: 545) as describing the ontology of *the individual one is*.[5] My engaged experience of the world and my appearance in the world are therefore, for Sartre, independent aspects of my existence. I am 'simultaneously for-itself and for-others' but neither of these aspects can be derived from the other one (B&N: 306).

The experience of shame, Sartre writes, reveals 'that our being along with its being-for-itself is also for-others'; shame is 'the cogito a little expanded' which 'reveals to us as a fact the existence of the Other and my existence for the Other' (B&N: 306). It is not just my 'being-for-others' that is revealed, then, not just 'my existence for the Other', but the very existence of 'the Other' itself. But this does not mean that shame infallibly reveals that someone is watching me. For the same experience can occur when I hear a rustle of branches and wrongly assume there is somebody there or when soldiers creep past a farmhouse they do not realize is empty. In such a case, 'the Other is present everywhere, below me, above me, in the neighbouring rooms, and I continue to feel profoundly my being-for-others' (B&N: 301). Mark Sacks reads this as claiming that the experience reveals absent human beings and hence the 'fundamental presence' of people in general. 'What I am experiencing', he writes, 'is that the world contains some such persons' (2005a: 292). This might seem rather mysterious: could I not have the same experience if, unbeknownst to me, all other people had been destroyed in some recent apocalyptic calamity? Given this possibility, we should say that other people are present in such experiences only in the sense that when one imagines an external observer one imagines a specific sort of external observer, such as a member of one's society or an enemy soldier, and this is informed by one's experience of other people (see Zahavi this volume, p. 221).[6]

If experience can manifest the Other without there being any other persons present or even in existence, we cannot understand the term 'the Other' here as referring primarily to other people. 'What I apprehend immediately when I hear the branches crackling behind me is not that there is someone there', Sartre writes; 'it is that I am vulnerable, that I can be hurt, that I occupy a place … in short, that I am seen' (B&N: 282). What is apprehended immediately, that is to say, is that my own perspective on the world is not the only one, and that I am an entity in the world as it is seen from such a perspective other than my own. The primary meaning of Sartre's term 'the Other' (l'Autrui) is consciousness of the world which is not my own consciousness of the world. This is why the Other is necessarily revealed along with my being-for-others (être-pour-autrui). Although he often uses the term 'the Other' to refer to another person, then, this is a derivative usage intended to highlight that the other person has a perspective that is distinct from one's own pre-reflective engagement in the world. Shame infallibly reveals that not all experience of the world need be my experience of the world, and thereby that there can be experiences of the world that include me as an external object of experience, but it does not infallibly reveal that anyone exists who has such experiences.

In revealing that I am an entity in the world seen from other perspectives, moreover, shame thereby reveals that I am my body. Although I am aware from the inside that I have a particular relationship with my body that I do not have with other bodies, that I can move my limbs directly but only move chairs and tables indirectly, this is not sufficient to reveal to me that I *am* that body, as Sacks points out (2005a: 286). What is manifest to the Other is not simply what my body is doing, but what I am doing. This requires that I am that body. 'It is that identity that is established, with all the immediacy of a blush' when I am caught spying through the keyhole, writes Sacks; 'what they have caught at it is not my body, but me, my self' (2005a: 287). For myself, within my own experience, Sartre claims, 'I shall remain forever a consciousness', whereas for the Other 'I have an outside' since for the Other 'I am seated as this inkwell is on the table' or 'I am leaning over the keyhole as this tree is bent by the wind' (B&N: 286). My body's posture is my posture; what the Other sees is me.

We are now in a position to see just which aspects of Sartre's account of shame are presupposed by his account of the behaviour of the waiter in bad faith. For the waiter presents himself as 'a being-in-itself of the café waiter' through his actions (B&N: 83). This requires that he understands his actions as *presenting himself*, rather than simply being effects that his decisions have on this particular body, and that he understands that there is an *external perspective* on the world to which such actions can present himself. This is rooted in the experience of shame. The assumption that people are watching him and are ascribing to him a fixed nature, on the other hand, is part of the project of bad faith and therefore is not something revealed in shame. Of course, some of the waiter's behaviour that Sartre describes will occur in the absence of any other person, such as his getting out of bed in the morning, sweeping the café before it is open, setting the coffee pot going. His clientele need not actually be present and demanding him to behave in this way, therefore. But even in their absence, he is acting under the abstract gaze of the Other which, as we have seen, will not be devoid of expectations and motivations but will rather have precisely those the waiter expects his potential witnesses to have. His absent clientele haunt the closed café.

We should agree, therefore, that the vignette of the waiter early in *Being and Nothingness* cannot be fully understood except in the context of aspects of our experience that Sartre does not explain until much later in the book through his analysis of shame. Together with the observation that Sartre's discussion of anguish cannot be fully appreciated except in the context of his existential psychoanalysis of feelings in general, which also appears towards the end of the book, this might seem to show that the waiter vignette is, in Eshleman's words, a 'misplaced chapter' that would be much better placed towards the end of *Being and Nothingness*. What this suggestion overlooks, however, is that much of Sartre's discussion in the book is to be understood within the framework of the theory of bad faith that is sketched in the example of the waiter and the other examples he places alongside it. Unless we read that early chapter as setting the context for the subsequent discussion, we cannot understand why the feeling of shame should involve the assumption that the other person is ascribing to one a fixed nature.

Moreover, given Sartre's theory that feelings are a function of the projects we are pursuing, the experience of the Other would not be aptly described as *shame* unless some dimension of it conflicted with some project. What is it about the revelation that I am my body and can be seen from perspectives other than my own that conflicts with my projects? Sartre does not give us any reason to think that we are each pursuing a project that is directly challenged by these aspects of the experience. But the ascription to me of a fixed nature which is outside of my control, on the other hand, clearly conflicts with the project of seeing myself as having a particular kind of fixed nature. So it seems that we cannot understand why this experience should have a negative affective tenor unless we see it as an experience occurring within the project of bad faith.

Thus it seems that Sartre's account of the alienation felt under the gaze of another person, the consequent claim that conflict is at the heart of intersubjectivity, and the conclusion that sexual and other interpersonal relationships are doomed are all strangely undermotivated unless we read him as describing awareness of the Other from within the project of bad faith. Sartre's account of our relations with one another is an account of the lives to which we are condemned by the project of bad faith. Reading the book in this way makes sense of Sartre's recommendation of a radical conversion to authenticity: such a conversion will liberate us, he thinks, from the difficulties detailed throughout *Being and Nothingness*. If this is the right way to read Sartre, then the discussion of the waiter is not misplaced at all: its early position is crucial to the argument of the book as a whole.

If we are to make sense of *Being and Nothingness* as a whole, therefore, the discussion of shame should be understood in the context of the theory of bad faith. We have already seen that the theory of bad faith depends in part on the phenomenological analysis of shame. So there is a threat here of conceptual circularity: if neither bad faith nor shame can be explicated without reference to the other one, then it seems that Sartre has not offered us a coherent theory after all. However, this threat is only apparent. For the aspect of the discussion of shame that presupposes the account of bad faith exemplified by the waiter is not one of the aspects presupposed by that account. The waiter vignette presupposes the waiter's awareness of his being-for-others, of the gaze of the Other, and that his actions present himself to that gaze. These aspects of Sartre's keyhole-spying example do not presuppose the theory of bad faith: they are essential to the phenomenology of shame entirely independently of whether one is in bad faith or not. What does depend on being in bad faith is the assumption that the other person will be ascribing to one a fixed nature. Sartre sees this assumption as underlying the alienation that he finds in our experience of shame and the conflict that he finds in our interpersonal relationships. While this assumption is at the heart of the project of bad faith, it is not derived from the experience of shame. That these aspects of his discussion of shame need to be teased apart is a result of his weaving his phenomenological analyses of the essential structures of experiences together with his existentialist critique of his surrounding culture.

The central tenet of Sartre's account of interpersonal relations, therefore, is internal to his theory of bad faith, while that account of bad faith relies on other aspects of his analysis of shame. Although there is no conceptual circularity here, there might seem to be an explanatory circularity. If social expectation is part of the causal explanation of bad faith, then how can it be that one's view of other people as ascribing one a fixed nature is itself a product of bad faith? To answer this, we need to distinguish the general background view that people in one's culture tend to see one another's behaviour as manifesting fixed dispositional properties from the particular occurrent belief that this other person or these other people now see this behaviour of mine as manifesting my fixed nature. The latter can be a product of bad faith while the former is not. Indeed, if bad faith is part of one's cultural fabric, then one will come to learn that people generally see one another this way as a result of growing up within that culture and relying on the people around one to help one to make sense of the world (see B&N: 544–5). Bad faith itself, of course, is not the recognition that people see one another this way; it results from the interiorization of this view of people into one's own outlook.

Once this view of behaviour is adopted, once one just sees behaviour as clearly manifesting fixed dispositional properties, one is liable to make the assumption that any given observer will read fixed dispositions off one's own behaviour. What is more, any evidence that behaviour should not be viewed in this way will, according to Sartre's theory of aversion, be experienced negatively; the reflective apprehension of freedom will be anguish. Relations with other people will be tainted with alienation due to one's realization that other people's understanding of one's fixed nature is beyond one's own control or even knowledge. If the view that people manifest fixed natures in their behaviour is culturally pervasive, moreover, then it would hardly be surprising that most people end up with this outlook. Bad faith would be the default position for anyone growing up in such a culture, though its perpetuation as one's outlook would involve persistence in trying to portray oneself as having some particular fixed nature, a project occasionally challenged by the awareness of one's freedom to start behaving in a whole different way.[7]

Notes

1 This production opened on 30 May 2007 at the Apollo Theatre in London. It was booked to run for an initial twelve weeks but closed after seven.

2 Anthony Manser has also argued that we should not understand the waiter as an illustration of bad faith. He is not denying the usual interpretation of the waiter's behaviour, however, but is rather arguing that this behaviour is a manifestation of what Sartre calls 'good faith', not what Sartre calls 'bad faith' (Manser 1987: 66). But this overlooks the fact that Sartre uses the term 'bad faith' to mean both the ascription of fixed natures to people and the more specific form of this that ascribes to oneself qualities that one does not in fact have. My claim here is only that the waiter is an example of bad faith in the broader sense. Manser shows only that he is not an example of bad faith in the narrower sense. For more on the various senses in which Sartre uses this phrase, see Webber 2009: chs 6 and 7.

3 This is not to imply that Sartre thinks of anguish as a common phenomenon, even though he does think of bad faith as an ongoing uninterrupted project and as widespread. Anguish occurs when we become reflectively aware of our freedom, but most of our lives are spent unreflectively engaged in our activities; 'the most common situations of our life', he writes, 'do not manifest themselves to us through anguish because their very structure excludes anguished apprehension' (B&N: 59). What is more, we have organised our world in such a way that we do not often need to reflect on the range of possibilities that really confront us: 'there exist concretely alarm clocks, signboards, tax forms, policemen, so many guard rails against anguish', ploys to cover over the fact that I am 'the one who gives its meaning to the alarm clock, the one who by a signboard forbids himself to walk on the flower bed or on the lawn' (B&N: 63).

4 For a more detailed argument in favour of distinguishing the 'human reality' Sartre discusses from our basic ontological structures in this way, see Webber 2009: ch. 8, esp. 107–10.

5 There is something puzzling about first of these quotations: the term 'pour-soi' is here capitalised in the original French edition (342), but not in the French edition with corrections by Arlette Elkaïm-Sartre (321), though 'For-itself' remains capitalised in the English edition corrected by the same person. By capitalising some but not all uses of this term, Sartre clearly means to indicate that he is using it in more than one sense. Perhaps the capitalisation is intended to indicate the entity that has being-for-itself (i.e. the person) whereas the absence of the capital is intended to indicate the kind of being it has (i.e. consciousness of the world). Alternatively, perhaps the capitalisation is intended to indicate its use in contrast with his other capitalised term 'the Other', in which case, if I am right about the meaning of 'the Other', it would seem to indicate the perspective one has on the world as opposed to a perspective not one's own. To decide on the meaning of the capitalisation directly, of course, we would need to be able to distinguish intended instances of it from occasional slips of the pen, but the puzzle over the sentence quoted casts doubt over whether we can do this with confidence. This capitalisation therefore fails to communicate the distinction it is intended to mark. Perhaps he should just have told us, just as he does tell us what some of his parentheses mean (e.g. B&N: 10, 305).

6 As it stands, this discussion of the writings of Sebastian Gardner and Mark Sacks in this area does not do justice to either their motivations or their arguments, since they make the claims that I discuss here in the context of articulating careful analyses of Sartre's critique of solipsism, an aspect of Sartre's

philosophy distinct from, though closely related to, the issue I am discussing, and their discussions of this are part of their wider interest in the transcendental aspects of his philosophy. While there is much to recommend these discussions, I do not fully agree with the accounts they give of Sartre's response to the problem of solipsism. Proper discussion of this disagreement, however, is for another time.

7 An early version of this paper was given at the 2009 Joint Conference of the Society for European Philosophy and Forum for European Philosophy. I am grateful to the organisers of the conference and participants of that session for helpful discussion. I am also grateful to Matthew Eshleman for comments on the penultimate draft.

13

PRE-REFLECTIVE SELF-CONSCIOUSNESS AND THE AUTOBIOGRAPHICAL EGO

Kenneth Williford

Concurring with Hubert Dreyfus's harsh, Heidegger-inspired assessment of *Being and Nothingness* as *Dreck* or 'muck', Bryan Magee once opined: 'I find it difficult to believe that Sartre will survive as a philosopher, though easy to believe that he might survive as a playwright or novelist' (1988: 276). Twenty-odd years later, Sartre the philosopher is alive and well. There has been a steady stream of studies of various aspects of Sartre's philosophy since Magee's pronouncement (e.g. McCulloch 1994; Wider 1997; Priest 2000; Zheng 2005; Webber 2009). And Magee might well have known that there have always been anglophone philosophers willing to engage with Sartre's work at some level (e.g. Chisholm 1969; Castañeda 1979; Rosenberg 1981; Evans 1982: 266). But one source of new vital powers that Magee probably could not have predicted was the resurgence of interest among analytic philosophers, cognitive psychologists, AI researchers, neuroscientists, and others in the problems of consciousness.

It is no surprise that this resurgence has led many students of consciousness to draw much from the deep wells of the Phenomenological tradition and, within that tradition, from Sartre's early phenomenological investigations (e.g. Dainton 2000: xv, ch. 2; Levine 2001: 173; Lloyd 2004: 256–60; Kriegel 2009: 176–7).[1] The resurgence has also helped make it possible for others who had long been impressed by aspects of Sartre's characterization of consciousness to 'come out' and admit the influence without the fear and academic self-and-other-loathing once associated with an interest in his work (e.g. McGinn 2002: 39–44). Finally, we should note that Dan Zahavi and Shaun Gallagher, riding the wave of this resurgence, have done more than anyone else to demonstrate the relevance of the Phenomenological literature, including Sartre's share in it, to issues in the cognitive sciences and the philosophy of mind (e.g. Zahavi 1999, 2005; Gallagher and Zahavi 2008).

195

In this vein, I argue that Sartre's phenomenological description of consciousness, subjectivity, and the ego in *The Transcendence of the Ego* remains compelling, and that Sartre's 'non-egological theory of consciousness' (Gurwitsch 1941) is profound, highly likely to be true, and, Sartrean excesses removed, in good resonance with contemporary neuroscientific thinking about consciousness, Antonio Damasio's in particular (Damasio 1999).

To make this case I must address the persistent tendency to misinterpret Sartre's account. Commentators, both favourable and unfavourable, have a tendency to regard Sartre's 'non-egological' account as a 'no-ownership' account of conscious experience (e.g., Zahavi 2005: 99–103; Butchvarov 1979: 252). Others have seen in it, and not without some justice, a root of the 'death' or 'decentring' of the subject played out in Structuralist, Post-structuralist, and Postmodernist French theorizing (e.g. Fox 2003: ch. 1). But the account in TE *does* incorporate the intuition of ownership and the intuition that there is, *in the relevant sense of the term*, a subject; that is, it incorporates the intuition that the conscious presence *of* something is also its presence *to* a conscious mind. Moreover, it incorporates ownership and subjectivity in a way that is better than its Cartesian or Husserlian competitors. It is Sartre's mode of expression, a mode of expression he adjusted in *Being and Nothingness*, that continues to mislead (B&N: 127, 259).

Husserl's ego

Sartre's primary target in *The Transcendence of the Ego* is, of course, the Husserl of the *Ideas I* and *Cartesian Meditations*. We should be careful not to caricature either Husserl or Sartre *qua* interpreter of Husserl. Sartre is well aware that Husserlian Phenomenology is not intended to be a metaphysic and that it aims at yielding transcendentally purified, eidetic descriptions. Insofar as it aims at describing lived conscious experience, it aims at bringing to light its essential features. But any putatively essential feature of consciousness will be subject to the tribunal of phenomenological reflection. By giving *The Transcendence of the Ego* the subtitle *A Sketch for a Phenomenological Description*, Sartre is clearly indicating that his claims will ultimately rest upon the givens of reflection, and not on *a priori* speculation.

Though some of his argumentation might seem to have metaphysical flavour to it, a closer look reveals that the arguments in question are of an entirely negative character: he will argue that there *need not be* a transcendental ego immanent in consciousness – it is not needed to account for the unity or individuality of consciousness, nor is it, if we reify it, a Kantian 'condition of possibility' for the unity of consciousness; and he will argue that there *could not be* such an ego immanent in consciousness. Both of these claims rest upon premises Sartre derives from a description of immediate experience: consciousness *comes* unified and individuated; and consciousness has no 'inhabitants' at all – there are no entities *within* consciousness; and it is inconceivable that there should be, but 'inconceivable' in the sense of transcendental phenomenology, namely, contrary to the very *sense* of our immediate experience of consciousness.

What Husserl claims to find upon phenomenological reflection is not, of course, to be literally assimilated to Cartesian substance metaphysics, in spite of certain superficial resemblances. The claims he makes are to be regarded as descriptions of lived experience and not metaphysical interpretations of that experience. But like Descartes's *res cogitans*, Husserl maintains that what he calls the 'pure' or 'transcendental' ego survives the *epoché* – the Husserlian version of Descartes's methodological doubt. This will mean, in a manner analogous to the Cartesian *Cogito*, that the positing of the existence of the ego cannot undergo suspension, cannot be 'neutralized' in phenomenological reflection. Thus, for Husserl, it is not a mere entity we represent, an object of thought or perception, rather it is internal to consciousness itself (1982: §§57, 80; 1950: §8).

He also regards the ego as remaining identical through time, as invariant vis-à-vis the variability of acts and the flow of the stream of consciousness, as the substrate of certain properties and dispositions, what Husserl calls 'habitualities', and as the source of decisions and acts. It is not a pure activity, on the Husserlian view, as it is, in a sense, both passive and active over time, both an I and a Me. Indeed, Husserl well describes cases in which the pure ego 'recedes', in terms of activity, and then 'steps back in', and he maintained that in attention shifting we very clearly see the ego at work and, in some cases, its spontaneity. In this sense, the ego could be said to 'stand behind' acts of attention shifting and decision-making, and other types of acts as well. It is from the ego that the 'ego-rays' (*Ichstrahle*) emanate and 'go out' towards objects. When, for example, I suddenly cease being absorbed in a movie I am watching and shift attention to the pizza I left in the oven, it is my ego that 'stands behind' that shift. But it is also *to* the ego that 'rays' from the objects of desire or absorption bounce back. Thus, whether in passivity or activity, the ego is, in a sense, the permanent seat of experience (1982: §§92, 122; 1950: §§12, 31, 32, 38, 47).

We should note as well that this ego is a 'transcendence in immanence'. It is a transcendence in that it cuts across many different experiences over time. That is to say, it is transcendent to any one of the particular acts or experiences in which it 'lives'. On the Husserlian view, this is so because it is fully the subject of these temporally distinct acts and experiences; and from any one such 'act-location' it can be aware of this fact about itself. The subject of my acts of thought and experience going on now is the very same subject of my acts of dreaming last night, for example, and I can be fully aware of this. Nonetheless, it is immanent; as such, it is immediately given without profiles in any act (though Husserl only says this explicitly, so far as I know, in *Ideas II*, §24, which Sartre did not have access to). Moreover, it is correlated with my individuality or particularity insofar as it grounds a unique perspective that could only be 'mine'. To put it in Zahavi's terms, my ego is the ground for my first-personal mode of givenness. Yours is the ground for yours (Zahavi 2005: 130–1; see also Husserl 1982: §57; 1950: §31).

Now, we should stress that Husserl does not argue that the pure ego is what 'accounts for' the unity of consciousness. Rather, he maintains that one just finds the pure ego in phenomenological description. When Sartre claims that the ego is not needed to account for the unity or individuality of lived experience, he is not claiming that Husserl had so argued. In accordance with the Husserl of the first edition of the *Logical Investigations* (1970: Inv. V, §4) and of *The Phenomenology of Internal Time-Consciousness* (1991: §39), Sartre maintains that the unity of consciousness is given independently of any ego – unless we just *mean* by 'ego' 'unified consciousness'. We can thus regard his arguments about the explanatory superfluity of the transcendental ego as addressing those who might, unlike Husserl, be inclined to argue in a metaphysico-explanatory vein for the existence of such an entity. If the unity and individuality of consciousness can be accounted for without the aid of this ego then, *given the ego's absence on the descriptive plane*, why posit it? 'It is certain' Sartre writes, 'that phenomenology need have no recourse to this unifying and individualising I' (TE: 6, translation modified).

The transcendental ego is *de trop*

Sartre will attempt to do justice to the unity of consciousness entirely in terms of the intentionality of lived experience. It is customary to think of the problem of the unity of consciousness as dividing into two: the problem of diachronic unity and the problem of synchronic unity (e.g. Dainton 2000: 25f.). To account for synchronic unity one must explain how it is that in a single, global episode of consciousness at a given time, one can incorporate the awareness of a multitude of objects via various modalities. You might see, hear, smell, feel, and think different things *simultaneously*. Sartre's account of synchronic unity has to be extrapolated from the little bit he says in *The Transcendence of the Ego* that has a bearing on the problem. He writes, 'consciousness is defined by intentionality. By intentionality it transcends itself; it unifies itself in escaping itself. ... The object is transcendent to the consciousnesses that seize it, and it is in it that their unity is found' (TE: 6, translation modified). How could this fact about intentionality incorporate the synchronic unity of consciousness?

It is one thing to maintain that intentionality, construed anti-psychologistically à la Husserl, gets us objectivity and thereby secures the possibility, as he suggests, of intersubjectivity and intrasubjective diachronic sameness of reference. It is another to think that it thereby incorporates our ability to be aware of a multiplicity of objects simultaneously. But I think we must recall how Sartre was already thinking of intentionality at the time. In 'Intentionality: A Fundamental Idea of Husserl's Phenomenology', Sartre energetically sketches the sort of radical phenomenological externalism and Heideggerian 'enworlded' holism that was to characterize his account of intentionality from then on.[2] He writes:

> You see this tree, to be sure. But you see it just where it is: at the side of the road, in the midst of the dust, alone and writhing in the heat, eight miles from the Mediterranean coast ... Consciousness and the world are given at one stroke: essentially external to consciousness, the world is nevertheless essentially relative to consciousness ... Being, says Heidegger, is being-in-the-world. One must understand this 'being-in' as movement. To be is to fly out into the world.
>
> (IHP: 4–5)

By intentionality, consciousness is a 'relation' to the world. This already means that consciousness is a 'relation' to an interconnected multiplicity. To be conscious of one object is already to be conscious of a multiplicity, even if this multiplicity remains only on the horizon. If anything is given, on this view, a world is given. And this implies that a differentiated unity is given. It is the object itself that individuates episodes of consciousness. If the objects are different, so are the episodes. But this means then that a whole variegated world is required for there to be even one episode of consciousness. If consciousness is by nature consciousness of a differentiated multiplicity in unity, then there is really no *further* problem at the abstract level about different modalities (sensory, etc.); that would just be further differentiation in unity. And this, seen from the point of view of *Being and Nothingness*, would just be a function of your particular type of embodiment and particular set of situations, your bodily facticity (see Longuenesse 2008).

Sartre addresses the diachronic unity of consciousness in *The Transcendence of the Ego* explicitly. He writes:

> It will be said that nonetheless a principle of unity in duration [dans la durée] is required for the continual flux of consciousnesses to be able to posit transcendent objects outside of itself. This is exactly right. But it is typical that Husserl, who studied this subjective unification of consciousnesses in *The Phenomenology of Internal Time-Consciousness*, never had recourse to any synthetic power of the I. It is consciousness that unifies itself and concretely so by a play of 'transversal' intentionalities which are the concrete and real

retentions of past consciousnesses. In this way consciousness perpetually refers back to itself, and whoever says 'a consciousness'
says the whole of consciousness. And this singular property
belongs to consciousness itself, whatever relations to the I it may
have in addition.

(TE: 6–7, translation modified)[3]

The diachronic unity of a stream of consciousness is thus to be accounted
for in terms of Husserlian retention (and protention: see IPPI: 75). The
present episode of consciousness retends the just past episode which
retended its just preceding episode, and so on as they trail off into the past.
Retention is an essential feature of all lived, intentional experience; it is not
something superadded to that experience. But as with the world-directed
intentionality just discussed, it will be that which is retended that does
some of the individuating work for an ongoing episode of consciousness.
My current, concrete episode of consciousness *could not be* what it is without that just past episode it retends. That elapsed or elapsing episode is part
of its very identity. And the retended episode would not have been what it
was without its retention of the episode that preceded it. This will mean
that the current episode depends for its identity on the entire chain of
retention, all the way back to the first episode in the chain, hence the
remark about the 'whole of consciousness'. If Sartre is right, one needs
only internal time-consciousness to account for the diachronic unity of the
stream of consciousness. No invariant ego, transcendent in immanence,
seems needed. There is a recurrent or invariant structure of non-positional
or pre-reflective self-consciousness here, but that is not a transcendent
quasi-thing-like *entity*; it is more like an ever-repeated *property*, the instances
of which are temporally linked.

But what of individuality? Couldn't we imagine two streams of consciousness that are, from their first-person points of view, phenomenologically qualitatively identical, even *modulo* a Sartrean-externalist
construal of intentionality? Time-consciousness might suffice for the intra-
stream unity; being-in-the-world might suffice for synchronic unity. But *ex
hypothesi* these two consciousnesses have literally the same mundane
objects. We are imagining, in effect, that my *Doppelgänger* is not in some
Putnamian Twin-Earth but right here, coinciding with me in every intentionally characterizable way. Never mind that this is physically impossible;
we are seeking a conceptual truth here. Neither retention nor world-
directed intentionality would now capture, phenomenologically or ontologically, the particularity of the two streams. We seem to need *something else*
to account for this. What could it be?

Sartre did not run unity and individuality together, as might be suggested
on a loose reading of him. On the egological theory he is imagining, the
transcendental ego is supposed to account for both. He writes:

Ordinarily it is believed that the existence of a transcendental I is justified by consciousness' need for unity and individuality. It is because all my perceptions and all my thoughts relate to this permanent seat [*foyer*] that my consciousness is *unified*; it is because I can say my consciousness and Pierre and Paul can speak of their consciousness that these consciousnesses are *distinguished from* each other.

(TE: 6, translation modified, emphases mine)

Evidently, he too will want to do justice to the individuality of consciousness but without any such 'permanent seat'. Unity alone is not deemed sufficient for this. The thought experiment above perhaps helps to illustrate why.

In this vein Sartre writes:

the individuality of consciousness derives evidently from the nature of consciousness. Consciousness (like Spinoza's substance) can only be limited by itself. It therefore constitutes a synthetic and individual totality entirely isolated from other totalities of the same type. And the I can evidently only be an *expression* (and not a condition) of this incommunicability and interiority of consciousnesses. We can thus respond without hesitating: the phenomenological conception of consciousness renders the unifying and individualising role of the I totally gratuitous. It is consciousness, on the contrary, that renders possible the unity and personality of my I. The transcendental I therefore has no *raison d'être*.

(TE: 7, translation modified)

This passage certainly demands interpretation. Commentators refer, in this connection, to Spinoza's definition of substance as that which is 'in itself and is conceived through itself, that is, that whose concept does not require the concept of another thing' (Spinoza 1985: *Ethics* Pt 1, def. 3). Coorebyter points out that the ultimate phrase in that definition could not possibly apply to consciousness *chez* Sartre precisely because consciousness depends upon something other than itself, both phenomenologically and ontologically, namely the world and, in *Being and Nothingness*, the In-itself (Coorebyter 2003: 180n18; see also Le Bon in TE: 57n20).

Perhaps the best we could do here is to point out that in order to have the concept of consciousness, one must *be* a consciousness, where this not a trivial claim. Of course if I were not a consciousness, I would never have the concept of anything. The relevant contrast, however, is this: I need not be, for example, a lump of Camembert or be a cactus to form the concepts of those things. But I get the concept of consciousness through living/being conscious experience itself and *only* in that way. I get the concept of it through being an instance of it. Moreover, we cannot directly think of consciousness in terms of any other concept. This is a relative of the generally conceded point that one could never arrive at an identification of consciousness with, for example, brain or computational processes or structures *a priori*. Our knowledge of it does not depend upon and does not analytically entail the application of any other concepts. In *this* sense, it is 'conceived through itself' – being a consciousness is non-trivially required for conceiving of it; and its concept does not require the concept of another thing. (Though, again, this is not quite right, because it must always be thought of in connection with its revealing of a world.) Somewhat similarly, on Spinoza's view, the concept of substance is basic and our thoughts of it require no other concepts (though one need not *be* a substance to have the concept).

But there are more disanalogies. Human consciousness is finite and admits of a multiplicity of instances, whereas Spinoza's substance is infinite and necessarily singular. Coorebyter claims that what is really common here is the impossibility of 'seeing' the contours or boundaries of oneself from the inside (2003: 180n18). To make a geometrical analogy, one might say that consciousness is like a finite but unbounded space while Spinoza's substance is like an infinite and unbounded one. From the inside, you see no walls or barriers to your consciousness (save, of course, the objectual centres of opacity), just as a person on a sphere might walk forever in what they take to be a straight Euclidean line. But this, even if true or apt, does not help us with our individuation problem. And Stephen Priest's remark (2000: 44), in connection with this passage, that 'it is intrinsic to its [consciousness'] nature that its only direct access is to itself and not to another consciousness', even if true, does not solve the difficulty. That one is *just this* individual is not accounted for by any of these ideas.

I think we should consider more carefully what we are asking for here. Once we have dispensed with property-dependent individuation (via spatio-temporal properties in particular), there is really very little that we can say. Take two protons. Consider them in the abstract, apart from their spatio-temporal relations (*per impossibile* perhaps). What would explain that proton A is proton A and not proton B? I think this a muddle-headed question. There is no *further* explanation of particularity. At some level, barring some form of Pythagoreanism, it is just a *brute fact* that A is *that* proton and B is *a different one*. We can, of course, postulate, in an ontological vein, bare particulars or, if we like properties instead of little things, haecceities, special individuating properties. But this is just gratuitous hypostatization. The protons are different. If we postulate more stuff that is different, we can always ask the same question: what differentiates these two bare particulars or these two haecceities? Of course, one might say, that is a wrong-headed question, because bare particulars and haecceities are precisely the things we postulate in order to account for the fundamental differentiation of things. The buck stops there. Fine. But this really is just to admit the point: there are distinct particulars in the world. And we should confess our ignorance about what it is, at the deepest ontological level, that accounts for that differentiation. And what goes for protons goes for streams of consciousness as well.

If we are good physicalists, then we might hold that what differentiates streams of consciousness is whatever physical facts, relations, or entities that differentiate brains and their processes. We need not postulate any special entities or properties *in* consciousness to do this. We need not postulate an ego-entity that is a particular. Again, we could always just ask what accounts for *its* particularity. It is not obvious that the buck should stop there. And we need not postulate special 'minenesses', essentially haecceities, like Sartréité or Husserlheit to *account* for Husserl's experiences being his or Sartre's being Sartre's. The 'first-personal mode of givenness', as we shall see, is well characterized by the self-manifestation of the stream, in Sartrean terms, by non-positional self-consciousness. We don't need anything else. Different self-manifesting streams will feel themselves to be distinct individuals. Streams of consciousness are individuated; we don't find any special, phenomenologically available individuators immanent in them. Whatever we make of Sartre's appeal to Spinoza here, he is certainly saying that streams of consciousness are, in fact, individuated by their very nature and that no ego is needed to account for this fact. Whether he is right about streams being individuated by their very nature or not, he is certainly right that postulating an ego to do this job would be gratuitous. There is no good *a priori* reason not to locate the individuality of a stream at the level of the stream itself. Two brutely differentiated streams of consciousness are no more and no less mysterious, *a priori*, than two brutely differentiated egos, whether we construe them as ego-particulars or ego-haecceities. We have it then that there need be no ego to account for the unity and individuality of consciousness. In those respects, it is *de trop*.

The transcendental ego is *impossible*

In addition to the argument from explanatory gratuitousness against an egological entity immanent in consciousness, Sartre has two important, and I think, with qualifications, compelling arguments against the very *possibility* of such a thing. The first argument is basically this: Consciousness is an insubstantial revealing of objects other than itself and of itself *insofar as* it is a revealing of those objects. The objects are centres of opacity and are thereby given as being *other* than consciousness. Consciousness is given to itself as an empty or translucent revealing of these *other* objects. Consciousness, moreover, is *completely* self-manifesting in the sense that it delivers up everything essential about itself to itself. He expresses this as follows: 'consciousness remains a "phenomenon" in the highly particular sense in which "to be" and "to appear" are one and the same' (TE: 8; see also STE: 30–2). If there were an ego immanent in consciousness, it would be a centre of opacity in consciousness, 'however formal and abstract one may suppose it to be' (TE: 8).[4] But there *can be no* centres of opacity in consciousness, given that it is self-given as, necessarily, 'nothing but light-ness and translucency' (TE: 9; see also IPPI: 6). Therefore, there *cannot be* an ego in consciousness (TE: 7–9).

Now, I think Sartre is not at all entitled to the idea that consciousness is *completely* self-manifesting. On the contrary, I think consciousness has no access to a great number of its essential properties. This idea of *complete* self-manifestation is at the root of a good many Sartrean moves and *insolu-bilia*. But in the present case the argument can be recast and more or less salvaged. We can agree with the phenomenological claim that we do not find a contracted centre of opacity in consciousness, even a very formal or pure one. But we will not be able to conclude from this that there *is* no such ego. But we will be able to conclude that, *if* there is, it is not some-thing we have conscious access to. It would have to be a special entity dwelling in the unconscious (see TE: 2). But then our desire to attri-bute to that entity the characteristics that belong solely to lived conscious experience (e.g. desiring, deciding, being spontaneous, shifting attention; see TE: 32–8) would be thwarted. Either it would be a consciousness too, presumably with its own ego (and off we go on a homuncular regress), or it would be more like a Lacanian, non-homuncular unconscious that we can characterize, to some extent, in intentional idioms but only in a Den-nettian as-if sort of way. The latter, for aught we know, might yield some explanatory dividends, but it is not a re-postulation of the sort of entity in question. The former, however, is a dead end. So, even if one relinquishes complete self-manifestation, one still has a plausible line of thought here.

The second argument depends on the distinction between immanence and transcendence that Phenomenologists commonly used to demarcate consciousness and its mode of givenness from transcendent objects and their mode of givenness (e.g. Husserl 1982: §41; TE: 13). Transcendent objects, and physical objects paradigmatically, are given via profiles or *Abschattungen*, while consciousness is not self-given in that way. It makes no sense to imagine turning an episode of consciousness over to see its under-side, etc. At best we can hold an experience in retention or memory and shift our focus from its theme to its horizon or margin (which technique Sartre makes use of in TE: 11–12), but this is not the same thing.[5] Importantly, givenness via profiles was a major component of the Phenomenological account of perceptual error and of the ineradicable dubitability of perceptual judgement. I can be mistaken in thinking that what I am seeing in the brush is a deer. This mistake can be found out after the accumulation of more profiles vis-à-vis the object. I might find out that it is a lunatic dressed in a deer hide and wearing antler-like branches on his head. Perceptual error is possible because the deer-construed profiles might coincide with the lunatic-construed profiles up to a point. But in the case of the self-givenness of consciousness at a time, this type of error is not possible, at least not if we are dealing with immediate reflection instead of the application of some sort of theory, sophisticated or rudimentary, to our experience. Once we have put those conceptual overlays aside, all the errors we are subject to are errors of attention from lack of due diligence and hasty generalizations based upon those errors.

This will mean that if we can be in error about something in a way that is genuinely analogous to perceptual error, then that object, even if it is not physical, gives itself via profiles. If it gives itself via profiles, then it is transcendent to consciousness and not immanent in it. The ego, Sartre argues, though it is not a physical object or a little invariant subject-spot, is like this. We can be wrong about it. We can attribute to it dispositions, abilities, and valuations it does not have. We can project, for example, that we will always be in love with so-and-so or hate so-and-so, and we can find ourselves wrong about that (TE: 22–3).

Sartre's view is that these kinds of mistakes ought not be possible if the ego were immanent in consciousness. If it were, then it would be given without profiles. And if it were given without profiles, one could not be wrong about it in that way. But one can be wrong about it in this way. So it must not be immanent. It must, rather, be a transcendent object *for* consciousness. The very fact that we can wonder with others about our loves and hates and other dispositions is an indication that the object we are concerned with is not something we have access to the way we have access to our episodes of consciousness (TE: 31–8, 43–4).

The ego can go *missing*

The ego is explanatorily impotent and, in fact, *could not be* a structure of consciousness, according to Sartre. But, as noted, these arguments ultimately rest upon the phenomenological fact that there are experiences in which the ego *is not given*. If we always found the ego upon appropriate reflection, then we would have to conclude that it is indeed inherent in consciousness. And the other arguments would have to be regarded as misguided. Thus Sartre offers a phenomenological description that is aimed at showing that the ego is often absent from our episodes of consciousness. He describes his just passed absorption in his reading and concludes:

> There is no doubt about the result: while I was reading, there was consciousness *of* the book, *of* the heroes of the novel, but the *I* was

not inhabiting this consciousness. It was only consciousness of the object and non-positional consciousness of itself. I can now make these athetically apprehended results the object of a thesis and declare: there was no *I* in the unreflected consciousness.

(TE: 11–12)

It is somewhat ironic that many people who object to the idea that consciousness always involves some form of self-consciousness adduce examples like this in support of their view (e.g. Tononi and Koch 2008: 240–1). Indeed, Sartre has been attractive to some writers and unattractive to others precisely because they have assimilated him too closely to Hume or Lichtenberg in this connection (Chisholm 1969; Butchvarov 1979: 251–2; 1998: 55; Zahavi 1999: 140; 2005: 101). Though some of Sartre's modes of expression invite this comparison, it should be clear from the above passage that Sartre is not asking us to envision consciousness *without subjectivity*. He is asking us just to note that often we are not conscious of any ego in the sense of an opaque seat or source, even if conceived of very minimalistically, of our dispositions, experiences, and actions. I think we must concede that he is indeed right about that. The descriptive point upon which Sartre's other arguments ultimately rest stands.

A ramification of this is that Sartre distinguishes sharply between subjectivity, conceived of as non-positional self-consciousness or the self-manifestation of the stream, and the ego. If one wants to *call* the former an egological structure or a 'sense of self', that is fine and merely terminological (see Zahavi 1999: 142). But Sartre's view has seemed mysterious to many and has been misunderstood by others precisely because they did not really comprehend that his account of subjectivity or 'presence to –' is in terms of non-positional self-consciousness. That notion could not be more fundamental to Sartre's view. Moreover, it is all we need, ultimately, to make sense of subjectivity at its root.

At present let me mention that philosophers have often been hobbled in their attempts at describing consciousness adequately because they have thought that their choice was between some sort of egological reflection theory of self-consciousness (whereby self-consciousness would involve both an attitude of reflection and a reference to a kind of homuncular I) and some sort of no-subjectivity view (whereby there could be ownerless episodes of consciousness, and, presumably, a world of objects appearing but not appearing *to* anything). Those who take the phenomenology of engagement and absorption to heart often argue for the latter and regard all modes of self-consciousness as derivative. Those who maintain that there is always some sense of self or subjectivity present in consciousness, always something *to which* the world appears, often argue for the former. Sartre offers us a third way.

The ego and the impersonal field

Perhaps more than anything else, what has misled readers of *The Transcendence of the Ego* is Sartre's claim that once the ego falls before the *epoché* the transcendental field is revealed as *impersonal* (TE: 46). And his Lichtenbergian-sounding construal of the 'pseudo-*Cogito*' ('there is consciousness of a chair' rather than 'I am conscious of a chair') encourages this same misunderstanding (TE: 16). But we must remember that he corrects this mode of expression in *Being and Nothingness*. He changes his mode of expression, *not* the real content of his view (see Coorebyter 2003: 211n58). After summarizing his view presented in *The Transcendence of the Ego*, he writes:

> [W]e need not conclude that the for-itself is pure and simple 'impersonal' contemplation. But the Ego is far from being the personalising pole of a consciousness without which it would remain in the impersonal stage; on the contrary, it is consciousness in its fundamental selfness (*ipséité*) which under certain conditions allows the appearance of the Ego as the transcendent phenomenon of that selfness ... [W]hat confers personal existence on a being is not the possession of an Ego – which is only the *sign* of the personality – but it is the fact that the being exists for itself as a presence to itself.
>
> (B&N: 127)

In both *The Transcendence of the Ego* and *Being and Nothingness*, Sartre maintains that the ego is an object for reflective consciousness and that consciousness is a unified, individuated, self-manifesting stream. Self-manifestation, again, is what Sartre calls non-positional or non-thetic self-consciousness. The terms 'non-thetic' and 'non-positional' are synonymous and derive ultimately from Husserl. According to Husserl consciousness of mundane objects in the natural, pre-phenomenological attitude, involves a 'positional' or 'thetic' character by which we spontaneously 'posit' something about the existential status of those objects. We encounter them as existing, as not-possibly-existing, as having-once-existed, as probably existing, etc., depending on the type of object in question (e.g. 1982: §§114, 115, 117, 122, 129, and *especially* 113 where Husserl seems to indicate *exactly* the notion of non-positional self-consciousness in its connection to time-consciousness; see also IPPI: 11–14). In the phenomenological attitude we are supposed to suspend or 'put in brackets' that spontaneous positing. Accordingly 'non-positional' and 'non-thetic' are meant to indicate that the pre-reflective mode of self-consciousness does not have a positing character to it. To posit and to encounter objectually are correlated, and positing is further correlated with different types of acts. Imagination involves one mode of positing, perception another. As I do not, pre-reflectively, take up any particular positing attitude toward my stream of lived experiences as they unfold engaged with the world, I do not posit that stream as a perceptual (imaginary, etc.) object (TE: 8).

Though the ego is an object for reflective consciousness, this does not mean that consciousness is devoid of a *subject* in the sense of a *that to which the objects of consciousness appear*. The phenomenological subject, in this sense, is just the stream of consciousness itself, and the ultimate origin of 'personality' is not to be found in a personal ego-entity, but in the self-manifesting stream of consciousness. The self-manifestation of the unified stream is sufficient for basic selfhood. We do not need some invariant entity. Instead what we have is an invariant, ever repeated *structure*.[6] What is truly extraordinary about this view is that it allows us to sublate or synthesize those competing intuitions about consciousness that have plagued philosophers for centuries and that persist today not only in philosophy but in neuroscience as well.

On the one hand, there has been the Humean tradition according to which there fundamentally is no self or sense of selfhood at all to be found in consciousness. As noted, Tononi and Koch represent this tradition within contemporary neuroscience. As also noted, some philosophers have been attracted to Sartre or repulsed by him precisely because they have located him in this Humean tradition. On the other hand, there is the Cartesian tradition that has always emphasized the fundamentality of selfhood to consciousness. Strange, isn't it, that Sartre has often been located in *that* tradition, often before being dismissed as a warmed-over Cartesian mutilator of Heidegger (see Dreyfus's comments in Magee 1988: 275)? Within neuroscience the Cartesian tradition found its most elaborate expression in the work of John Eccles. But it should be evident that Sartre does not fit easily into either of these traditions. He does not eliminate the sense of selfhood from consciousness, as we have seen. Yet he is not a substantialist, and does indeed 'eliminate' the ego-entity, the homunculus, the Cartesian spectator from consciousness. He represents a passage between the Scylla of conscious experiences without an owner and the Charybdis of a Cartesian substantial homunculus (in all of its varieties). In contemporary neuroscience, this Sartrean position, I'll briefly argue in the final section, is occupied by Antonio Damasio.

The competing traditions are based on two genuine intuitions that seem to be in tension with one another. On the one hand, my lived experiences seem to be *relational* in the sense that they offer me a world that stands over against my consciousness. I am conscious of a world and that world *is not* my consciousness of it. It is *for me*, but it is *not me* (TE: 7–8). On the other hand, if like Hume I go looking for myself under the misconception that there should be some sort of *entity* I could identify myself with and contrast with the world of objects, I can find no such thing. The Sartrean view resolves this impasse: the world of objects is not the consciousness before which they appear, and we are indeed always aware of something that contrasts with those objects; but it is not some separable entity among those objects, it is just that very consciousness itself. In being non-positionally self-conscious, in having this reflexive (but not reflective) structure, consciousness can always experience the world as standing over against it without having to find a contrasting *entity*.

Conclusion: Sartre neuralized?

I claimed that Damasio's view of consciousness, at the neuro-phenomenological level, meshes extremely well with the Sartrean 'third way'. Like Sartre, Damasio regards all consciousness as involving self-consciousness or, as he likes to put it, 'a sense of self in the act of knowing' (1999: 19). This sense of a 'core self' is essential to what Damasio calls 'core consciousness'. It is not to be construed as either a reflective self-consciousness or consciousness of some sort of homunculus or ego in the Sartrean sense – what Damasio calls the 'autobiographical self'. Rather, core consciousness corresponds very well to Sartre's notion of non-positional self-consciousness. 'The sense of self which emerges in core consciousness is the *core self*', writes Damasio, 'ceaselessly re-created for each and every object with which the brain interacts' (1999: 17). Damasio also has a notion corresponding to the ego *à la* Sartre. According to Sartre we spontaneously 'constitute' an ego for ourselves on the basis of patterns in pre-reflective experience and our facticity (TE: 21–41). Something similar could be said for Damasio's autobiographical self. 'The autobiographical self depends on systematised memories of situations in which core consciousness was involved in the knowing of the most invariant characteristics of an organism's life – who you were born to, where, when, your likes and dislikes, the way you usually react to a problem or a conflict, your name, and so on' (Damasio 1999: 17; see also 173, 196). Sartre and Damasio both recognize that the autobiographical self or ego is not involved in core consciousness or non-positional self-consciousness as such, is subject to variation and evolution over the course of one's life and subject to various pathological deviations, and tends nevertheless towards unity and stability in order to carry out its practical function (Damasio 1999: 225–6; compare TE: 47–8). Though their preferred vocabularies are quite different, there is a deep phenomenological insight that Damasio and Sartre share.

If this is correct, then in attempting to 'naturalize' phenomenology or find the neural correlates of consciousness, we should explore the class of mathematical models that allow us to describe massively integrated dynamical systems that are, at the same time, uroboric or 'self-engulfing'. Perhaps there is a mathematical framework that would allow us to adequately capture the phenomenologically invariant temporality, multifaceted unity, and self-mirroring structure of consciousness. If we had such a framework, perhaps we could, by finding the relevant structural isomorphism, bridge the gap between consciousness as lived and the brain as an object of empirical science.[7]

Notes

1 Among those works I include the brief 1939 article, 'Intentionality: A Fundamental Idea of Husserl's Phenomenology', *The Imagination* (1936), *The Transcendence of the Ego* (1937), *Sketch for a Theory of the Emotions* (1939), *The Imaginary* (1940), *Being and Nothingness* (1943), and the lecture, published in 1948, 'Consciousness of Self and Knowledge of Self'.

2 Sartre was writing this article around the same time that he was writing *The Transcendence of the Ego* (see Coorebyter 2003: 9). Of course, Husserl well recognized this 'horizonal' structure of lived experience.

3 Coorebyter (2003: 179n15) points out that Sartre should have said 'longitudinal' or 'horizontal' intentionality (Husserl's *Längsintentionalität*) instead of 'transversal' intentionality (Husserl's *Querintentionalität*). The former, as Brough puts it, is 'the flow's intending of itself in its flowing' (in Husserl 1991: 84n). The latter is the intending of the temporality of immanent acts of consciousness, e.g. perceivings, rememberings, and, correlatively, the intending of the temporality of the transcendent objects of those acts, e.g. the duration of a heard tone. However, this slip does not hurt Sartre's case. On the Husserlian view these two aspects of time-consciousness are inseparable; there is a 'play' of the one if and only if there is a 'play' of the other.

4 That is an important qualification from both Kantian and Husserlian points of view. Husserl's pure or transcendental ego, while not the Kantian formal *Ich denke*, is conceived of as stripped of all its empirico-mundane content. Husserl also did not conceive of the pure ego as like a 'fixed idea' a little invariant sensory quality or set of persistent mental acts (1982: §57). Sartre was well aware of this.

5 Thanks to Harry Reeder here.

6 I do not mean by 'structure' what a neuroanatomist would mean. I mean, roughly, 'complex, articulated property'; and it could be a property that is only instantiated in a very dynamic process. By 'entity' I mean, roughly, 'a thing that is, relatively speaking, static, and not a process'. In my use of these terms, an invariant pattern in e.g. the flow of a swirling liquid could be called a 'structure', while a stone in the water would be called an 'entity'. Thanks to David Rudrauf here.

7 This paper is dedicated to the memory of Denny Bradshaw who first piqued my interest in Sartre's early phenomenological works. I would like to thank Harry Reeder, Dan Zahavi, David Rudrauf, Tomis Kapitan, Panayot Butchvarov, Antonio Damasio, Louis Sandowsky, Gregory Landini, Uriah Kriegel, Jonathan Webber, Anthony Hatzimoysis, Katherine Morris, and an audience at The University of Texas at Arlington for comments, questions, criticisms, and discussions pertaining to this paper or the material in it. And thanks to Celia Stigall for help with the bibliography.

14

SHAME AND THE EXPOSED SELF

Dan Zahavi

On many standard readings, shame is an emotion that in an accentuated manner targets and involves the self in its totality. In shame, the self is affected by a global devaluation: it feels defective, objectionable, condemned. The basic question I wish to raise and discuss is the following: What does the fact that we feel shame tell us about the nature of self? What kind of self is it that is affected in shame?

Shame and self-reflection

My point of departure will be the work of Michael Lewis. Lewis is not only the author of a highly influential monograph entitled *Shame: The Exposed Self*, he is also the author of numerous articles and book chapters on shame and self-conscious emotions in various handbooks and standard reference works dealing with these topics.

Lewis starts out by arguing that emotions come in many different forms and shapes. Emotion research has spent much time investigating what Ekman called the basic six: joy, fear, sadness, surprise, anger and disgust. Allegedly these emotions emerge early in human development, they have a biological basis, a characteristic facial expression, and are culturally universal. It is fairly obvious, however, that these basic or primary emotions do not exhaust the richness of our emotional life. Think merely of more complex emotions like embarrassment, envy, shame, guilt, pride, jealousy, remorse or gratitude. According to Lewis, one useful way of classifying the different emotions is by operating with a distinction between self-conscious and non-self-conscious emotions. Whereas primary emotions do not involve self-consciousness, the more complex emotions do (Lewis 2007: 136). Indeed on Lewis's account, the latter group of emotions involve elaborate cognitive processes, they all come about through self-reflection or introspection (Lewis uses these concepts interchangeably), they all involve and require the concept of self. Thus, a developmental presupposition for experiencing such emotions is that the child is in possession of a self-concept or a self-representation, which according to Lewis only happens from around eighteen months of age.

211

In order to assess Lewis's theory it is necessary to say a few words about his terminology. Lewis basically operates with a distinction between subjective self-awareness and objective self-awareness.[1] On Lewis's account all living systems from the simplest to the most complicated regulate and monitor themselves. Some of the examples he provides concern the way a body tracks the level of CO_2 in its blood, or the way in which T-cells differentiate themselves from foreign protein (Lewis 2003: 279). For Lewis this self-regulation and self–other differentiation requires a certain amount of subjective self-awareness, but for Lewis we are here dealing with a form of self-awareness that is unconscious (Lewis 1992: 16, 27).[2] All living systems possess subjective self-awareness, only very few attain the level of objective self-awareness which denotes a much higher representational complexity. The moment this level is attained, however, experiences and emotions become conscious. Only from that moment on are they like something to or for us. Thus, on Lewis's account, it is only when we consciously reflect upon ourselves, only when we direct our attention inwards and internally attend to our own mental states as objects of attention, that they become conscious (Lewis 1992: 29). Lewis illustrates this idea with the following example. A loud noise may put me in a state of fright. But I only consciously experience the state of fright if I reflect upon it. Prior to reflection, the fright remains unconscious. Considered from a developmental point of view, Lewis claims that prior to the emergence of objective self-consciousness, i.e. before the infant develops a concept of self and an objective self-representation, the infant might have emotional states, but none of these states are conscious (Lewis 2000: 273–4), just as it doesn't have any other conscious experiences.

Lewis goes on to distinguish two groups of self-conscious emotions. Both groups involve self-exposure and objective self-consciousness, i.e. self-reflection. But whereas the first involves non-evaluative exposure, the second involves both self-exposure and evaluation. The first group includes embarrassment, empathy, and envy and emerges around eighteen months. The second group emerges around thirty-six months, it includes shame and guilt and requires the ability to appropriate and internalize standards, rules, and goals and to evaluate and compare one's behaviour vis-à-vis such standards (Lewis 2007: 135).

Let me quickly summarize Lewis's basic claim. On his view, increasing cognitive capacities allow for objective self-awareness and thereby for self-conscious emotions like embarrassment, empathy, and envy. When joined with an even more complex cognitive capacity for standards, rules, and goals, self-conscious evaluative emotions like pride, shame, and guilt emerge.

There is much one could take issue with here. Let me focus on Lewis's very distinction between primary and secondary emotions. Lewis writes:

I suggest that emotions can be classified in relation to the role of the self. The elicitation of fear, joy, disgust, surprise, anger, sadness and interest does not require introspection or self-reference. Therefore, let us consider these emotions as one set. The elicitation of jealousy, envy, empathy, embarrassment, shame, pride, and guilt does require introspection or self-reference. These emotions constitute another set. ... Thus, I propose that the difference between primary and secondary emotions is that the secondary emotions involve self-reference. Secondary emotions will be referred to as *self-conscious emotions*; shame is a self-conscious emotion.

(Lewis 1992: 19–20)

But is it really true that primary emotions are non-self-conscious, and that they lack a reference to self? I think this claim can be disputed in at least two ways. The first way is to endorse a notion of pre-reflective self-consciousness, and to argue that our experiential life is characterized by an ongoing sense of self (see Zahavi 2005). If one accepts this line of thinking, it makes no sense to single out the complex emotions as self-conscious emotions, since all emotions, in so far as they are experienced first-personally by the subject, are self-conscious. Of course, Lewis might object that emotions like fear, anger, and joy are not consciously experienced by the subject, at least not prior to being taken as objects of reflection, which only happens from when the child is around eighteen months of age. But I have to admit that I find this view absurd, especially if we consider that Lewis would also have to deny that infants (and animals) can consciously experience pain, exhaustion, frustration, etc. After all, according to Lewis our mental states only become conscious the moment they are introspectively taken as objects. In that sense, objective self-consciousness is a precondition for consciousness. But by arguing in this manner, Lewis is committed to the view that animals and infants who lack higher-order representational skills will also lack phenomenal experiences.

It is not difficult to detect the influence of both theory-theory and higher-order representational theory in Lewis's considerations. This combination is not unique. For comparison, consider Gallup's work on mirror self-recognition. On several occasions, Gallup has argued that conscious experience necessarily presupposes self-awareness. Either one is aware of being aware, or one is unaware of being aware, and the latter amounts to being unconscious (Gallup 1985: 638). In continuation of this line of thought, Gallup then claims that organisms that lack the ability to monitor their own mental states are mindless (1982: 243, 245), and that although most organisms behave *as if* they are conscious and minded (1982: 242), prior to the emergence of self-awareness as evidenced from their ability to pass the mirror self-recognition task, they lack conscious experience, and only possess unconscious sensations and pains, etc. (1985: 638). This

conclusion has rather dramatic implications not only for our ascription of an experiential life to infants, but also to all those animals that remain incapable of recognizing their own mirror image.

But back to Lewis. The second way to question Lewis's distinction is by arguing that emotions – to an even larger extent than perceptions or cognitions – are self-referential and self-involving. Consider that we respond emotionally to that which matters to us, to that which we care about, to that towards which we are not indifferent. In that sense, one might argue that emotions involve appraisals of what has importance, significance, value, and relevance to oneself. This doesn't merely hold true for complex emotions like guilt, shame, or pride, but certainly also for emotions like joy, disgust, anger, and fear. Don't misunderstand me. I am not denying that there are interesting differences between emotions like anger and fear, and emotions like shame and repentance. I just don't think the relevant difference is whether or not the emotions in question are self-conscious or self-referential.

But where then should one search for the difference? A possibility would be to claim that the different types of emotions are self-involving in different ways. Consider again, the title of Lewis's book, *Shame: The Exposed Self.* This is how Lewis explains the subtitle:

> The subtitle of this book is *The Exposed Self.* What is an exposed self and to whom is it exposed? The self is exposed to itself, that is, we are capable of viewing ourselves. A self capable of self-reflection is unique to humans.
>
> (Lewis 1992: 36)

In short, Lewis defines the exposure in question as one of being exposed to oneself. That is, when he talks of the exposed self, he is referring to our capacity for self-reflection. But is this not to basically miss the crucial point? Compare by contrast the following remark by Darwin: 'It is not the simple act of reflecting on our own appearance, but the thinking what others think of us, which excites a blush' (Darwin 1965: 325).

Others in mind

Let me turn to an alternative account that specifically argues that shame rather than merely being a self-reflective emotion, an emotion involving negative self-evaluation, is an emotion that reveals our relationality, our being-for-others. I am of course thinking of the account that Sartre offers in *Being and Nothingness.*

One of Sartre's central claims in that book is that consciousness is essentially characterized by intentionality. Consciousness is as such consciousness *of* something. Sartre also claims, however, that each and every intentional experience exists in such a way that it is implicitly self-given, or as Sartre puts it, it is 'for itself'. This self-givenness of experience is not simply a quality added to the experience, a mere varnish; rather for Sartre the very *mode of being* of intentional consciousness is to be *for-itself* (*pour-soi*), that is, self-conscious (B&N: 10; see Zahavi 1999). When speaking of self-consciousness as a permanent feature of consciousness, Sartre is, how-ever, not referring to what we might call reflective self-consciousness. Reflection (or higher-order representation) is the process whereby con-sciousness directs its intentional aim at itself, thereby taking itself as its own object. According to Sartre, however, this type of self-consciousness is derived; it involves a subject–object split, and the attempt to account for self-consciousness in such terms is, for Sartre, bound to fail. It either gen-erates an infinite regress or accepts a non-conscious starting point, and he considers both options unacceptable (B&N: 8).

According to Sartre, the right alternative is to accept the existence of a pre-reflective and non-objectifying form of self-consciousness. To put it differently, on his account, consciousness has two different modes of givenness, a pre-reflective and a reflective. The first has priority since it can prevail independently of the latter, whereas reflective self-consciousness always presupposes pre-reflective self-consciousness. So to repeat, for Sartre pre-reflective self-consciousness is not an addendum to, but a con-stitutive moment of the original intentional experience. If I consciously see, remember, know, think, hope, feel or will something, the experience in question is not like nothing to me, I am not self-blind, rather it is given to me in a non-objectifying, tacit manner.

This is Sartre's basic account. In the third part of *Being and Nothingness* Sartre modifies and complicates matters insofar as he argues that there is a type of self-consciousness that is intersubjectively mediated, i.e. which has the other as its condition of possibility. Sartre initially argues that there are modes of consciousness which although remaining strictly for-itself, i.e. characterized by pre-reflective self-consciousness, nevertheless points to a very different type of ontological structure. More specifically he makes the somewhat enigmatic claim that there are modes of consciousness which although they are mine nevertheless reveal to me a being which is my being without being-for-me (B&N: 245). To better understand what Sartre is up to, let us consider the example he himself introduces, namely the feeling of *shame*.

According to Sartre, shame is a form of intentional consciousness. It is a shameful apprehension of something, and this something happens to be myself. I am ashamed of what I am, and to that extent shame also exem-plifies an intimate self-relation. As Sartre points out however, shame is not primarily and originally a phenomenon of reflection. I can reflect upon my feeling of shame, but I feel shame prior to reflecting upon it. Shame is, as he puts it, 'an immediate shudder which runs through me from head to foot without any discursive preparation' (B&N: 246). Indeed and more significantly, in its primary form shame is not a feeling I can simply elicit on my own through reflection, rather shame is shame of oneself before the other (B&N: 246, 312). It presupposes the intervention of the other, and not merely because the other is the one before whom I feel ashamed, but also and more significantly because the other is the one that constitutes that of which I am ashamed. I am ashamed of myself, not qua elusive first-person perspective, but qua the way I appear to the other. Thus although shame exemplifies a self-relation, we are on Sartre's account dealing with a mediated form of self-relation, one where the other is the mediator between me and myself.

To feel shame is – if ever so fleetingly – to accept the other's evaluation; it is to acknowledge that I am that object that the other looks at and judges. In being ashamed, I accept the judgement of the other. I *am* the way the other sees me (B&N: 246, 287). Sartre's central claim is consequently that for shame to occur there must be a relationship between self and other where the self cares about the other's evaluation. Moreover, according to Sartre it makes no difference whether the evaluation of the other is positive or not, since it is the objectification as such that is shame-inducing. As he writes:

> Pure shame is not a feeling of being this or that guilty object but in general of being *an* object; that is, of *recognizing myself* in this degraded, fixed and dependent being which I am for the Other. Shame is the feeling of an *original fall,* not because of the fact that I may have committed this or that particular fault but simply that I have 'fallen' into the world in the midst of things and that I need the mediation of the Other in order to be what I am.
>
> (B&N: 312)

Varieties of shame

There are many details of Sartre's analysis that call for further clarification, and his account has not gone unchallenged. Let me first consider a few important differences between his account of shame and an earlier phenomenological analysis, namely the one we find in Max Scheler's long 1913 essay 'Scham und Schamgefühl'.

In contrast to Sartre, Scheler emphasizes the need for a differentiation between several distinct forms of shame. Sartre only discusses *honte,* but French has the distinction between *honte* and *pudeur,* whereas German has the distinction between *Schande* and *Scham.* Both meanings can be found in the definitions of shame provided by the *Oxford English Dictionary.* The OED distinguishes the painful emotion arising from the consciousness of something dishonouring or disgraceful in one's own conduct from our sense of shame, i.e. our perception of what is improper or disgraceful. If one accepts this differentiation (and other relevant distinctions such as the one between discretion shame, disgrace shame, anticipatory shame, conformity shame, etc.), one would have to reject the idea that shame is a negative and repressive emotion *per se*, one we should aim to remove from our lives (see Schneider 1987). As already Plato pointed out in the *Laws*, shame is what will prevent man from doing what is dishonourable (647a). Similarly, a sense of shame might also be what allows us to be tactful, to respect the integrity and privacy of others.[3] On his part, Scheler distinguishes the extremely painful experience of repenting shame (*Schamreue*), a burning shame that is backward looking and full of piercing sharpness and self-hatred, from the protecting shame of the blushing virgin which, on his view, is characterized by lovely warmth (Scheler 1957: 140). Moreover, he argues that the occurrence of shame testifies to the presence of a certain self-respect and self-esteem; it is only because one expects oneself to have worth that this expectation can be disappointed and give rise to shame (Scheler 1957: 141; see G. Taylor 1985: 80–1). By comparison, the very notion of shamelessness indicates that the possession of a sense of shame is a moral virtue.[4]

Another important difference is that while Scheler would agree with Sartre that shame is a self-involving emotion, he explicitly rejects the claim that shame is essentially a social emotion, one that by necessity involves others (Scheler 1957: 78). Rather for Scheler, the central feature of shame is that it concerns a tension between our aspirations and ideals on the one hand and our awareness of our finitude and helplessness on the other (1957: 68), and he argues that there is a self-directed form of shame which is just as original as the shame one can feel in the presence of others (1957: 78). For obvious reasons, Scheler didn't discuss Sartre's concrete analysis, but a more recent and related criticism of Sartre's emphasis on the role of the other can be found in Gabriele Taylor's by now classical contribution *Pride, Shame, and Guilt: Emotions of Self-Assessment*.

Taylor initially argues that Sartre's account of shame is too simplistic in that it only covers a limited range of cases (1985: 59). I would to some extent agree with this assessment, just as I also think that Sartre's analysis could have profited from a more meticulous differentiation between the members of the so-called shame-family of emotions – shame, embarrassment, humiliation, etc. In addition, however, she also raises two more specific objections. She first claims that Sartre is wrong in arguing that shame necessarily entails that the observer is critical of the agent, since positive praise might under certain circumstances also be shame-inducing, and she furthermore denies that shame always entails that the subject in question adopts and accepts the evaluation of the observer (G. Taylor 1985: 60). Here I would disagree, however. After all, as we have just seen, Sartre's point isn't that the gaze has to be critical in order to be shame-inducing;

rather it is its objectifying character that is decisive. As for the claim that one can feel shame when faced with the other's evaluation, even if one doesn't accept or share the evaluation, one kind of example that allegedly would support this view is the following: when giving mouth-to-mouth respiration to a girl after you have saved her from drowning, you are accused by passers-by of taking advantage of the girl. If this episode were shame-inducing, it might precisely constitute a case where you are shamed by the other's evaluation although you don't share it and know it to be false. However, I think it would be more correct to classify the example as a case of embarrassment than of shame. Why? Because (disgrace) shame in contrast to embarrassment is crucially linked to a decrease of self-esteem, and I don't think the situation in question would occasion such a decrease. To feel ashamed is to feel unworthy, is to feel that the negative assessment of the other is deserved. If one didn't care about the other's opinion, if her (lack of) recognition didn't matter to one, if one held her opinions in contempt, she wouldn't be able to shame us. As already Aristotle points out in his *Rhetoric*, the people we feel shame before are those whose opinion of us matters to us (1384a25).

If we turn to Taylor's positive account, she argues that shame is crucially related to a shift in the agents' perspective on himself or herself; a shift that specifically occasions the realization of an adverse discrepancy between the agent's assumptions about himself till now and the perspective offered by a more detached observer (G. Taylor 1985: 66). According to Taylor, this shift is typically brought about by the realization that one is or could be the object of another's attention. In contrast to Sartre, however, the other is for Taylor merely a means to this shift. Because although the adverse *judgement* – and for Taylor shame is a rather sophisticated type of self-consciousness in that it amounts to a reflective self-evaluation (1985: 67) – is brought about by the realization of how one's position is or may be seen from an observer's point of view, there is in the final self-directed judgement no reference to such a point of view. The final judgement concerns oneself only. One is degraded absolutely and not just relative to a specific observer or audience (G. Taylor 1985: 68). This latter point is important since it allows for the continuation of the feeling of shame even after a change of situation or context. And for Taylor this points to one of the important differences between shame and embarrassment. In embarrassment the focus is on the agent's appearance to others, on the impression he makes on others in a given situation. Given that the concern is always with one's own position vis-à-vis others, embarrassment is a more social emotion than shame. But this is also what, according to Taylor, makes it a less painful and shattering experience. Given that the focus is merely on how one presents oneself in a specific context vis-à-vis a given audience, the embarrassment can be alleviated by changing the situation and context, whereas shame concerns an absolute failure, an adverse judgement of the person as a whole, which is why it typically persists even after the shame-inducing situation has changed or ceased (G. Taylor 1985: 70–6).

Although Taylor in the course of her treatment can point to examples of shame where the social dimension is less perspicuous, although she can come up with counter-examples that don't easily fit Sartre's model – for instance, by referring to an artist who feels ashamed because his last work doesn't match the quality of his earlier creations (G. Taylor 1985: 58) – this doesn't in and of itself show that Sartre's account fails to capture a central type of shame. Indeed, I think one problem with Taylor's account is that she commits the same kind of mistake as Sartre, and offers us an account with too few distinctions.

Let us take the case of a person who has done something he or she believes shouldn't be done (or failed to do something he or she believes ought to be done). In such a situation, one might indeed feel ashamed afterwards. One might feel guilty about the specific deed in question, but one might also feel ashamed of simply being the kind of person who could do (or fail to do) such a thing. For a concrete and somewhat extreme example, consider a case discussed by Hutchinson. It concerns Léopard, who committed atrocities against innocent individuals during the Rwanda genocide. Several years later, Léopard is interviewed while in prison, and he recounts how he has subsequently come to feel deep shame – despite the fact that this has led to mockery and ridicule from his comrades (Hutchinson 2008: 141–3). It would be far-fetched to explain Léopard's shame as the result of his comrades' negative evaluation. But should we then conclude that we here have a form of shame that isn't socially mediated, that doesn't involve others? I don't think the answer to that question is a straightforward yes, and I will come back to that in a moment. For now, however, I just want to contrast this kind of repenting, self-reflective shame with the following examples of shame:

1   When writing your latest article, you make extensive use of passages found in an essay by a little known and recently deceased scholar. After your article has been published, you participate in a public meeting where you are suddenly accused of plagiarism. You emphatically deny it, but the accuser – your departmental nemesis – produces incontrovertible proof.

2   You are still living at your parents' place and have invited a friend home from school. When he arrives, your friend, who is black, is greeted with a racial slur by your father.

3   You are ridiculed by your peers when you show up at a high-school party in out-of-fashion clothes.

4   You apply for a position, and have told your friends that you are sure to get it, but after the job interview, you are informed by the hiring committee that you simply aren't qualified for the job.

5 You have reached old age, but you spend considerable time applying make-up and dressing nicely in order to keep up appearance. One morning, however, you receive an unexpected and unwelcome early morning call from visitors who see you before you have managed to make yourself presentable.

If we consider these examples, how plausible is it to claim that others are quite accidental to the emotion in question and that the very same experience of shame could have occurred in a private setting? I don't find such a suggestion plausible at all. Consider also the phenomenal differences. I am not denying that a failure to live up to one's own standards might be shame-inducing, but the accompanying feeling of unease, self-disappointment or even self-loathing, strikes me as quite different from the acute feeling of shame we experience when faced with others. In the latter case, there is a characteristic narrowing of focus. You cannot carefully attend to details in the environment while being subjected to that kind of shame. Rather, the world recedes and the self stands revealed. As Nietzsche puts it in *Daybreak*:

> The feeling 'I am the mid-point of the world!' arises very strongly if one is suddenly overcome with shame; one then stands there as though confused in the midst of a surging sea and feels dazzled as though by a great eye which gazes upon us and through us from all sides.
>
> (Nietzsche 1997: 166)

This exposure is accompanied by an urge to hide and disappear, to become invisible, to sink into the ground. It is hardly insignificant that shame has frequently been associated with nakedness and that the etymology of the word 'shame' can be traced back to the pre-Teutonic term for cover.[5]

In order to capture this acute experience of shame it is, however, not enough to just focus on the fact that the shamed subject is thrown back upon itself. As Seidler points out, and I think this constitutes an essential insight: 'Das Schamsubjekt ist "*ganz bei sich*" und gleichzeitig "*außer sich*"' (2001: 25–6). This, I think, is also Sartre's basic idea. In his analysis of the different ontological dimensions of the body, Sartre argues that the gaze of the other disrupts my control of the situation (B&N: 289). Rather than simply existing bodily, rather than simply being absorbed in my various projects, I become aware of my body's facticity and being-there. I become aware that my body is something on which others bear points of view. This is why Sartre speaks of my body as something that escapes me on all sides and as a perpetual 'outside' of my most intimate 'inside' (B&N: 375). To 'be embarrassed by one's own body' is, as Sartre continues, an inaccurate expression. The shy person is not embarrassed by his body as it is for himself, but as it is for the other. And when the shy person longs to be

220

invisible and disappear, it is not his body-for-himself which he wants to annihilate, but the alienating dimension of the body-for-the-other (B&N: 377).

More generally speaking, Sartre takes shame to involve an existential alienation. I would agree with this. In some cases the alienating power is a different subject, and Sartre's description of our pre-reflective feeling of shame when confronted with the gaze of the other is an example of this. In other cases, the feeling of shame occurs when we sit in judgement on ourselves. But in this case as well, there is a form of exposure and self-alienation, a kind of self-observation and self-distancing.

As should be clear from what I have said so far, I am not denying that you can feel ashamed when you are alone. And of course, Sartre would not deny it either. After all, one of his most famous illustrations of the effect of the gaze, concerns the example of the voyeur who is looking through the keyhole, and who suddenly hears steps. He shudders as a wave of shame sweeps over him, but when straightening up, and looking down the corridor, he realizes that it was a false alarm. There was nobody there (B&N: 301). Sartre's interpretation of this is not that shame is after all something I can attain on my own. Rather he argues that the feeling of shame refers me to the other-as-subject, and that the other-as-subject can be present, even when the other-as-object is absent. There are various things to be said for and against this analysis.[6] For now, I just want to emphasize that Sartre concedes that one can feel shame when alone. But as even Bernard Williams points out – who is otherwise known for having argued contra Kant that shame *can be* an autonomous emotion – to overlook the importance of the imagined other is just silly (Williams 1993: 82).[7] In most cases where the shame-experiencing subject *de facto* is physically alone and not in the presence of others, he or she will have internalized the perspective of another, he or she will have others in mind, to use Rochat's phrase (Rochat 2009). There might be an imagined interlocutor or the anticipated presence of an audience, and even in those situations where such an audience is missing, we shouldn't overlook the fact that our personal standards are reflections of societal values and that others influence the development and formation of our own norms and values. Finally even if one could argue that the kind of shame you might feel when failing to meet your own standards is not socially mediated in any direct fashion (it is not as if you only feel shameful because you fear being found out or fear losing face) the question remains whether this kind of intrapersonal shame is not always subsequent to (and perhaps even conditioned by) the interpersonal form of shame. This would be the view, not only of some developmental psychologists, but also of, say, Levinas.[8] Whatever the reply to that specific question turns out to be, however, I think the preceding discussion has shown that it is quite questionable whether the self-relation we find in shame is as self-contained and inward-directed as Gabriele Taylor and Michael Lewis claim. I would consequently dispute the claim that interpersonal shame can be reduced to or explained on the basis of intrapersonal shame.

Lewis has explicitly denied that the issue of public failure has any relevance for the emotion of shame. Rather he defines shame as an intense negative emotion that is elicited when one experiences failure relative to a standard, feels responsible for the failure, and believes that the failure reflects a damaged self (Lewis 1998: 126–7). But one problem with such a definition that focuses exclusively on an individual's own negative self-assessment is that it becomes difficult to differentiate shame from other negative self-evaluations, such as self-disappointment or self-criticism. Another problem with this highlighting of our visibility to ourselves is that it simply doesn't do justice to those undeniably social forms of shame which are induced by a deflation and devaluation of our public appearance and social self-identity, by the exposure of a discrepancy between who we claim to be and how we are perceived by others.[9]

Let me add one further comment concerning the relation between embarrassment and shame. Harré has argued that whereas shame is occasioned by the realization that others have become aware that what one has been doing has been a moral infraction, embarrassment is occasioned by the realization that others have become aware that what one has been doing has been a breach of convention and the code of manners (Harré 1990: 199). We might readily agree that embarrassment is less shattering and painful than shame, that it is more obviously related to awkward social exposure (due to an open fly button, a loud stomach noise, inappropriate clothing, etc.) than to the violation of important personal values and that it in contrast to shame, which can be long-lasting and backward looking, is context-bound, short-lived, and typically strikes quickly and by surprise. But Harré's definitions and neat distinction are clearly inadequate. Not only doesn't he distinguish between different kinds of shame, he also puts too much emphasis on an actual audience, and finally, the sharp distinction between moral infraction and breach of convention is questionable. As a case in point, consider the following vignette reported by Jacoby: A boy had been on a field trip with his class and was on a train on the way back. He got acute diarrhoea, but since the toilet was occupied, he eventually defecated in his pants; something that was noticed and ridiculed by the entire class (Jacoby 1994: 7). As Jacoby goes on to explain, this episode turned out to be a quite traumatic experience for the child, and even as a grown-up he remained deeply affected by it. It seems wrong to categorize this experience as a momentary feeling of embarrassment, but on the other hand, it doesn't seem plausible to categorize it either as a moral transgression. Although, one can be ashamed of moral infractions, one can certainly also be ashamed of things that have nothing to do with ethics. Indeed shame doesn't have to be brought about by something one wilfully does. One can feel ashamed of one's red hair, one's weight, or one's skin colour.

Thus, rather than linking shame and embarrassment to an infraction of moral values and social conventions respectively (an attempt that also flies in the face of the fact that the same event can be felt as either shameful or embarrassing by different people), a more plausible demarcation criterion is to link shame, but not embarrassment, to a decrease of self-esteem. This would also match well with a perceptive observation by Galen Strawson: whereas past embarrassments can furnish funny stories to tell about oneself, past shames and humiliations do not (Strawson 1994).

Back to self

Let me return to the question I started out with: What does the fact that we feel shame tell us about the nature of self? What kind of self is it that is affected in shame?

To answer that question, let us return to Sartre. Whereas Sartre in *The Transcendence of the Ego* characterized non-egological consciousness as *impersonal*, he went on to describe this view as mistaken in both *Being and Nothingness* and in his important 1948 article 'Consciousness of Self and Knowledge of Self'. Although no ego exists on the pre-reflective level, consciousness remains personal because consciousness is, at bottom, characterized by a fundamental self-givenness or self-referentiality which Sartre called *ipseity*:

> Thus, the Ego appears to consciousness as a transcendent in-itself, as an existent in the human world, not as *of* the nature of consciousness. Yet we need not conclude that the for-itself is a pure and simple 'impersonal' contemplation. But the Ego is far from being the personalizing pole of a consciousness which without it would remain in the impersonal stage; on the contrary, it is consciousness in its fundamental selfness [*ipséité*] which under certain conditions allows the appearance of the Ego as the transcendent phenomenon of that selfness.
>
> (B&N: 127)

When speaking of ipseity, Sartre is referring to something quite basic, something characterizing consciousness as such. It is something that distinguishes my very mode of existence and, although I can fail to articulate it, it is not something I can fail to be. As he also wrote, 'pre-reflective consciousness is self-consciousness. It is this same notion of self which must be studied, for it defines the very being of consciousness' (B&N: 100).

I have a lot of sympathy for this basic idea, and I have sought to defend a primitive experiential notion of self in a number of previous publications (Zahavi 2005, 2007, 2009). The point I wish to make now, though, is that a study of shame can demonstrate the limitations of this minimal notion of self. Shame manifests our exposure, vulnerability, and visibility and is importantly linked to such issues as concealment and disclosure, sociality and alienation, separation and interdependence, difference and connectedness. The shamed self is a more complex (and complicated) self than the experiential self. I would consequently argue that the presence of self-conscious – or, to use Reddy's recent and quite apt term, self-other-conscious (Reddy 2008: 145) – emotions such as shame illustrates the need for adopting a multidimensional account of self, i.e. an account that recognizes that the self is a multifaceted phenomenon and that various complementary accounts must be integrated if we are to do justice to its complexity.

Perhaps you are still wondering precisely what I have in mind. Maybe a reference to Mead can make matters more clear. In *Mind, Self and Society*, Mead argued that the self is not something that exists first and then enters into relationship with others, rather it is better characterized as an eddy in the social current (Mead 1962: 182), and he explicitly defined self-consciousness as a question of becoming 'an object to one's self in virtue of one's social relations to other individuals' (Mead 1962: 172). For Mead, the problem of selfhood is fundamentally the problem of how an individual can get experientially outside itself in such a way as to become an object to itself. Thus, for Mead, to be a self is ultimately more a question of becoming an object than of being a subject. In his view, one can only become an object to oneself in an indirect manner, namely by adopting the attitudes of others on oneself, and this is something that can only happen within a social environment (Mead 1962: 138).

If one compares Mead and Sartre there are of course some marked differences between the two. Whereas Mead distinguishes sharply between consciousness and self-consciousness, and even claims that prior to the rise of self-consciousness we experience our own feelings and sensations as parts of our environment rather than as our own (Mead 1962: 171), Sartre would argue that our experiential life is characterized by a primitive form of self-consciousness from the very start. Despite this important difference, however, both of them highlight the extent to which certain forms of self-experience are constitutively dependent upon others. They call attention to the dramatic way our awareness and adaptation of the other's attitude towards ourselves contribute to the constitution of self.

Much more could and should be said about shame. Indeed, what I have offered so far barely scratches the surface of this exceedingly complex and intricate emotion. Are emotions like shame, for instance, among the distinctly human emotions, in that they require language, culture, and norms to find their full expression and articulation? It is hardly insignificant that these emotions are more culture specific than the basic emotions, and that a cultural perspective is indispensable for an understanding of the full complexity of these emotions. To mention an example, Chinese is supposed to contain 113 shame-related terms, and has for instance special terms for 'losing face', 'truly losing face', 'losing face terribly', 'being ashamed to death', 'being so ashamed that even the ancestors of eight generations can feel it' (Edelstein & Shaver 2007: 200).

Time doesn't permit me to discuss these issues in any further detail. Let me end with a simple question of my own concerning the relation between language and shame. Sartre argues that a linguistic self-description inevitably entails the attempt to grasp oneself through the eyes of others (B&N: 377). As he puts it, language is not just something added on to my being-for-others, but expresses my being-for-others in an original way, because it confers a significance upon me that others have already found words for (B&N: 394–5). A question worth pursuing is to what extent full-blown (disgrace) shame necessarily presupposes language-use or whether it might exist in prelinguistic forms. This is where a closer look at the developmental literature would be appropriate; something that in any case would be also be required if one were to assess the accuracy of Lewis's claim concerning the late emergence of shame (see Draghi-Lorenz et al. 2001).

Notes

1 Lewis occasionally distinguishes two levels of subjective self-awareness, namely reflexive subjective self-awareness and representational subjective self-awareness, but these two levels differ only in terms of complexity (see Lewis 1992: 9).

2 I think it would have been much better if Lewis had spoken of non-conscious self-regulation and self-differentiation rather than of unconscious subjective self-awareness – I find it nonsensical to attribute subjective self-awareness to leucocytes – but let me not dwell on this disagreement.

3 Izard has argued that shame has two functions. It sensitizes the individual to the opinions and feelings of others and thus facilitates a degree of social conformity and social responsibility. Just think, for instance, of the teenager who carefully selects his clothing in order to avoid being shamed by his peers. To that extent it increases the permeability of the boundaries of the self. At the same time, Izard also takes shame to play a significant role in the development of self-control and autonomy (Izard 1977: 418).

4 Scheler even argues that this dimension of shame is a requirement of civilization. It is the inhibiting effect a sense of shame exercises over libido that allows us to transcend auto-eroticism and seek sexual interaction with others (1957: 111). To put it differently, shame is a condition of possibility for the erotic interest in others and therefore for the survival of the species.

5 As Sartre remarks, modesty and the fear of being surprised in a state of nakedness are only a symbolic specification of original shame; the body symbolizes our defenceless state as objects. To put on clothes is to hide one's object-state; it is to claim the right of seeing without being seen; that is, to be a pure subject (B&N: 312).

6 When Sartre advances the claims that the look is merely the concrete occasion of my original being-for-others (B&N 441), that the Other is present everywhere as that through which I become an object, and that this fundamental relation to

the Other is the condition of possibility for my particular experience of the concrete Other (which is why the concrete encounter with a particular Other is described as a mere empirical variation of my fundamental being-for-others (B&N: 303–4)), it is difficult not to reproach him for advocating the very kind of apriorism that he was criticizing in Heidegger's account of *Mitsein* (for a more extensive criticism, see: Zahavi 1996: 114–17; Hartmann 1983: 102; Theunissen 1984: 238–9). More generally speaking, although there are many insights to be found in Sartre's analysis of intersubjectivity, there is also a good deal to disagree with. This would include Sartre's excessively negative assessment and characterization of our encounter with others.

7 As Williams continues, the internalized other need not be a particular individual, or the representative of some socially identified (significant) group, rather the other may also be identified in ethical terms. He might be conceived as one whose reactions I would respect. Some might claim that if the other is identified in such terms, then he is no longer an other. But as Williams argues, this is the wrong conclusion. Although the other doesn't have to be an identifiable individual, he is still potentially somebody rather than nobody and somebody other than me (Williams 1993: 84).

8 Levinas has argued that it is the encounter with the other which conditions and makes possible the unnatural movement of reflection. Levinas sees reflection as a suspension of the natural spontaneity. It makes my thought detach from itself and join itself as if it were other to itself. But as he points out, this movement cannot arise out of nothing. It needs an impulse from without. For Levinas, this impulse comes from the ethical encounter with the other, who interrupts and disrupts my tranquillity by putting me into question (1998: 146).

9 The social dimension is, of course, also quite manifest in the intricate phenomenon of vicarious shame.

BIBLIOGRAPHY OF SARTRE'S
WORKS CITED

All quotations from Sartre's work in this volume are taken from the translations listed here except where indicated otherwise. All page citations are to the English editions, except where it is indicated that there is no English edition. Works are listed in order of original publication and preceded by the identifying acronyms used in this volume.

TE: *The Transcendence of the Ego: A Sketch for a Phenomenological Description.*
Translated by Andrew Brown. London and New York: Routledge, 2004. Translation of *La transcendance de l'ego: Esquisse d'une description phénoménologique*, Paris: Vrin, 1965. First published in *Recherches Philosophiques* 6 (1936–7): 85–123.

N: *Nausea.*
Translated by Robert Baldick. Harmondsworth: Penguin, 1965. Translation of *La nausée*, Paris: Gallimard, 1938.

IHP: Intentionality: A Fundamental Idea in Husserl's Phenomenology.
Translated by Joseph Fell. *Journal of the British Society for Phenomenology* 1, no. 2 (1970): 4–5. Translation of 'Une idée fondamentale de la phenomenology de Husserl: L'Intentionnalité', first published in *La Nouvelle Revue Française* 304 (janvier 1939): 129–31, then collected in *Situations I: Critiques littéraires*, Paris: Gallimard, 1947.

TW: *The Wall.*
Collection of short stories. Translated by Andrew Brown. London: Hesperus. First published as *Le Mur*, Paris: Gallimard, 1939. Includes previously unpublished short stories 'Erostrate' [Herostratus] and 'L'Enfance d'un chef' [The Childhood of a Leader] and the following previously published: 'Le Mur' [The Wall], *La Nouvelle Revue Française* 286 (juillet 1937): 38–62; 'La Chambre' [The Bedroom], *Mesures* 3 (15 janvier 1938): 119–49; 'Intimité' [Intimacy] *La Nouvelle Revue Française* 299 (août 1938): 187–200 and 300 (septembre 1938): 381–406.

F: Faces.
Translation by Richard McCleary. In *The Writings of Jean-Paul Sartre*, vol. 2, edited by Michel Contat and Michel Rybalka, Evanston IL: Northwestern University Press, 1974. Translation of 'Visages', *Verve* 5–6 (1939): 43–4.

STE: *Sketch for a Theory of the Emotions.*
Translated by Philip Mairet. 2nd edn. London and New York: Routledge, 2002. Translation of *Esquisse d'une théorie des emotions*, Paris: Hermann, 1939.

IPPI: *The Imaginary: A Phenomenological Psychology of the Imagination.*
Translated by Jonathan Webber. London and New York: Routledge, 2004. Translation of *L'Imaginaire: Psychologie phénoménologique de l'imagination*, revised by Arlette Elkaïm-Sartre, Paris: Gallimard, 1986. Original edition published by Gallimard in 1940.

B&N: *Being and Nothingness: An Essay in Phenomenological Ontology.*
Translated by Hazel Barnes. Rev. edn. London and New York: Routledge, 2003. Translation of *L'Être et le néant: Essai d'ontologie phénoménologique,* revised by Arlette Elkaïm-Sartre, Paris: Gallimard, 1994. Original edition published by Gallimard in 1943.

TF: The Flies.
Translated by Stuart Gilbert. In *Altona and Other Plays: Altona, Men without Shadows, The Flies,* by Jean-Paul Sartre, Harmondsworth: Penguin, 1987. Translation of *Les mouches,* Paris: Gallimard, 1943.

HC: Huis Clos.
Translated by Stuart Gilbert. In *Huis Clos and Other Plays,* by Jean-Paul Sartre, London: Penguin, 2000. Translation of *Huis clos,* Paris: Gallimard, 1944.

AR: *The Age of Reason.*
Translated by Eric Sutton, Harmondsworth: Penguin, 1986. Translation of *L'Âge de raison,* Paris: Gallimard, 1945.

TR: *The Reprieve.*
Translated by Eric Sutton, Harmondsworth: Penguin, 1986. Translation of *Le sursis,* Paris: Gallimard, 1945.

EH: *Existentialism Is a Humanism.*
Translated by Carol Macomber. New Haven CT: Yale University Press, 2007. Translation of *L'Existentialism est une humanisme,* 2nd edn, Paris: Gallimard, 1996. Original edition published by Nagel in 1946.

A&J: *Anti-Semite and Jew.*
Translated by George J. Becker, New York: Schocken Books, 1948. Translation of *Réflexions sur la question juive,* Paris: Morihien, 1946.

CM: Calder's Mobiles.
Translated by Chris Turner. In *The Aftermath of War (Situations III),* by Jean-Paul Sartre, London: Seagull Books, 2008. Translation of 'Les Mobiles de Calder', first published in a catalogue for an exhibition of Alexander Calder's mobiles in 1946, then collected in *Situations III: Lendemains de guerre,* Paris: Gallimard, 1949.

CSKS: Consciousness of Self and Knowledge of Self.
Translated by Mary Ellen and Nathaniel Lawrence. In *Readings in Existential Phenomenology,* edited by N. Lawrence and D. O'Connor (Englewood Cliffs NJ: Prentice-Hall, 1967). Translation of 'Conscience de soi et connaissance de soi', *Bulletin de la Société Française de Philosophie* 42, no. 3 (1948): 49–91.

BO: Black Orpheus.
Translated by S. W. Allen. Paris: Présence Africaine, 1976. Translation of 'Orphée Noir', Préface to *Anthologie de la nouvelle poésie nègre et malgache de langue française,* edited by Léopold Sédar Senghor, Presses Universitaires de France: 1948.

IS: *Iron in the Soul.*
Translated by Eric Sutton, Harmondsworth: Penguin, 1986. Translation of *Le mort dans l'âme,* Paris: Gallimard, 1949.

CDR1: *Critique of Dialectical Reason,* vol. 1: *Theory of Practical Ensembles.*
Translated by Alan Sheridan-Smith. Edited by Jonathan Rée. London: Verso, 1982. Translation of *Critique de la raison dialectique: Précédé de questions de méthode,* Paris: Gallimard, 1960.

UP: The Unprivileged Painter.
Translated by Chris Turner. In *Portraits (Situations IV),* by Jean-Paul Sartre, London: Seagull Books, 2009. Translation of 'Le peintre sans privilèges', first published in a catalogue for an exhibition of paintings by Robert Lapoujade in 1961, then collected in *Situations IV: Portraits,* Paris: Gallimard, 1964.

WE: The Wretched of the Earth.
Translated by Azzedine Haddour, Steve Brewer, and Terry McWilliams. In *Colonialism and Neocolonialism (Situations V)*, by Jean-Paul Sartre, London: Routledge, 2001. Originally published as the Préface to *Les damnés de la terre*, by Frantz Fanon, Paris: Maspéro, 1961.

W: *Words.*
Translated by Irene Clephane. Harmondsworth: Penguin, 1967. Translation of *Les mots*, Paris: Gallimard, 1964. First published in two parts in *Les Temps Modernes* 209 (octobre 1963): 577–649 and 210 (novembre 1963): 769–834.

E&L: L'Ecrivain et sa langue.
An interview with Pierre Verstraeten. In *Situations IX: Mélanges*, by Jean-Paul Sartre, Paris: Gallimard, 1972. First published in *Revue d'Esthétique* 18 (juillet –décembre 1965): 306–34. (As yet unavailable in English.)

FI: *The Family Idiot: Gustave Flaubert, 1821–1857.*
Translated by Carol Cosman. 5 vols. Chicago and London: University of Chicago Press, 1981–93. Translation of *L'Idiot de la famille: Gustave Flaubert de 1821 à 1857*, 3 vols, Paris: Gallimard: 1971–2.

IRPG: An Interview with Jean-Paul Sartre.
Interview by Michel Rybalka, Orestes Pucciani, and Susan Gruenheck (Paris, 12 and 19 May 1975). Translated by Susan Gruenheck. In *The Philosophy of Jean-Paul Sartre*, edited by Paul Arthur Schilpp, Library of Living Philosophers, La Salle IL: Open Court, 1981.

WD: *War Diaries: Notebooks from a Phoney War 1939–40.*
Translated by Quintin Hoare. London: Verso, 1984. Translation of *Les carnets de la drôle de guerre: Novembre 1939 – mars 1940*, Paris: Gallimard, 1983. A new edition has since been published in French, edited by Arlette Elkaïm-Sartre, which includes the previously unpublished Notebook 1 (Paris: Gallimard, 1995).

NE: *Notebooks for an Ethics.*
Translated by David Pellauer. Chicago: University of Chicago Press, 1992. Translation of *Cahiers pour une morale*, Paris: Gallimard, 1983.

BIBLIOGRAPHY OF OTHER
WORKS CITED

Alain [Emile-Auguste Chartier]. 1974. *The Gods*. New York: New Directions.

Anderson, Thomas C. 1993. *Sartre's Two Ethics: From Authenticity to Integral Humanity*. Chicago: Open Court.

Aristotle. 1984. *The Complete Works of Aristotle*. Edited by Jonathan Barnes. Princeton: Princeton University Press.

Armstrong, David M. 1968. *A Materialist Theory of Mind*. London: Routledge & Kegan Paul.

Ayer, A. J. 1954. Freedom and Necessity. In Philosophical Essays, by A. J. Ayer. New York: St. Martin's Press.

Bales, Eugene R. 1971. Act Utilitarianism: Account of Right-making Characteristics or Decision-making Procedures? *American Philosophical Quarterly* 8: 257–65.

Bar-On, Dorit. 2004. *Speaking My Mind*. Oxford: Oxford University Press.

Barthes, Roland. 1972. *Mythologies*. Edited and translated by Annette Lavers. London: Paladin.

Beauvoir, Simone de. 1962. *The Prime of Life*. Translated by Peter Green. London: Penguin.

——1976. *The Ethics of Ambiguity*. Translated by Bernard Frechtman. New York: Citadel Press.

——2004a. Pyrrhus and Cineas. In *Philosophical Writings*, by Simone de Beauvoir, edited by Margaret A. Simons with Marybeth Timmermann and Mary Beth Mader. Urbana and Chicago: University of Illinois Press.

——2004b. A Review of *The Phenomenology of Perception* by Maurice Merleau-Ponty. In *Philosophical Writings*, by Simone de Beauvoir, edited by Margaret A. Simons with Marybeth Timmermann and Mary Beth Mader. Urbana and Chicago: University of Illinois Press.

——2004c. Introduction to an Ethics of Ambiguity. *Philosophical Writings*, by Simone de Beauvoir, edited by Margaret A. Simons with Marybeth Timmermann and Mary Beth Mader. Urbana and Chicago: University of Illinois Press.

——2009. *The Second Sex*. Translated by Constance Borde and Sheila Malovany-Chevallier, London: Jonathan Cape.

Bergmann, Frithjoff. 1982. Sartre on the Nature of Consciousness. *American Philosophical Quarterly* 19: 153–61.

Bergson, Henri. 1910. *Time and Free Will: An Essay on the Immediate Data of Consciousness*. Translated by Frank Lubecki Pogson. London: George Allen & Unwin.

——1911. *Laughter: An Essay on the Meaning of the Comic*. Translated by Cloudesley Brereton and Fred Rothwell. London: Macmillan & Co.

——1977. *The Two Sources of Morality and Religion*. Translated by R. Ashley Audra and Cloudesley Brereton. Notre Dame: University of Notre Dame Press.

Bernasconi, Robert. 2006. *How to Read Sartre*. London: Granta.

Biggs, Victoria. 2005. *Caged in Chaos: A Dyspraxic Guide to Breaking Free*. London and Philadelphia: Jessica Kingsley Publishers.

Billington, Michael. 2007. Review of Kean at the Apollo Theatre, London. *Guardian*, 31 May.

Biro, John. 1991. Consciousness and Subjectivity. In *Consciousness: Philosophical Issues*, edited by Enrique Villanueva. Atascadero: Ridgeview Publishing.

——1993. Consciousness and Objectivity. In *Consciousness: Psychological and Philosophical Essays*, edited by Martin Davies and Glynn Humphreys. Oxford: Blackwell.

——2006. A Point of View on Points of View. *Philosophical Psychology* 19: 3–12.

Breslin, James. 1998. *Mark Rothko: A Biography*. Chicago: University of Chicago Press.

Bürger, Peter. 2007. *Sartre: Eine Philosophie des Als-ob*. Frankfurt: Suhrkamp.

Busch, Thomas. 1990. *The Power of Conscious and the Force of Circumstance in Sartre's Philosophy*. Bloomington: Indiana University Press.

Butchvarov, Panayot. 1979. *Being qua Being: A Theory of Identity, Existence, and Predication*. Bloomington: Indiana University Press.

——1998. *Skepticism about the External World*, Oxford: Oxford University Press.

Byrne, Alex. 2005. Introspection. *Philosophical Topics* 33: 79–104.

——2010. Knowing That I Am Thinking. In *Self-knowledge*, edited by Anthony Hatzimoysis. Oxford: Oxford University Press.

Campbell, Gerard. 1977. Sartre's Absolute Freedom. *Laval Théologique et Philosophique* 35: 61–91.

Caro, Mario De. 2004. Is Free Will a Mystery? In *Naturalism in Question*, edited by David Macarthur and Mario De Caro. Boston: Harvard University Press.

Castañeda, Hector-Neri. 1979. Philosophical Method and Direct Awareness of the Self. *Grazer Philosophische Studien* 7/8: 1–58.

Chaitin, Gregory. 1975. Randomness and Mathematical Proof. *Scientific American* 232, no. 5: 47–52.

——2001. *Exploring Randomness*. London: Springer-Verlag.

Chalmers, David. 2003. Consciousness and Its Place in Nature. In *The Blackwell Guide to Philosophy of Mind*, edited by Stephen Stich and Ted Warfield. Oxford: Blackwell, pp. 102–42.

Chappell, Timothy. 2007. Integrity and Demandingness. *Ethical Theory and Moral Practice* 10: 255–65.

Charmé, Stuart Z. 1991. *Vulgarity and Authenticity: Dimensions of Otherness in the World of Jean-Paul Sartre*. Amherst: University of Massachusetts Press.

Chisholm, Roderick. 1969. On the Observability of the Self. *Philosophy and Phenomenological Research* 30: 7–21.

Clarke, Laura Hurd and Meredith Griffin. 2008. Visible and Invisible Ageing: Beauty Work as a Response to Ageism. *Ageing and Society* 28: 653–74.

Clearwater, Bonnie. 2007. *The Rothko Book*. London: Tate Publishing.

Contat, Michel and Michel Rybalka. 1974. *The Writings of Jean-Paul Sartre*. Vol. 1: A Bibliographical Life. Translated by Richard McCleary. Evanston IL: Northwestern University Press.

Coorebyter, Vincent de. 2000. *Sartre face à la phénoménologie*. Brussels: Ousia.

——2003. Introduction et notes. In *La transcendance de l'ego et autres textes phénoménologiques*, by Jean-Paul Sartre, introduits et annotés par Vincent de Coorebyter. Paris: Vrin.

Cox, Gary. 2006. *Sartre: A Guide for the Perplexed*. London: Continuum.

Currie, Gregory and Ian Ravenscroft. 2002. *Recreative Minds*. Oxford: Oxford University Press.

Daigle, Christine. 2005. *Le nihilisme est-il un humanisme? Étude sur Nietzsche et Sartre*. Sainte-Foy, Canada: Presses de l'Université Laval.

——2007. A Sartrean Phenomenological Ethics. In *Phenomenology 2005*. Vol. 4: *Selected Essays from North America*, edited by Lester Embree and Thomas Nenon. Bucharest: Zeta Books.

Dainton, Barry. 2000. *Stream of Consciousness: Unity and Continuity in Conscious Experience*. London: Routledge.

Damasio, Antonio R. 1999. *The Feeling of What Happens: Body and Emotion in the Making of Consciousness*. New York: Harcourt Brace & Co.

Darwin, Charles. 1965. *The Expression of the Emotions in Man and Animals*. Chicago: University of Chicago Press.

Davis, Kathy. 1995. *Reshaping the Female Body: The Dilemma of Cosmetic Surgery*. London and New York: Routledge.

Dennett, Daniel C. 1991. Real Patterns. *Journal of Philosophy* 88: 27–51.

Detmer, David. 1986. *Freedom as a Value*. La Salle IL: Open Court.

——2008. *Sartre Explained*. Peru IL: Open Court.

Doeuff, Michèle Le. 1991. *Hipparchia's Choice: An Essay Concerning Women, Philosophy, Etc.* Translated by Trista Selous. Oxford: Blackwell.

Draghi-Lorenz, Riccardo, Vasudevi Reddy, and Alan Costall. 2001. Rethinking the Development of 'Nonbasic' Emotions: A Critical Review of Existing Theories. *Developmental Review* 21: 263–304.

Drew, Sharon. 2005. *Developmental Co-ordination Disorder in Adults*. Chichester: John Wiley & Sons.

Edelstein, Robin S. and Phillip R. Shaver. 2007. A Cross-cultural Examination of Lexical Studies of Self-conscious Emotions. In *The Self-conscious Emotions: Theory and Research*, edited by J. L. Tracy, R. W. Robins, and J. P. Tangney. New York: Guilford Press.

Elkins, James. 2001. *Pictures and Tears: A History of People Who Have Cried In Front of Paintings*. New York: Routledge.

Eshleman, Matthew. 2008a. The Misplaced Chapter on Bad Faith, or Reading *Being and Nothingness* in Reverse. *Sartre Studies International* 14: 1–22.

——2008b. Bad Faith Is Necessarily Social. *Sartre Studies International* 14: 40–7.

Evans, Gareth. 1982. *The Varieties of Reference*. Oxford: Oxford University Press.

Fanon, Frantz. 1986. *Black Skin, White Masks*. Translated by Charles Lam Markmann. London: Pluto.

Fischer, John, Robert Kane, Derk Pereboom, and Manuel Vargas. 2007. *Four Views of Free Will*. Oxford: Blackwell.

Føllesdal, Dagfinn. 1981. Sartre on Freedom. In *The Philosophy of Jean-Paul Sartre*, edited by Paul Arthur Schilpp. La Salle IL: Open Court.

Fox, Nik Farrell. 2003. *The New Sartre: Explorations in Postmodernism*. London: Continuum.

Fraassen, Bas van. 2004. Transcendence of the Ego: The Non-existent Knight. *Ratio* 17: 453–77.

Freud, Sigmund. 1913. *Totem and Taboo*. Reprinted in *The Standard Edition of the Complete Psychological Works of Sigmund Freud*, vol. 13. London: Hogarth Press.

Fuchs, Thomas. 2003. The Phenomenology of Shame, Guilt and the Body in Body Dysmorphic Disorder and Depression. *Journal of Phenomenological Psychology* 33: 223–43.

Gagné, Patricia and Deanna McGaughey. 2002. Designing Women: Cultural Hegemony and the Exercise of Power among Women Who Have Undergone Elective Mammoplasty. *Gender and Society* 616: 814–38.

Gallagher, Shaun and Dan Zahavi. 2008. *The Phenomenological Mind: An Introduction to Philosophy of Mind and Cognitive Science*. London: Routledge.

Gallup, Gordon G. 1982. Self-awareness and the Emergence of Mind in Primates. *American Journal of Primatology* 23: 237–48.

——1985. Do Minds Exist in Species Other Than Our Own? *Neuroscience and Biobehavioral Reviews* 94: 631–41.

Gardiner, Patrick. 1977. Sartre on Character and Self-knowledge. *New Literary History* 9: 65–82.

Gardner, Sebastian. 2005. Sartre, Intersubjectivity, and German Idealism. *Journal of the History of Philosophy* 42: 325–51.

——2006. Sartre, Schelling, and Onto-theology. *Religious Studies* 42: 247–71.

——2009. *Sartre's Being and Nothingness*. London: Continuum.

Gertler, Brie. 2001. Introspecting Phenomenal States. *Philosophy and Phenomenological Research* 63: 305–28.

——2010. Self-knowledge and the Transparency of Belief. In *Self-knowledge*, edited by Anthony Hatzimoysis. Oxford: Oxford University Press.

Gilman, Sander L. 1999. *Making the Body Beautiful: A Cultural History of Aesthetic Surgery*. Princeton: Princeton University Press.

——2004. *Fat Boys: A Slim Book*. Lincoln and London: University of Nebraska Press.

Goldman, Alvin. 1993. The Psychology of Folk Psychology. *Behavioral and Brain Sciences* 16: 15–28.

Goodman, Nelson. 1976. *Languages of Art*. Indianapolis: Hackett Publishing Co.

——1978. *Ways of Worldmaking*. Indianapolis: Hackett Publishing Co.

Gordon, Lewis R. 1995. *Bad Faith and Antiblack Racism*. Atlantic Highlands NJ: Humanities Press.

Gothlin, Eva. 2002. Lire Simone de Beauvoir à la lumière de Heidegger. *Les Temps Modernes* 619 (juin–juillet): 53–77.

Groot, A. D. de. 1965. *Thought and Choice in Chess*. The Hague: Mouton & Co.

Gurwitsch, Aron. 1941. A Non-Egological Conception of Consciousness. *Philosophy and Phenomenological Research* 1: 325–38.

Haddour, Azzedine. 2006. Fanon dans la théorie postcoloniale. *Les Temps Modernes* 635–6 (novembre 2005–janvier 2006): 136–58.

Haji, Ishtiyaque. 2005. Libertarianism, Luck, and Action Explanation. *Journal of Philosophical Research* 30: 321–40.

Hampshire, Stuart. 1975. *Freedom of the Individual*. Princeton: Princeton University Press.

Harcourt, Edward. 1998. Integrity, Practical Deliberation and Utilitarianism. *Philosophical Quarterly* 48: 189–98.

Harman, Gilbert. 2009. Skepticism about Character Traits. *Journal of Ethics* 13: 235–42.

Harré, Rom. 1990. Embarrassment: A Conceptual Analysis. In *Shyness and Embarrassment: Perspectives from Social Psychology*, edited by W. Ray Crozier. Cambridge: Cambridge University Press, pp. 181–204.

Hartmann, Klaus. 1983. *Die Philosophie J.-P. Sartres*. Berlin: De Gruyter.

Hatzimoysis, Anthony. 2010. Introduction. In *Self-knowledge*, edited by Anthony Hatzimoysis. Oxford: Oxford University Press.

Heidegger, Martin. 1962. *Being and Time*. Translated by John Macquarrie and Edward Robinson. Oxford: Blackwell.

Heter, T. Storm. 2006. Authenticity and Others: Sartre's Ethics of Recognition. *Sartre Studies International* 12: 17–43.

Hollier, Denis. 1999. Mosaic: Terminable and Interminable. *October* 87: 139–60.

Holton, Richard. 2002. Particularism and Moral Theory: Principles and Particularisms. *Aristotelian Society Supplementary Volume* 76: 191–209.

——2009. Determinism, Self-efficacy, and the Phenomenology of Free Will. *Inquiry* 52: 412–28.

Hopkins, Robert. 1998. *Picture, Image and Experience*. Cambridge: Cambridge University Press.

——2006. With Sight Too Much in Mind, Mind Too Little in Sight? *Philosophical Books* 47: 293–305.

Horstmann, Rolf-Peter. Forthcoming. Fichte's Anti-sceptical Programme: On the Anti-sceptical Strategies in Fichte's Presentations of the Doctrine of Science 1794 to 1801/2. In *The Transcendental Turn*, edited by Mark Sacks, Sebastian Gardner, and Matthew Grist.

Hurka, Thomas. 2001. *Virtue, Vice and Value*. Oxford: Oxford University Press.

Husserl, Edmund. 1950. *Cartesian Meditations*. Translated by Dorion Cairns. Dordrecht: Kluwer Academic Publishers.

——1970. *Logical Investigations*. Translated by J. N. Findlay. London: Routledge.

——1982. *Ideas Pertaining to a Pure Phenomenology and to a Phenomenological Philosophy: First Book*. Translated by F. Kersten. Dordrecht: Kluwer Academic Publishers.

——1989. *Ideas Pertaining to a Pure Phenomenology and to a Phenomenological Philosophy: Second Book*. Translated by Richard Rojcewicz and André Schuwer. Dordrecht: Kluwer Academic Publishers.

——1991. *On the Phenomenology of the Consciousness of Internal Time (1893–1917)*. Translated by John Brough. Dordrecht: Kluwer Academic Publishers.

Hutchinson, Phil. 2008. *Shame and Philosophy: An Investigation in the Philosophy of Emotions and Ethics*. Basingstoke: Palgrave Macmillan.

233

Inwagen, Peter van. 1983. *An Essay on Free Will*. Oxford: Clarendon Press.

———2002. Free Will Remains a Mystery. In *Oxford Handbook of Free Will*, edited by Robert Kane. Oxford: Oxford University Press.

Izard, Carroll E. 1977. *Human Emotions*. New York: Plenum Press.

Jacoby, Mario. 1994. *Shame and the Origins of Self-esteem: A Jungian Approach*. London: Routledge.

Jacquette, Dale. 2006. Intention, Meaning, and Substance in the Phenomenology of Abstract Painting. *British Journal of Aesthetics* 46: 38–58.

Jewell, Edward A. 1936. Art review. *New York Times*, 20 December.

Kaelin, Eugene. 1982. *An Existential Aesthetic: The Theories of Sartre and Merleau-Ponty*. Madison: University of Wisconsin Press.

Kandinsky, Wassily. 1977. *Concerning the Spiritual in Art*. Translated by M. T. H. Sadler New York: Dover Publications.

Kane, Robert. 1999. *The Significance of Free Will*. Oxford: Oxford University Press.

———2007. Libertarianism. In *Four Views of Free Will*, edited by John Fischer, Robert Kane, Derk Pereboom, and Manuel Vargas. Oxford: Blackwell.

Kaw, Eugenia. 2003. Medicalization of Racial Features: Asian American Women and Cosmetic Surgery. In *The Politics of Women's Bodies*, edited by Rose Weitz. Oxford: Oxford University Press.

Kidd, Chad. 2009. The Irresistible Itch: Review of *Personal Responsibility: Why It Matters*. A. Brown. 2009. *London Review of Books* 31, no. 23: 9–10.

Kriegel, Uriah. 2009. *Subjective Consciousness: A Self-representational Theory*. Oxford: Oxford University Press.

Kritzman, Laurence D. 1995. Critical Reflections: Self-portraiture and the Presentation of Jewish Identity in French. In *Auschwitz and After: Race, Culture and the Jewish Question in France*, by Laurence D. Kritzman. London: Routledge.

Kruks, Sonia. 1991. Simone de Beauvoir: Teaching Sartre about Freedom. In *Sartre Alive*, edited by Ronald Aronson and Adrian van den Hoven. Detroit: Wayne State University Press.

———1995. Simone de Beauvoir: Teaching Sartre about Freedom. In *Rereading the Canon: Feminist Interpretations of Simone de Beauvoir*, edited by Margaret Simons. University Park, PA: The Pennsylvania State University Press, pp. 79–95.

Levinas, Emmanuel. 1998. *Of God Who Comes to Mind*. Stanford: Stanford University Press.

Lewis, Michael. 1992. *Shame: The Exposed Self*. New York: The Free Press.

———1998. Shame and Stigma. In *Shame: Interpersonal Behavior, Psychopathology, and Culture*, edited by Paul Gilbert and Bernice Andrews. New York: Oxford University Press.

———2000. The Emergence of Human Emotions. In *Handbook of Emotions*, 2nd edn, edited by Michael Lewis and Jeannette M. Haviland-Jones. New York: Guilford Press.

———2003. The Development of Self-consciousness. In *Agency and Self-awareness*, edited by Johannes Roessler and Naomi Eilan. Oxford: Oxford University Press.

———2007. Self-conscious Emotional Development. In *The Self-consciousness of Emotions: Theory and Research*, edited by Jessica L. Tracy, Richard W. Robins, and June Price Tangney. New York: Guilford Press.

Lloyd, Dan E. 2004. *Radiant Cool: A Novel Theory of Consciousness*. Cambridge MA: MIT Press.

Locke, John. 2008. *An Essay Concerning Human Understanding*. Edited by Pauline Phemister. Oxford: Oxford University Press.

Longuenesse, Béatrice. 2008. Self-consciousness and Self-reference: Sartre and Wittgenstein. *European Journal of Philosophy* 16: 1–21.

Lundgren-Gothlin, Eva. 1994. Simone de Beauvoir and Ethics. *History of European Ideas* 19: 899–903.

Lyon, William. 1986. *The Disappearance of Introspection*. Cambridge MA: MIT Press.

Magee, Bryan. 1988. *The Great Philosophers: An Introduction to Western Philosophy*. Oxford: Oxford University Press.

Manser, Anthony. 1987. A New Look at Bad Faith. In *Sartre: An Investigation of Some Major Themes*, edited by Simon Glynn. Aldershot: Avebury Press.

Marcuse, Herbert. 1983. *From Luther to Popper*. Translated by Joris de Bres. London: Verso.

Martin, Thomas. 1999. Sartre, Sadism, and Female Beauty Ideals. In *Feminist Interpretations of Jean-Paul Sartre*, edited by Julien S. Murphy. University Park: Pennsylvania State University Press.

Mazis, Glen A. 1983. A New Approach to Sartre's Theory of Emotions. *Philosophy Today* (Fall): 183–99.

McCulloch, Gregory. 1994. *Using Sartre: An Analytical Introduction to Early Sartrean Themes*. London: Routledge.

McDowell, John. 1979. Virtue and Reason. *Monist* 62: 331–50.

——1984. Wittgenstein on Following a Rule. *Synthese* 58: 325–63.

McGill, V. J. 1949. Sartre's Doctrine of Freedom. *Revue Internationale de Philosophie* 3: 329–42.

McGinn, Colin. 2002. *The Making of a Philosopher: My Journey through Twentieth-century Philosophy*. New York: HarperCollins.

Mead, George H. 1962. *Mind, Self and Society: From the Standpoint of a Social Behaviorist*. Chicago: University of Chicago Press.

Mellor, D. H. 1978. Conscious Belief. *Proceedings of the Aristotelian Society* 78: 87–101.

Memmi, Albert. 1962. *Portrait of a Jew*. New York: Orion.

Merleau-Ponty, Maurice. 1962. *The Phenomenology of Perception*. Translated by Colin Smith. London: Routledge.

——1964. *The Visible and the Invisible*. Translated by Alfonso Lingis. Evanston IL: Northwestern University Press.

Mill, John Stuart. 1961. *Auguste Comte and Positivism*. Ann Arbor: University of Michigan Press.

Moi, Toril. 1994. *Simone de Beauvoir: The Making of an Intellectual Woman*. Oxford: Blackwell.

Moran, Richard. 2001. *Authority and Estrangement: An Essay on Self-knowledge*. Princeton: Princeton University Press.

Morris, Katherine. J. 2003. The Phenomenology of Body Dysmorphic Disorder. In *Nature and Narrative: An Introduction to the New Philosophy of Psychiatry*, edited by Bill Fulford, Katherine Morris, John Sadler, and Giovanni Stanghellini. Oxford: Oxford University Press.

——2008. *Sartre*. Oxford: Blackwell.

——2010. The Phenomenology of Clumsiness. In *Sartre on the Body*, edited by Katherine J. Morris. London: Palgrave Macmillan.

Morris, Phyllis. S. 1976. *Sartre's Concept of a Person*. Amherst: University of Massachusetts Press.

——1999. Sartre on Objectification: A Feminist Perspective. In *Feminist Interpretations of Jean-Paul Sartre*, edited by Julien S. Murphy. University Park: Pennsylvania State University Press.

Morriston, Wesley. 1977. Freedom, Determinism, and Chance in the Early Philosophy of Sartre. *Personalist* 58: 236–48.

Morton, Adam. 1996. Folk Psychology Is Not a Predictive Device. *Mind* 105: 119–37.

Nagel, Thomas. 1974. What Is It Like To Be A Bat? *Philosophical Review* 83: 435–50.

Nahmias, Eddy, Steven Morris, Thomas Nadelhoffer, and Jason Turner. 2004. The Phenomenology of Free Will. *The Journal of Consciousness Studies* 11: 162–79.

Neta, Ram. 2010. The Nature and Reach of Privileged Access. In *Self-knowledge*, edited by Anthony Hatzimoysis. Oxford: Oxford University Press.

Nietzsche, Friedrich. 1974. *The Gay Science, with a Prelude in Rhymes and an Appendix of Songs*. Translated by Walter Kaufmann. New York: Vintage Books.

——1997. *Daybreak: Thoughts on the Prejudices of Morality*. Translated by R. J. Hollingdale. Cambridge: Cambridge University Press.

Owens, David. 2010. Deliberation and the First Person. In *Self-knowledge*, edited by Anthony Hatzimoysis. Oxford: Oxford University Press.

Peacocke, Christopher. 1985. Imagination, Experience and Possibility: A Berkeleian View Defended. In *Essays on Berkeley*, edited by John Foster and Howard Robinson. Oxford: Oxford University Press.

——1998. Conscious Attitudes, Attention and Self-knowledge. In *Knowing Our Own Minds*, edited by Crispin Wright, Barry Smith, and Cynthia Macdonald. Oxford: Oxford University Press.

Perec, Georges. 1990. A Man Asleep. Translated by Andrew Leak. In *Things: A Story of the Sixties and A Man Asleep*. London: Harvill.

Perna, Maria Antonietta. 2003. Bad Faith and Self-deception: Reconstructing the Sartrean Perspective. *Journal of the British Society for Phenomenology* 34: 22–44.

Pfänder, Alexander. 1967. *The Phenomenology of Willing and Motivation*. Evanston IL: Northwestern University Press.

Phillips, D. Z. 1981. Bad Faith and Sartre's Waiter. *Philosophy* 56: 23–31.

Phillips, Katharine. 1986. *The Broken Mirror: Understanding and Treating Body Dysmorphic Disorder*. Oxford: Oxford University Press.

Plato. 1961. *The Collected Dialogues of Plato*. Princeton: Princeton University Press.

Portwood, Madeleine. 1996. *Developmental Dyspraxia: A Practical Manual for Parents and Professionals*. Durham: Durham County Council.

Priest, Stephen. 2000. *The Subject in Question: Sartre's Critique of Husserl in The Transcendence of the Ego*. London: Routledge.

Reddy, Vasudevi. 2008. *How Infants Know Minds*. Cambridge MA: Harvard University Press.

Renaut, Alain. 1993. *Sartre, le dernier philosophe*. Paris: Grasset.

Richmond, Sarah. 2007. Sartre and Bergson: A Disagreement about Nothingness. *International Journal of Philosophical Studies* 15: 77–95.

Robinson, William. 2005. Thoughts without Distinctive Non-imagistic Phenomenology. *Philosophy and Phenomenological Research* 70: 534–62.

Rochat, Philippe. 2009. *Others in Mind: Social Origins of Self-consciousness*. Cambridge: Cambridge University Press.

Rosenberg, Jay. 1981. Apperception and Sartre's Pre-reflective Cogito. *American Philosophical Quarterly* 18: 255–60.

Rosenblum, Robert. 1975. *Modern Painting and the Northern Romantic Tradition: Friedrich to Rothko*. San Francisco: Harper & Row.

Rothko, Mark. 2004. *The Artist's Reality: Philosophies of Art*. New Haven CT: Yale University Press.

Rothko, Mark and Miguel López-Remiro. 2006. *Writings on Art*. New Haven CT: Yale University Press.

Russell, Bertrand. 1912. *The Problems of Philosophy*. Oxford: Oxford University Press.

——1921. *The Analysis of Mind*. New York: Humanities Press.

Sacks, Mark. 2000. *Objectivity and Insight*. Oxford: Clarendon Press.

——2005a. Sartre, Strawson and Others. *Inquiry* 48: 275–99.

——2005b. The Nature of Transcendental Arguments. *International Journal of Philosophical Studies* 13: 439–60.

——2005c. Kant's First Analogy and the Refutation of Idealism. *Proceedings of the Aristotelian Society* 106: 113–30.

Santoni, Ronald. 1995. *Bad Faith, Good Faith, and Authenticity in Sartre's Early Philosophy*. Philadelphia: Temple University.

——2008. Is Bad Faith Necessarily Social? *Sartre Studies International* 14: 23–39.

Scheler, Max. 1957. *Schriften aus dem Nachlass*. Vol. 1: *Zur Ethik und Erkenntnislehre*. Bern and Munich: Francke Verlag.

Schelling, Friedrich Wilhelm Joseph von. 2001. *Ages of the World*. Translated by Judith Norman. Ann Arbor: University of Michigan Press.

Schneider, Carl D. 1987. A Mature Sense of Shame. In *The Many Faces of Shame*, edited by Donald L. Nathanson. New York: Guilford Press.

Seidler, Gunther. 2001. *Der Blick des Anderen: Eine Analyse der Scham*. Stuttgart: Klett-Cotta.

Shoemaker, Sydney. 1994. Self-knowledge and 'Inner Sense'. Lecture II: The Broad Perceptual Model. *Philosophy and Phenomenological Research* 54: 271–90.

Sibley, Frank. 1959. Aesthetic Concepts. *Philosophical Review* 68: 421–50.

Spinoza, Benedictus de. 1985. *The Collected Works of Spinoza*. Vol. 1. Translated and edited by Edwin Curley. Princeton: Princeton University Press.

Strawson, Galen. 1994. Don't Tread on Me. *London Review of Books* 16, no. 19: 11–12.

——1995. Libertarianism, Action, and Self-determination. In *Agents, Causes, and Events: Essays on Indeterminism and Free Will*, edited by T. O'Connor. New York: Oxford University Press.

Stroud, Barry. 1968. Transcendental Arguments. *Journal of Philosophy* 65, no. 9: 241–56.

Suleiman, Susan. 1995. The Jew in Sartre's *Réflexions sur la question juive*: An Exercise in Historical Reading. In *The Jew in the Text*, edited by Linda Nochlin and Tamar Garb. London: Thames & Hudson.

——1999. Rereading Rereading: Further Reflection on Sartre's 'Réflexions'. *October* 87: 129–38.

Taylor, Gabriele. 1985. *Pride, Shame, and Guilt: Emotions of Self-assessment*. Oxford: Clarendon Press.

Taylor, Paul. 1981. Imagination and Information. *Philosophy and Phenomenological Research* 42: 205–23.

Theunissen, Michael. 1984. *The Other: Studies in the Social Ontology of Husserl, Heidegger, Sartre and Buber*. Translated by Christopher Macann. Cambridge MA: MIT Press.

Thomas, Alan. 2005. Reasonable Partiality and the Agent's Personal Point of View. *Ethical Theory and Moral Practice* 8: 25–43.

——2006a. Reconciling the Transparency of Consciousness with the Ubiquity of Self-Awareness. Presented to the conference: Association for the Scientific Study of Consciousness – 10. Oxford, 23–6 June.

——2006b. *Value and Context: the Nature of Moral and Political Knowledge*. Oxford: Oxford University Press.

——2008. The Genealogy of Epistemic Virtue Concepts. *Philosophical Papers* 37: 345–69.

——2009. Consequentialism, Integrity and Demandingness. In *The Problem of Moral Demandingess: New Philosophical Essays*, edited by Timothy Chappell. Basingstoke: Palgrave Macmillan.

——Forthcoming. Another Particularism: Reason, Status and Defaults. *Ethical Theory and Moral Practice*.

Tononi, Giulio and C. Koch. 2008. The Neural Correlates of Consciousness: An Update. *Annals of the New York Academy of Sciences* 1124: 239–61.

Walton, Kendall. 1978. Fearing Fictions. *Journal of Philosophy* 75: 5–27.

——1990. *Mimesis as Make-Believe*. Cambridge MA: Harvard University Press.

Walzer, Michael. 1995. Preface. In *Anti-Semite and Jew*, by Jean-Paul Sartre, translated by George J. Becker, new edn. New York: Schocken Books.

Wang, Stephen. 2006. Reason and the Limits of Existential Freedom: Why Sartre Is Not a Voluntarist. *Philosophy Today* (Fall): 338–48.

Webber, Jonathan. 2009. *The Existentialism of Jean-Paul Sartre*. New York: Routledge.

Wider, Kathleen. 1997. *The Bodily Nature of Consciousness: Sartre and Contemporary Philosophy of Mind*. Ithaca NY: Cornell University Press.

Williams, Bernard. 1985. *Ethics and the Limits of Philosophy*. London: Fontana.

——1993. *Shame and Necessity*. Berkeley: University of California Press.

——2004. *Truth and Truthfulness: An Essay in Genealogy*. Princeton: Princeton University Press.

Wollheim, Richard. 1973. Imagination and Identification. In *On Art and the Mind: Essays and Lectures*, by Richard Wollheim. London: Allen Lane.

——1984. *The Thread of Life* Cambridge: Cambridge University Press.

——1987. *Painting as an Art*. Cambridge MA: Harvard University Press.

——1999. *On the Emotions*. New Haven CT: Yale University Press.

Zahavi, Dan. 1996. *Husserl und die transzendentale Intersubjektivität: Eine Antwort auf die sprachpragmatische Kritik*. Dordrecht: Kluwer Academic Publishers.

——1999. *Self-awareness and Alterity: A Phenomenological Investigation*. Evanston IL: Northwestern University Press.

——2002. Intersubjectivity in Sartre's *Being and Nothingness*. *Alter* 10: 265–81.

——2005. *Subjectivity and Selfhood: Investigating the First-Person Perspective*. Cambridge MA: The MIT Press.

——2007. Self and Other: The Limits of Narrative Understanding. In *Narrative and Understanding Persons*, edited by Daniel Hutto. Cambridge: Cambridge University Press.

——2009. Is the Self a Social Construct? *Inquiry* 52: 551–73.

Zheng, Yiwei. 2002. Sartre on Authenticity. *Sartre Studies International* 8: 127–40.

——2005. *Ontology and Ethics in Sartre's Early Philosophy*. Lanham MD: Lexington Books.

INDEX

Abraham, Karl: 121.

abschattungen: 98 n5, 204. *See also*
  perspective.

action: 26–27, 31–47, 85, 86, 131–32, 150,
  151, 163–64, 166–79, 180–85, 190–91, 206.

addiction: 128.

Adler, Alfred: 86, 121, 122.

aesthetics: 15–30, 102, 108, 110,
  112, 113, 116–17, 130–31, 136–39, 142 n1.

affectivity: 23–30, 110–17, 155, 186, 191. *See
  also* aesthetics; anguish; disgust; emotions;
  shame.

Age of Reason, The: 123–24, 126–27, 128.

Alain (Emile-Auguste Chartier):
  14–149, 151, 154, 156, 159 n3.

alienation: 7, 9, 73–75, 79, 83–84,
  87–88, 133, 134, 161–79, 181,
  191–92, 221, 224.

analogon: 20–30, 105–6, 108.

Anderson, Thomas C.: 6.

anguish: 5–6, 13, 42, 44, 74, 83,
  87, 122, 128, 185–87, 190, 192, 193 n3.

anthropology: 147, 149, 151, 153, 154.

Anti-Semite and Jew: 1, 7–8, 13, 73–76,
  84–85, 87–88, 138–39.

anxiety: 3, 42. *See also* anguish.

Aristotle: 171, 218.

Armstrong, David M.: 98 n1.

art: *See* painting.

attraction: 102, 112.

authenticity: 1–14, 74–76, 78, 81–82, 85, 86,
  87, 168, 169, 170, 175, 177, 184, 186–88,
  191.

Ayer, A. J.: 47 n4.

bad faith: 1–6, 11–13, 14 n3, 38, 42,
  76, 81, 122–27, 152, 155, 157–59, 167–70,
  172, 178 n4, 179 n15, 180–94.

Bales, Eugene: 176.

Balzac, Honoré: 121.

Barnes, Hazel: 47 n11, 90.

Bar-On, Dorit: 98 n3.

Barthes, Roland: 120.

Beauvoir, Simone de: 1–2, 8–14, 121, 147,
  155–56.

Being and Nothingness: 1–14, 31–47,
  48–72, 73–75, 87–88, 98 n1 n2,
  90–99, 115–16, 118–29, 130–44, 146, 148,
  152, 154, 156–59, 160 n10, 161–79,
  180–94, 195, 196, 199, 201, 207, 210 n1,
  214–16, 220–21, 223, 225, 225 n5 n6.

being-for-itself: *See* for-itself.

being-for-others: *See* interpersonal relations.

being-in-itself: *See* in-itself.

being-in-the-world: 2–3, 9–10, 73, 80, 86,
  155, 199, 200.

belief: 15–16, 22–23, 26, 27, 29, 42–43, 44,
  51–52, 54, 62–63, 92–95, 98 n4, 98–99 n5,
  116, 148–49, 150, 152, 157, 164, 169, 170,
  186, 192, 219.

Bergmann, Frithjoff: 178 n6.

Bergson, Henri: 133–36, 148, 151, 154, 159
  n2.

Bernasconi, Robert: 184, 187.

Biggs, Victoria: 135, 139.

Billington, Michael: 181.

Biro, John: 178 n7.

Black Orpheus: 73–74, 78–82, 87–88.

body dismorphic disorder (BDD): 134, 135,
  138, 143 n9.

body, the: 75, 79, 82, 84–88, 104–5, 123,
  124, 130–44, 149, 152, 154, 158, 190, 191,
  211–26. *See also* embodiment.

Breslin, James: 15, 30.

Bürger, Peter: 62.

Busch, Thomas: 42.

Printed in Great Britain
by Amazon